Intentional Living and Giving

WHAT OTHERS ARE SAYING ABOUT THE AUTHOR &

Intentional Living And Giving

This new book on biblical stewardship is refreshing, compelling, convicting, and absolutely on point. Please read *Intentional Living and Giving* and let God use it to expand your life and His work for the glory of God. I've known Larry as a friend for years and worked with him in raising funds. He walks his talk and has helped tens of thousands of people learn these truths and put them to work.

Dr. Ron Jenson, international speaker and author of multiple books, Rancho Bernardo, CA

In *Intentional Living and Giving* Larry O'Nan unlocks the secrets of giving within the broader context of biblical stewardship. Understanding O'Nan's concepts on biblical stewardship will greatly multiply your influence in the kingdom of God, making you a much better instrument of blessing to many others. *Intentional Living and Giving* is just the resource you need for the optimization of your God-given resources and opportunities.

Prof. Delanyo Adadevoh, president, International Leadership Foundation

Stewards are required to be faithful! For five decades, on several continents, Larry O'Nan has helped many individuals, and numerous organizations become faithful stewards. In *Intentional Living and Giving*, Larry applies that experience and the wisdom of scripture to help the reader lay a solid foundation and create their personal strategy for achieving faithful and effective stewardship.

David L. Orris, SR, Leadership consultant and retired publishing executive, Springfield, MO

For twenty-five years, Larry O'Nan worked in the trenches with me as my Board Chair, building the foundations of the National Network of Youth Ministries. He was a mentor to me in many ways, but especially in modeling the principles and practices of biblical stewardship."

Paul Fleischmann, president emeritus, National Network of Youth Ministries, San Diego, CA

Intentional Living and Giving could be one of the most difficult you read but the potential results are new joy and freedom. Understanding these principles could start a revolution in homes, churches, and communities across the globe. This book is a deep devotional study and a practical handbook to a new way of living. If you allow God to use these thoughts, He will touch you in your deepest places as He reshapes your Christian worldview and every aspect of how you live life.

Astrid Murfut, communications specialist, Agape Europe Partner Development, Strasbourg, France

I have known Larry for over fifty years and have seen the impact that the teachings in *Intentional Living and Giving* have made on people's lives. It speaks truth from God's Word and not from an earthly perspective. Change is tough. Applying the principles in what Larry is sharing will change you. It is SO WORTH IT. It is an honor to recommend *Intentional Living and Giving* to you!

Elvin Ridder, president of Management Development Associates, Cary, NC

Intentional Living and Giving has quickly become the primary resource for my current and new staff in fund development. For over five decades, Larry O'Nan has proven to be one of the most brilliant minds in teaching biblical lifestyle stewardship and fund development coaching and training. This amazing book chronicles O'Nan's personal journey from a fundraising neophyte to a master of the art for development. His principles are practical and extremely applicable for any believers that want to be used by God. This is a must-read.

Jim Dempsey, director of Ministry Development, Cru U.S. Ministries

Intentional Living and Giving is challenging, practical, and a pleasure to read. Larry O'Nan's experience shines through, and his stories keep you wanting more. The applications at the end of each chapter help the reader turn thought and conviction into action. Great content for sharing with others through sermons or seminars.

Dr. Dave Hine, founder of World Ministries, Leesburg, Florida

Over twenty-five years ago, as an inexperienced national director for Campus Crusade Ethiopia, I attended Larry's teaching on lifestyle stewardship. What he taught ignited a strong conviction in me to boldly raise up lifestyle stewards in Ethiopia that would lead the Ethiopia ministry toward indigenous sustainability and increased fruitfulness. Based on what I learned, I led my team to develop twenty-three ways of contextually relevant fundraising strategies that enabled us to fund initiatives through local sources. Regardless of your profession or your possessions, applying the principles outlined in *Intentional Living and Giving* will ignite the same fire in you that was ignited in me.

Dr. Bekele Shanko, president or GACX (Global Alliance for Church Multiplication), Global vice president for Cru Global Church Movements, Orlando, FL

Larry O'Nan invites readers to consider biblical giving and receiving by focusing on God's heart rather than wallets. *Intentional Living and Giving* is more than just seeing biblical principles—it is about seeing God. In addition to its solid theological foundation, *Intentional Living and Giving* contains gripping stories of God moving in the lives of everyday people. It's a fun read.

Leo Mullarky, Cru Campus, Riverside, CA

In today's ultra-materialistic society, our compass bearing is often dragged towards a life of getting, self-interest, and personal accumulation. In *Intentional Living and Giving* Larry offers a radical alternative, based on God's view of the possessions He has entrusted to our care. Larry's explanation of the biblical principles of stewardship and generosity, along with very practical pointers to help us live out these principles in our daily lives, will give your compass a completely new direction, aiming you towards God's nature and His purposes for your life.

Myles Wilson, author, *Funding the Family Business,* Bangor, Ireland

I have watched Larry bless churches for almost thirty years. His work will help you raise up stewards for the ministry God has given you. It may also challenge you as it has challenged me!

Dr. Paul M. Reinhard, founder of JumpStart Mentor Training

Larry O'Nan's book, *Intentional Living and Giving*, is thought-provoking and eloquently presents the meaning of living for God's purpose. What is our purpose on earth, how do we balance the purpose that we set for ourselves as opposed to balancing the purpose that God requires of us? What is truly our endgame? *Intentional Living and Giving* is perfect for all who are "undernourished spiritually."

Karen DiCarlo, CEO of Santa Claus Inc., San Bernardino, CA

Larry O'Nan has been one of the leaders who has invested immensely in helping believers here in Africa grow in maturity and generosity. Larry became a friend and mentor. What he imparted to me I am now imparting to others as I train and mentor young believers to apply God's principles of biblical lifestyle stewardship in the Horn of Africa.

Steve Sandagi, ministry partner development coach,
East Africa/Horn of Africa

In *Intentional Living and Giving,* Larry O'Nan is handing us extraordinary keys to some of the most important locks in our lives. Imagine being plugged into God's unlimited resources and not choosing to live by that grace! The exercises at the end of each chapter will make you think hard. But the good news is, it is a liberating work as we lay down our lives for Jesus and ask Him to be the source for our lives.

Leendert de Jong, partnership development trainer
and coach, Utrecht, The Netherlands

Years ago, I met Larry O'Nan—we both worked for Christian ministries helping them develop resources. Larry was the expert; I was finding my way. Larry's expertise was founded on solid Biblical principles. In *Intentional Living and Giving*, Larry continues to build on those Biblical concepts to help people understand the freedom that God wants us to have in giving. *Intentional Living and Giving*will challenge and strengthen your spiritual walk.

Peter Torry, church health director (retired),
Transformation Ministries, Upland, CA

Regardless of where a person finds themselves on their faith journey, the principles shared in this book will connect with the heart, mind, and soul. Larry O'Nan takes biblical stewardship concepts that he has researched and taught for decades and packages them for today's Christ-follower. Beyond solid theology, he helps guide the reader through the application of spiritual truths. Having sat under his teaching, I can recommend it.

Larry Buck, associate director of Development
The Jesus Film Project

Intentional Living and Giving will help liberate you from spiritual bondage, just as I experienced 30 years ago. As I began to understand my role as a steward, my heart, spirit, and mind were propelled to an unexpected new purpose for living.

But, more importantly, it led me to co-teach more than 63,000 Christians in German-speaking Europe about biblical lifestyle stewardship. I was also blessed to challenge dozens of marketplace leaders in Europe to trust God more by willingly giving away substantially more of their riches than they ever dreamed possible—generosity led to freedom from bondage.

Horst Reiser, Team Leader for Partner Development,
Agape Europe. Zurich, Switzerland

Intentional LIVING *and* GIVING

LARRY O'NAN

NASHVILLE

NEW YORK • LONDON • MELBOURNE • VANCOUVER

Intentional **LIVING** *and* **GIVING**

Discovering Purpose, Igniting Abundance, and Thriving as a Steward of God's Blessing

Published in New York, New York, by Morgan James Publishing. Morgan James is a trademark of Morgan James, LLC. www.MorganJamesPublishing.com

Proudly distributed by Publishers Group West®

ISBN 9781636983042 paperback
ISBN 9781636983059 ebook
Library of Congress Control Number: 2023944504

Cover and Interior Design by:
Chris Treccani
www.3dogcreative.net

Dedication

Intentional Living and Giving is dedicated to you!

You are about to join hands with a host of others
on a life-transforming adventure.
This is going to radically change your life—
as well as impact the lives of countless others.

Many partners have helped make this book a reality.
They, too, have learned the secrets of giving themselves away.

They hope you will also experience
life transformation through intentional living and giving.

Welcome to the team!
Soon you too will be an Authorized Wealth Distributor.
So glad you are also embarking on this journey!

—*Larry*

Contents

The Backstory to Intentional Living and Giving

THE FREEDOM TO FAIL

Every book has a backstory. If you like back stories, you will want to read what follows. You will learn why I initially wrote *Giving Yourself Away* in 1984 and what motivated me to write this book today.

If you want to get to the meat of *Intentional Living and Giving*, skip this backstory and dive into the book. I believe it will be instrumental in transforming your life forever. This is what happened to me when I began to learn and experience what I am about to share.

MY JOURNEY BEGINS.

In June of 1972, I unexpectedly found myself out of a job. For five years, I provided leadership to the growing music ministry of Campus Crusade for Christ—expanding from one performing group to eight traveling teams. One responsibility was to oversee the recruiting of forty-nine performing groups for Explo 72. Due to some reorganization following Explo 72, I found I needed to find another place within the ministry to use my giftings and strengths.

In late August of 1972, I was asked to assume responsibility for a fund-raising strategy that would help fund many international ministry projects of the ministry. I had no clue about fund development—and I soon learned that neither did anyone else in this international ministry. There was no department for me to take over. No staff. No plan. No manual of instructions. I did not step into someone else's shoes who knew what they were doing.

"YOU HAVE THE FREEDOM TO FAIL."

One afternoon I went to an appointment with Steve Douglass, the recently appointed vice president of the ministry. Before my meeting I met a new staff guy for the first time. He joined me for my meeting. He was also looking or a place to serve. He and his wife had raised their full support faster than anticipated and now wanted to get to work. Steve had a significant funding problem that needed some solution. He had something to show us.

Steve explained a dilemma to us. He showed us thirty boxes of pledge cards that he had brought back from Explo 72—fourteen weeks earlier. Over 90,000 teenagers had made a financial pledge for international ministry expansion one evening at the Cotton Bowl. The pledge commitment totaled just over $1.7 million. The pledges had been collected, counted, boxed, and then given to Steve for safekeeping. His challenge to us was quite simple: find a way to follow up on this commitment and see what we could collect.

As we looked at thirty sealed boxes Steve said. "You can take these boxes to another office and figure out what should be done." After he prayed for us my colleague and I began removing boxes from Steve's office. He had just invited us to tackle the impossible.

Over the next hour, the two of us took our baby steps toward learning the foundational tactics of fundraising as we opened boxes. We had no coach to guide us. There was no plan to follow. As we began opening boxes, I recalled my senior leader saying to me about a year earlier when I was facing a daunting challenge: "Go for it! You have the freedom to fail."

One thing was clear to us: If we did not find a way to follow up on this $1.7 million pledge, no one else was going to come along behind us to solve this challenge.

We formulated a plan and then began to work our plan. Over the following six months we began seeing results. Within a year, our pioneering efforts actually ended up exceeding the initial pledge amount by over $200,000. What we were doing was working.

YOU CAN GO IF YOU PAY FOR IT.

In early 1973 my colleague and I requested permission to attend a gathering of individuals with similar funding responsibilities for other Christian nonprofits. I requested that the ministry pay for this trip but was told that no funds were available for such a risky and unnecessary venture. My colleague and

I were given permission to attend if we covered all of our expenses from our personal staff accounts. We decided we had to go!

For four days we networked, listened to peers about their experiences, heard of successes and failures, and gained new insights as we met with about 100 individuals with like-minded funding challenges for their Christian colleges and nonprofit ministries. This experience led to raising significantly more funding for the international ministry needs.

Because of thirty boxes of very old fundraising pledge cards, began we were set on a mission to resource ministry funding needs. I recruited other men and women to join us. As a team we began to see that raising partners to help fund ministry expansion was truly a ministry.

MORE FUNDING IS NEEDED—AND NOW.

Between 1974 and 1976, Campus Crusade embarked on a national evangelism initiative called Here's Life America—with the catchphrase, *I found it; you can find it too!* Funding was needed to resource the 180 cities sponsoring evangelistic city-wide campaigns. I was tasked with developing and implementing the Here's Life Budget Campaign plan to ensure that each city could meet the needed funding goals to resource all that was required for success. Nothing of this nature had been attempted before. What we implemented worked.

In less than twenty-four months this city-by-city initiative realized over $13 million in local giving through the 180 city funding campaigns. While I knew I had the freedom to fail, this was not a failure!

A BILLION DOLLARS.

Because of the nationwide success of the *I Found It!* city-focused campaigns there was now worldwide interest in replicating this success in cities throughout the world. Considerably more funding was needed to help resource culturally adapted evangelism and discipleship strategies.

Campus Crusade for Christ's president, Dr. Bill Bright, boldly proposed that an initiative to raise one billion dollars be launched to help fund a number of worldwide evangelism and discipleship initiatives. A funding goal of one billion dollars was unheard of in the Christian community! The need was to seek financial commitments that would be given within three to ten years—no long-term deferred commitments. The idea was to challenge 1,000 financial partners—that we called History's Handful—to commit to giving one million dollars or more within a few years to to help fulfill the Great Commission.

In early 1977 a reputable and seasoned consulting firm with global experience in capital campaigns was retained to help bring direction and process to this billion-dollar vision. An extensive feasibility study was undertaken. When the ministry leaders met for a report of findings and recommendations I was asked to attend. The findings and proposed plan they were to present would directly impact what my young development team was already doing.

The firm confirmed to ministry leadership that the billion-dollar goal could be achieved IF the right strategies were implemented. However, they identified one major barrier to the campaign's success: central to success was the ministry formulating a biblically sound theology of stewardship and then proactively helping broader the body of Christ to see the possibility of also experiencing generosity. Campus Crusade could be the catalyst in opening the floodgates of biblical stewardship and encourage exceptional generosity from believers, all ministries would benefit.

Campus Crusade leaders believed funding for ministry expansion was needed now but they were not excited about launching a new stewardship initiative. Time was pressing and they did not have the time, passion, or inclination to define a new "theology of stewardship." The consulting firm was firm. This biblical teaching on stewardship was central to launching a successful billion-dollar funding initiative.

The discussion was intense. Someone suggested I be assigned to look into the implications and how this would work for the ministry. This assignment was not given to me because of my qualifications. It just seemed reasonable that the leader of the team assigned to oversee fund development should look into this matter. With this assignment delegated to me, the discussion moved to other aspects of the proposed campaign. I jotted the new directive on my pad. I had no clue as to what to do. All I knew was that soon and somehow, I needed to define a proposal. I wrote at the bottom of the page: "Go for it! You have the freedom to fail."

SURPRISED BY WHAT I LEARNED.

A few weeks later, I began to do a bit of research on what was meant by stewardship. To my surprise, I found very little teaching anywhere on the subject. What did exist was very limited in scope and even, at times, deceptive. Campus Crusade was known for outstanding discipleship material, but the excellent materials did not focus on teaching lifestyle stewardship.

In my research, I did find a "new teaching" that was called "prosperity theology." A number of Word of Faith ministry leaders were just beginning to realize the power of financial manipulation that could be achieved by focusing on personal prosperity. By preaching a warped view of stewardship, they were finding they could raise millions of dollars. This "new truth" was beginning to generate unprecedented giving from individuals who were willing to give a lot, to hopefully get a lot more! The teachers of this doctrine were reaping riches from faithful and gullible followers that wanted God to do something big for them. The focus was on getting from God rather than stewarding for God and generously giving from the resources that He provided. I knew that something was wrong with this me-centered message.

As I began a serious study about what the Bible said about this subject seriously, I realized that stewardship in scripture was not an afterthought. It was core to the message and was threaded throughout the Bible. God introduced these principles with his desires and expectations in the first two chapters of Genesis. I was frankly amazed at how much the Bible actually had to say about giving, receiving, stewardship, and accountability to the Owner of everything. The clear mandate was to steward what God owned and manage His possessions wisely and effectively.

I found others that were getting into this subject in a serious way. I connected with early pioneers like Larry Burkett (Christian Financial Concepts), Jim Jackson (Christianomics), Ron Blue, Howard Dayton (Compass), and a number of other authors. This was before ministries like Crown, Compass, or Peace University were established. I began studying, networking, and collecting all I could find about the subject without Google's help. Search engines today will direct one to thousands of resources—the good and the bad. Not so in early 1977.

This stewardship study had significant implications. If a host of believers understood the principles of biblical stewardship, this could be a game changer for the Body of Christ. Generosity could be released. The hurting world could be blessed. God's plan of responsible stewardship needed to be threaded into all that we were doing to raise resources. How to achieve this became the question.

STEPS AND STAGES IN GROWTH.

My team of leaders were beginning to see ourselves on a mission to encourage lifestyle stewardship. This new insight influenced everything we did to raise funding for ministry programs. Over the following thirteen years, we launched specialized departments to achieve specific outcomes. We were no longer seeking to raise money. Rather we were raising up stewards that would give God's resources in His mission. This was a game-changer in our thinking.

We revamped how staff undertook ministry partner development so that they could raise their personal support with greater success. We developed an intentional process that focused on stewardship, prayer, and building lasting partnerships that would sustain long-term ministry. The changes we introduced are still influencing missionary support raising worldwide for hundreds of ministries.

We created a direct mail department that focused on using mail to communicate needs to stewards. Another team partnered with private foundations. Another team specialized in partnering with churches. Representatives were recruited to work with major funding partners. A team was tasked with hosting weekend events where we could communicate vision and invite guests to give generously. Another team was charged with hosting over 100 faith-promise dinners a year in cities across the U.S. The Cru Foundation was established as a separate organization to help stewards with legacy giving. To support this expansion, we established a team that focused on administration, management, and tracking results. By 1986 this team included over 110 staff working in these nine development disciplines.

TEACHING OTHERS ALSO.

We began looking for ways to teach financial partners what we were learning by hosting weekend seminars. Each weekend we hosted a training we saw seventy-five to 125 couples attended to learn about living an abundant stewardship lifestyle. We encouraged them to become Authorized Wealth Distributors—giving God's resources to meet the needs of others.

Life transforming stories were being reported. These weekends helped attendees with a new understanding and purpose for living. They were no longer living and giving out of necessity or obligation. They were eagerly investing as stewards in what God had entrusted to them.

The message we taught was twofold: choose to live a biblical lifestyle as stewards and live life empowered by the Holy Spirit. We always provide an opportunity to generously participate financially in a ministry opportunity, but the focus was on life change rather than how much was needed or how much we could raise on a weekend.

Word spread about what was happening. Soon I was traveling to Latin America, Europe, Africa, and Asia to share biblical principles of fund development and generous biblical giving. My goal was to establish beachheads where funding could be raised and stewardship taught in any culture.

A door of opportunity unexpectedly opened for me in January 1984. This allowed me to step back from managing the fund development process and focus my attention on developing a book and study guide on lifestyle stewardship. *Giving Yourself Away* was released in October 1984.

HELPING OTHERS BECOME LIFESTYLE STEWARDS.

Intentional Living and Giving is an updated release of what my team and I learned and I initially wrote about in 1984. The core message is the same, but the content has been revised and edited for a new generation of new stewards. I hope you will grasp the significance of lifestyle stewardship. You can help others learns these life-changing principles. These pages can help jumpstart you on your journey as a generous steward.

YOU ARE NOT ALONE!

Today many thousands from many diverse cultures are choosing to be generous stewards. The message continues to thrive. I meet transformed stewards all the time.

Yet, while many are thriving, I realize that many millions of believers are living defeated lives. Many feel sidelined. They do not realize that God created them for a relationship and their purpose is to be a trustworthy steward. They do not understand that they were born again to thrive. I pray that you will grasp this truth personally and want to help others find joy, transformation, and freedom. Lives can be changed, and healing can come to a broken world as you become an Authorized Wealth Distributor.

Go for it! Take a risk. And remember, as you do, **you have the freedom to fail**.

PART ONE

DISCOVERING THE PLAN

We make a living by what we get.
We make a life by what we give.
WINSTON CHURCHILL

Chapter 1
PENNIES FROM HEAVEN

All of God's people are ordinary people who have been made extraordinary by the purpose He has given them.
—OSWALD CHAMBERS

The sleepy town of Grand Junction, Colorado, awoke on Thanksgiving Day 1947 to a fresh batch of white snow. The crisp, cool air and clear skies gave little indication of the blizzard conditions that had plagued a carload of California radio celebrities the previous night as they lumbered over 300 miles of snow-stormed, icy, winding roads from Salt Lake, Utah. The unexpected late fall snowstorm had grounded the party's private plane.

These celebrities had left warm and sunny Southern California to fly to Grand Junction for a special Thanksgiving Day dedication of a church bell—a bell that had become, to at least 224,581 people, a symbol of hope and faith in the future. For one woman it was to be the fulfillment of her heart's desire.

In that year, 1945, Grand Junction had been experiencing a time of building and growth after World War II. This was also true of Columbus Community Church, a small new nondenominational church just south of town, which had started in the basement of a schoolhouse. The church was the fulfillment of a dream of a few dedicated women in the Orchard Mesa community to reach neighborhood children with the good news of Jesus.

Though small nondenominational churches have always been considered bad financial risks, this had not dampened the spirits of the few members and their young pastor, his wife, and their three-year-old son. One farmer donated land. Initiating a church-building project, they undertook an innovative approach that would involve the community. Church members went door to door through the area around the church, asking rural neighbors to donate the price of one or more concrete bricks that would be used in the construction of the little church. By taking the initiative with neighbors and friends, they soon found they had the needed funds raised to build a single-room white church building debt-free, with a forty-foot-high steeple pointing heavenward.

The fund drive proved remarkably successful, getting the whole community involved in giving both money and hours of loving labor. On August 3, 1946, the community friends and members crowded into the new sanctuary to hear the young preacher deliver the dedication sermon.

In his sermon, the pastor referred to the focal point of the little community church: the white steeple and an empty belfry topped by a simple white cross. He explained that no funds were available to obtain a bell. His one remaining desire was for a bell to ring on Sunday mornings to call the rural community to worship.

At the dedication of the new church another pastor friend for the city was present to assist. That night he told his own congregation of the church dedication he had attended and of the one remaining need—a bell for the belfry.

Mrs. Helma Weber was present that evening. As her preacher spoke, God translated that new little church's need for a bell into Mrs. Weber's own personal heart's desire. While traveling home after the service, she felt that desire begin to grow, and as she turned into her driveway, she decided she must take **action**—first to pray and then to write a letter!

Among the forerunners of today's popular television giveaway shows heard in that area was the first nationally syndicated daily radio program, "Heart's Desire." It was broadcast by the Mutual Network stations and hosted by Uncle Ben Alexander (who later became a co-star on the TV series, *Dragnet*). Each day Uncle Ben encouraged his radio audience to drop him a letter, telling him of their heart's desires.

Helma Weber felt she now had a genuine, God-given heart's desire. So, late that Sunday evening, she wrote to Uncle Ben and told him about her desire to help provide a bell for a little country church in Colorado. As she completed the letter, she prayed, then sealed the letter and mailed it to Uncle Ben in Hollywood, CA the next morning.

Her letter caught the attention of the radio team. Later reflecting upon that moment, Uncle Ben commented, "I knew right then and there that the listeners of our program would want to help give that bell."

On the next radio show, Uncle Ben read Helma Weber's letter, inviting his listeners from across America to give. He set only one limitation: the maximum contribution any individual could make was one cent!

And give, listeners did! Pennies poured in! Interest grew. The news media carried the message worldwide, and soon pennies began arriving from other countries. Uncle Ben began calling them "pennies from heaven." Each letter contained a penny or more, and each penny seemed to have a special story behind it. In a sense, each was a gift from the heart.

There was a penny from a toddler who went without candy and dessert. Three Norwegian pilots each sent his "good luck penny" with the prayer that peace would always ring over our nation.

There were pennies from the family who thanked God for their miraculous escape from a train wreck; a penny from a mother to thank God for her newborn son; and a penny from a nurse, her symbol of participation in service to humanity. Also in the same batch of mail was a penny sent by a mother who found her gift in the chubby palm of her son after a hit-and-run driver ran him down. There was a letter from a little orphan girl who prayed, "No one ever hearing that bell will ever be as lonely as I am." Another letter contained 185 pennies—but the letter closed with 185 signatures.

Some listeners, in order to get around the one-cent restriction, contributed on behalf of anyone and everyone they could think of. Two clowns (Fritz and Witz) and their trick dogs sent in nine cents—one cent for each of their dogs and for themselves. One woman sent in a penny for each state she had lived in or traveled through. One man sent in "a penny for myself, a penny for the fellow who forgot, a penny for the one who put it off, a penny for the one who lost the address, and a penny for Ben Alexander."

Creative listeners found loopholes in the contribution limitation, and the pennies kept coming. People gave because they wanted to—no one HAD to. The accumulation of pennies bought the copper and paid the craftsman to mold and pour a special copper bell, similar to those hanging in mission towers of churches in the Southwestern states. On the bell was inscribed:

> Luke 2:14: "Glory to God in the highest and on Earth, peace good will toward all men." Into this bell has gone the

> pennies and prayers of 224,581 Americans of over 30 denominations, from every county in every state of the nation.

Finally, the bell was completed, shipped by private plane to Grand Junction, and proudly installed in a specially built log cabin bell house, constructed by donated labor as members of the church hauled trees from the nearby mountains, hand stripped them, and carefully laid them in place. The bell never made it to the empty belfry in the little steeple; the thousands who gave their pennies to purchase the bell wanted to see *their* bell!

On that icy Thanksgiving morning, Mrs. Helma Weber and 2,000 other community members bundled up and came to hear the "Heart of America" bell ring for the first time. Uncle Ben and his radio team made it over the dangerous highway from Salt Lake just in time to do an on-location "Heart's Desire" broadcast from a makeshift wooden platform in front of the little church. While the live audience waited, thousands also tuned in by radio to hear the first ring of the bell that had become their symbol of hope and peace.

The bell rang. Major newspapers gave front-page coverage of the special event. Even *True Romance* magazine carried a story of one couple's shattered lives put back together through the ringing of the bell. Governors of 32 states responded with letters and telegrams of congratulations.

Because one woman **stepped out** and took action, a God-given desire was **planted** in her heart, and 224,581 people—if only for a moment in time—gave an expression of themselves for something they viewed as important.

Why did Mrs. Weber write a letter to Ben Alexander? Why did Uncle Ben choose her letter to be read to the nation over the thousands that he no doubt received? Why did 224,581 people choose to send one penny to help buy a bell for a little rural church tucked away in the hills of western Colorado?

There are six important reasons why you and I would also have sent our penny. Let's take a look at why we are motivated to respond to needs we see around us. As we do, let's keep in mind this basic fact: You and I need to give far more than any cause needs to receive from us. God, as we will see later, made us this way.

Because we are rather complex in our thinking processes, it is important to keep in mind that not all motivations are present every time we decide to give. Let me begin by asking you some soul-searching questions.

DO YOU GIVE BECAUSE YOU WANT TO BE IN PARTNERSHIP WITH A WORTHY CAUSE?

Let's face it; we gain satisfaction from feeling a part of a worthy cause. Two or more people working in harmony can indeed accomplish more than one person working alone. Some years ago, *Life* magazine released a photo story about a Midwestern farmer and his family who lived next to a massive wheat field. The first photo showed the farmer and his wife panic-stricken as they realized their young son was missing—nowhere to be found near the security and safety of the farmhouse.

The second photo indicated that the news of the missing boy had spread to the community. Neighbors had come to help search for the bow. The photo showed the confusion and distress of the people as they wandered with no direction, seeking to find the lost lad.

The third photo showed that someone had taken leadership after hours of fruitless searching. The small rural community had been organized into a human chain, each person locking hands with another, and together sweeping up and down the rows of tall ripe wheat. Each person assumed responsibility for the specific area immediately in front and to each side of him. They now had a defined plan to search for the boy.

The last photo expressed heartbreak and sorrow. The father was pictured kneeling over the body of his son as those in the search party looked on in sad disbelief. Yes, they found the boy, but their effort in partnership occurred too late. He had died from exposure.

The only words in this photo feature were those of the grieving father as he looked up at the other: "I only wish we had joined hands sooner."

A partnership involves joining together, locking hands in total cooperation, and moving with singleness of purpose to meet an objective. Helma Weber's request for a bell for the little country church created a sense of partnership with those who gave their pennies, each doing his part. Without partnership, the Heart of American Bell would not have rung on Thanksgiving Day of 1947.

DO YOU GIVE TO MEET A NEED?

Seldom, if ever, does our human nature stimulate us to act without knowledge of a need. Knowing of a need is the first step toward us responding.

Many years ago, I served as chairman for a building addition for my local church. Over a period of about two years, and in the midst of a recession, the moderately sized congregation gave over $150,000. We built only as we had the available cash. When the building was dedicated, the money abruptly stopped coming. Why? In the minds of those who had given, the need had been met.

After the dedication of the "Heart of America" bell in November 1947, America quit sending pennies. Why? You guessed it—there was no motivation to give. The need no longer existed.

DO YOU GIVE TO REPRESENT YOUR COMMITMENT TO A CAUSE WHEN YOU OTHERWISE COULD NOT PARTICIPATE?

When I joined the staff of Campus Crusade for Christ in 1966, an elderly lady made a commitment to be a part of my support team through a monthly contribution of $15. She then told me why she had decided to give.

"Larry," she said, "you are doing something that I cannot do. You are going to be talking to young people of a generation different from mine. I would not know what to do or what to say, and I don't have the physical energy I had when I was in college. You are doing something I cannot do, so I want to help you in the only way I can—through my prayers and my limited finances."

Let me tell you, those were sobering words to hear. She was trusting me to do what she was unable to do. Every month she faithfully sent in her gift. Even with her limited income, she never missed giving for 216 months—totaling $3,240.

I'm sure that the majority of those who gave their pennies to help purchase that bell in 1947 gave with a sense of vicarious participation. They wanted to feel a part of helping meet a need. Their gift was helping make a difference. Today we see the same type of involvement through GoFundMe campaigns. By our nature, we want to be involved.

DO YOU GIVE TO SATISFY YOUR OWN SELF-WORTH?

Have you found yourself feeling "good" inside because you gave something you had—your time, your skills, your money, or personal possessions—to help meet a need?

Sad to say, many thousands of people give only with the motivation of maintaining a positive self-image. Many give because they feel it just would "look bad" if they didn't want to help.

One man confided to me some years ago, "I give to my favorite charities and donate time to worthy community projects so I have something to talk about. I would love to be free from the obligation to help; but I guess if I didn't give something, I would have trouble living with myself."

DO YOU GIVE AS AN EXPRESSION OF GRATITUDE?

The one who gives with the sole motivation of expressing gratitude is rare indeed today. This person basically is saying, "I'm just thankful that I am able to help. I have been given so much, this is the least I can do."

I'm a preacher's kid. In fact, I'm the son of that young preacher who pastored that rural congregation in Grand Junction, Colorado. I remember one old gentleman who attended that little church. Mr. West was a regular. Every Sunday he drove up to church in an old Model A Ford that he kept in tip-top shape and so clean you could eat your dinner off the hood.

Mr. West's health was good, but his wife was sick most of the time. His daughter, Ruth, was badly crippled by polio. Even though he and his family did not have much of the world's wealth, Mr. West was in love with the Lord Jesus and with life itself. I can still hear him say, "I can't give my God enough; He's been so good to me. He loves me so."

How many people, I wonder, who sent in pennies for the bell gave their penny out of gratitude to Jesus?

DO YOU GIVE BECAUSE OF THE BLESSING YOU WILL RECEIVE?

I wish more people realized that blessing returns to the giver when something is given away. As a result of giving, God is able to give to the giver much more—a multiplied return on that which was given.

"I can't afford not to give, Larry," one friend said with a sparkle in her eyes. "God can bless me only if I'm giving away what He's given to me. I don't want to turn God's blessings off, so I'm going to be what He wants me to be—a pipeline that carries His love to others!"

DO YOU GIVE TO BE REMEMBERED?

Once while visiting Washington, DC, I visited the National Cathedral. While admiring the Cathedral and learning of its history, I noticed that almost everything in the Cathedral was memorialized, in memory of a loved one.

You may have no interest in being memorialized with a monogrammed quilted kneeling cushion placed in the National Cathedral. But maybe you **would** like that friend to remember your good cooking as he cuts a slice of your freshly baked bread or piping hot pie. Otherwise, you simply would have left it on his doorstep with an anonymous note that read, "I'm thankful for you."

DO YOU GIVE TO ACHIEVE SECURITY?

Soon after my wife and I purchased our first home, the families of our block began a Neighborhood Watch program. We committed ourselves as a group to watch out for one another's property and to be alert to any activity that might be harmful to any of us. Although we were not giving money to one another, we were committed to giving an eye or ear to what was going on around us. Why? Our security is at stake. As neighbors, we believe that if we give to one another, we can have a safer place to live.

Over my professional career, I've met many men and women that were blessed with exceptional wealth and have chosen to give substantial sums for evangelism and discipleship. I recall one man who was exceptionally generous commenting to me, "Larry, this is the only place I see to give my money. If I don't do all I can to change the hearts of people through a relationship with Jesus Christ, our world has no hope. I want a safe place where my grandchildren can grow to be adults. I am giving to protect their future. I believe that unless society is changed from the inside out, there will be no security for the next generation."

DO YOU GIVE FOR TAX ADVANTAGES?

For over twelve years, I provided leadership to various funding initiatives on behalf of Campus Crusade for Christ. I've noticed at one particular time of the year that strange things happen: between December 15–31!

This is when contributions of the strangest amounts are received—checks like the one for $5,242.50. Why? The end of the tax year was fast approaching, and the contributor had learned from his accountant that to be in a lower tax bracket, he needed to give just that much more.

Whatever their motivation for giving, when 224,581 radio listeners heard of the need for the church bell, they were willing to do something about it—in this case, send "just one penny."

But the "Heart's Desire" radio show was heard by **millions,** so why didn't more of the listeners send in their penny? What caused some to give and others not to give? Could it be that many who heard of the plan to give a penny thought, "Well, my gift won't help much," or "Sorry, Uncle Ben, I haven't got a penny to spare."

WHY WE DON'T GIVE

Could it be that the reason many of us fail to give is that we are not free to give? Is it possible that our preoccupation with things around us has paralyzed our ability to do what we know we should do?

It is sometimes easy to get caught up in the bondage of our circumstances. We become paralyzed by our preoccupation with our own needs, forgetting the needs of others. Those are the times when even giving a penny can be a burden.

Have you ever stopped to consider seriously what it would take to change things around you? Let's face it, even if we are declared "more than conquerors" by the One who loved us, we tend to forget there are needs to be met and a world to be reached. We can easily become indifferent to needs within our reach.

Today, there are now more than eight billion other people on this small planet. As many as half of these have never yet heard the name of Jesus—or if they heard the name, have no clue that he is the answer to their emptiness. If these people lined up in a single file line, the line would circle the earth over fifty times and increase in length to over thirty miles every day. These are people who have never had the opportunity to say yes to God's love. They are unaware that a relationship with Jesus is the answer to their confusion and sense of lostness. Helping them find the answer to their empty lives is within our reach. We are positioned to make a difference if we really want to.

ARE WE IMPACTING THE WORLD?

I'm afraid today we are preoccupied with our own affairs to such an extent that we fail to think about God's purpose for us and for others. Today almost everything we do is about meeting our personal needs. We in America spend hundreds of millions annually on technology that is outdated within five years. Today over 122.4 million televisions are plugged in the homes of Americans and tens of thousands of these are using power over eight hours a day to satisfy boredom. The more we watch the more depressed we get. More money is spent each year on chewing gum and on dog food in the United States than on mission outreaches and helping others.

We are undernourished spiritually. We have become "junk food" Christians by default. If we are lucky, we spend less than seven minutes a day in prayer. Our pastors spend an average of thirty minutes a day praying for people and their identified needs. We intend to spend time reading the Bible but rarely get to it because of life interruptions. We want to be good role models to others but miss the mark. We have become a secular society and feel we can survive without daily spiritual nourishment. We have forgotten our core guidelines reflected in the Ten Commandments. Here is a better test for you: Can you list at least five right now?

WHAT'S THE PROBLEM?

It's not money. It's not ability. It's not technology. The problem is self-centeredness and bondage to circumstances and self-seeking pursuits. We end up being responders, rather than planners. We are reactive rather than proactive. We live for the hour, forgetting we have a purpose and a plan we should be following. We allow our emotions and cravings for comfort to focus us on our own needs—and wants, rather than on being sensitive to what we are created to be.

The late Dr. Richard Halverson, chaplain of the US Senate between 1981 and 1995, was asked by reporters for *Christianity Today* in the mid-1980s if he felt the church demonstrates a healthy exception to the "self-seekers" that surround it. His response was sobering to me then—and even more so today:

> *I wish I could believe that. Instead, I think the so-called worldliness of even conservative evangelicals is far more subtle than it was 25 to 50 years ago. We are badly infected with secularism, with the materialism that says, "Live for the now." Generally speaking, the people of God today are living to get as much as they can out of life on this side of the grave. The eternal reference we profess in our theology we deny in our practice.*
>
> *For example, if you could pin people down, I think you would find very few longing for the return of Christ. His return now would instead constitute an interruption in our plans. Of course, if we had to choose, we wouldn't choose "the now" instead of eternity, but that's why the problem is so subtle. We are living without an eternal frame of reference and not even realizing it.*
>
> *As a result, there is very little kingdom-of-heaven interest. There is no real longing for an "awakening." God is sovereign in all these things, but to the extent that conditions have to be met for God to send an awakening like the past great revivals, I think all the conditions have been met except one:*

the desire on the part of God's people for an awakening that would issue in righteousness, in selflessness, and in authentic piety.[1]

This was in the mid-1980s! I see that things have changed—we have sunk even deeper into empty self-seeking and a quest for personal fulfillment. Our preoccupation with life **now** is keeping us from experiencing what God has planned for us.

JOIN THE ADVENTURE!

If you find yourself in Dr. Halverson's description, then I invite you to join me in an adventure to discover how to be free from our bondage to selfishness, and free to care, free to reach out to others, and free to help meet the needs of others. You can be free to give yourself away. This is an adventure that will lead you into a lifestyle of generosity and giving. Could this be what is missing in your life?

Mrs. Helma Weber was free in 1946. Because of her freedom, God was able to entrust to her a desire that ultimately impacted more than a quarter of a million people—and our nation, if only for a moment in time, was able to focus upon hope in the midst of selfish despair.

Little became much when she placed it in the Master's hand.

Has God already transferred a desire from His heart to yours? What are you doing with what He has already given to you? Before beginning this adventure, take a few moments to right now and focus your attention on the last page of this chapter. This page is reserved for your reflection. This will help you unlock new freedom, This is your Key to Abundant Living.

At the end of each chapter, you will find a page designed to help you process what you just read. I hope you will take a few minutes at each **Key to Abundant Living.** Pause and reflect on what you just read. This will help you distill and prepare you for what God has planned for you. Respond to the questions or the requests provided. You will gain a lot from these pauses.

Key To Abundant Living

UNLOCKING YOUR LIFE OF CONTENTMENT

Write down a desire you believe God has laid upon your heart. Describe the what, where, when, and how.

What have you learned or experienced so far toward making this desire a reality?

What one idea was especially helpful to you in this chapter?

What would you say are the three main reasons you currently give?

In what areas of your life would you like to experience growth?

Chapter 2
WHERE YOU FIT

O divine Master
Grant that I may not so much
Seek to be consoled as to console;
To be understood as to understand;
To be loved as to love;
For it is in giving that we receive;
It is in pardoning that we are pardoned; and
It is in dying that we are born to eternal life.
—SAINT FRANCIS OF ASSISI (1181—1226)

It had been a long, exhausting week for my associate and me. We were completing our sixth straight day of teaching in Mexico. We knew very little Spanish, and our class of nineteen Latin American leaders from twelve countries knew very little English. Consequently, we found ourselves mentally exhausted after six ten-hour days of teaching technical material and coaching the learners through an interpreter.

That day I dismissed the class early. They, too, were ready for a break. As soon as the last member of the class was out of the room, Ricardo and Renee (the two young Mexican men who had been assigned to assist us) came in to get us. We had become close friends, even though language often limited our ability to communicate. Both men were in love with Jesus and demonstrated His love to us. They wanted us to experience the wonders of their homeland.

"Time for dinner," Renee announced. That sounded like a good idea! In my mind, I pictured a quiet little cafe near the square in downtown Cuernavaca, where we could relax for an hour and then retire. But my idyllic vision exploded when Ricardo announced, "We have a special evening planned. We are going to Mexico City."

My heart sank! I wanted to say no, but I did not want to offend my friends. Soon my associate and I were in the back seat of an old VW Bug; and after an hour's drive, we came to the outskirts of the world's largest city at the time. As we talked in a combination of limited English and more limited Spanish, Ricardo and Renee began to show us the sights. They were proud of their homeland!

Much later—after a break for dinner—we were on a walking tour in the heart of the city. My associate and I followed our two friends, with no idea where we were going.

Without warning, we made an abrupt turn into an alley and, within minutes, entered a large church. The Saturday night mass was in progress, with close to 2,000 worshipers in attendance.

I was hesitant to barge in, but our two hosts seemed unconcerned about disrupting the service. We entered the sanctuary, and there I came face to face with the most beautiful giant wall murals I had ever seen. Each enormous painting illustrated one aspect of the life of the patron saint of Mexico, St. Francis of Assisi. I forgot that we were likely interrupting worship and stared in amazement at those dramatic works of art.

To the Mexican people, St. Francis of Assisi represents just the opposite of what the materialistic world offers them today. He was a man of great wealth and influence; but because he was passionately concerned for others, he chose to give away all he had to help meet others' needs.

As I viewed the massive murals, I could not help but remember the prayer of St. Francis that sums up the spirit of this man. This prayer opens this chapter.

"Come, come, we must be going," Ricardo's voice brought me back to reality. He and Renee took the lead, and we walked across the front of the church and out the door as the priest was delivering his evening message to the full sanctuary of worshipers in attendance.

We followed our guides another three or four blocks. It was then we learned that we were going for a ride—straight up to the top of the tallest building in Mexico City at the time. In minutes, our perspective on things drastically changed. Now we were looking down on the millions of city lights of the fourth-largest city in the world—from a thirty-two-story vantage point. As far as our eyes could see lights that shone like diamonds against black velvet.

Ricardo led me to a specific spot on the observation deck. As we stood together looking out into the darkness, Ricardo quietly said, "It was while standing right here that God called me to help take His Gospel to every person in my country. I gave Him my life on this spot, asking Him to use me in any way He saw fit."

Within three minutes, I encountered two examples of the true biblical teaching of giving and receiving, a teaching that usually is greatly misunderstood. Francis of Assisi prayed that he would seek to give himself, rather than be a greedy taker. Ricardo expressed his dedication to giving his life so that Mexico might know his Savior.

As we rode the elevator back to the hustle and bustle of life on the street, I now knew why I was in Mexico City that night. God wanted me to grasp the significance of what it means to give yourself away.

But wait! Doesn't this giving business deal with just finances—our money? Sad to say, the vast majority of people believe that. Giving encompasses much more than being generous financially.

In our fast-paced, automated tech society, "giving" (even among Christians) has become identified almost solely with the "ol' buck." But according to God's perspective, giving deals with every aspect of **life.** Ricardo recognized this. St. Francis of Assisi, over 800 years ago, recognized this. Everything we have is to be given away. Too often, our bondage to material possessions and desires of the world limits us in our ability to give as we were designed to do.

Jesus had a lot to say about giving and receiving. In fact, He spoke more about our relationship to material possessions, time, and talents than about any other topic. Of the thirty-eight recorded parables of Jesus, nineteen of them concern our use of money, property, time, skills, and our relationships with others as we deal with these God-entrusted possessions.

Other New Testament writers caught what Jesus was saying. One verse in five in the New Testament relates to this subject. Over 1,000 passages in the Bible deal with personal prosperity and the use of possessions. Are you aware that there are 1,565 Bible verses that deal with the subject of giving alone?[2]

Why is it, then, that we are not taught more about giving? I think the key reason is confusion and misunderstanding of Scripture. Most pastors have never been schooled in the biblical basis of giving and receiving. Somewhere along the line, the truth on stewardship became so twisted that "Stewardship

Sunday" today related to "the yearly budget push." In most churches today giving means appealing for and collecting money to fund the operation.

Do you know what's happened? Satan has slipped in his worldly definition of stewardship on us. He has twisted the truth. He is a masterful deceiver. As a result, we are neutralized and ineffective stewards. We are right where Satan wants us—doing only enough to get by and living selfish, defeated lives that attract virtually no one to the greatest Giver of all.

How did we get into this mess, anyway? To gain perspective on our preoccupation with possessions, we need to go back to the beginning.

What is the first chapter of Genesis all about? Yes, you are right—creation. But let's look more closely again. God is creating heaven and earth, but He is doing far more. The first chapter of Genesis is packed full of God dynamically **giving of Himself.** When God gives, confusion and chaos are transformed into purpose and meaning: "In the beginning, God created the heavens and the earth. The earth was formless and empty, and darkness covered the deep waters. And the Spirit of God was hovering over the service of the waters" (Genesis 1:1–2).

God was giving of Himself in the expression of creation, and nothingness took on form and purpose. Open your favorite translation to Genesis 1 and 2 and see what a giving God did. When God began giving, things began to happen:

- God made light and then divided the light from the darkness.
- God made the sky by separating vapor and **giving** the earth water.
- God made dry land by **giving** water-defined parameters.
- God **gave** life to the land; at His word, life designed to reproduce appeared.
- God **gave** order to the heavens by **giving** instructions; see verse14, 15.
- God **gave** life to the sky and oceans by His command in verse 20.
- God **gave** the gift of reproductive life to the earth by His command in verse 24.

In six days, a perfect world was given form and purpose because God gave. God was pleased with his giving, but something was missing. He needed a manager who would oversee His creation. The pinnacle of God's expression of giving Himself is found in Genesis 1:26–27 when God the Father spoke to God the Son:

Then God said, "Let us make human beings in our image, to be like us. They will reign over the fish in the sea, the birds in the sky, the livestock, all the wild animals in the earth, and the small animals that scurry along the ground."

So God made human beings in his own image.
In the image of God he created them;
male and female he created them like his Maker.

God gave His very nature and heart to human beings. He gave mankind the responsibility and the authority to manage His creation. We were created with a purpose: to be stewards of the gifts of God's creation.

In making man "like his Maker," God gave him those characteristics that reflected His nature and His personality. He made man as an extension of Himself, with the authority to make wise decisions, the ability to reflect His Spirit, to reproduce after his kind, to faithfully serve as a steward, and to have a personal relationship with the King.

God gave mankind a world that was made to sustain itself. It was a world of perfection and abundance. There were no "seconds," no rejects. No sin. God created the world with the ability to bear fruit and be replenished the earth.

What a deal! Imagine living in a perfect environment. Not too hot. Not too cold. Not too dry. Not too humid. No weeds. No back-breaking labor. Imagine an abundance of everything to meet every need, want, or desire. What a place! We can't even begin to describe such an environment because all we know about the choice that was made in Genesis 3. Perfection was shattered.

God was giving of Himself and operating according to His plan. He knew what He was doing. God wasn't surprised that the first days of creation were such a success. His standard was generous perfection.

Yes, God had a plan! Let's briefly examine five characteristics of His plan:

1. **God's plan is timeless.** Because we live our lives governed by God's gift of time, we cannot begin to imagine living outside of time. Time has limitations. God has no limitations. From God's view, there is no beginning or end. Does the thought of eternity sometimes baffle you? It baffles me. From my view, it looks almost frightening.

   God is already living in eternity—that's home to Him. When God gave His creation the gift of time, it was to help regulate activity. The gift of time allowed God's creation to be all He planned it to be.

2. **God's plan is built on a foundation of TRUTH.** What God says and does can be trusted. Truth is not relative to God. He does not change His mind when circumstances change. He is always the same. Truth is central to God's character. He is steadfast, firm, constant, loyal, and faithful. Truth flows from His very being.

   Moses described God's truth by saying: He is the Rock; his deeds are perfect. Everything he does is just and fair. He is a faithful God who does no wrong; how just and upright he is! (Deuteronomy 32:4).

   He is the God of truth. His Word is full of commitments and promises to us. We can put our confidence in His Word.
3. **God's plan is based on giving.** The entire Bible is a record of God giving of himself. The record shows He is a giver. God gave, and heaven and earth were formed. God gave life to Adam and gave him a beautiful mate. Even when Adam and Eve blew it, He gave them clothing, shelter, and protection. His ultimate gift is expressed by Jesus in John 3:16.

   God promised this gift in Genesis 3:15. And God's promises will redeem mankind and give him victory over the deceiver, Satan. Isn't it interesting that achieving this victory demanded He gives the life of His Son? As you study God's Word, you will find He never stops giving. Giving is core to his nature. He gives—and expects us to do so as well.

   We are the only part of His creation that can short-circuit giving! Every created gift of creation was designed to give or recreate—it has no choice. Plants give and receive; animals give and receive. Even man, as long as he lives, cannot stop giving out carbon dioxide and receiving oxygen. God designed all creation to operate by the principle of circulation. Giving first and receiving as a result of giving is as basic to life as breathing! Because we have the gift of free will, we as humans can choose not to give.
4. **God's plan is characterized by agape love.** Tucked away in the book of Deuteronomy 7:7–8, we find why God brought the children of Israel out of the land of Egypt. His agape love motivated Him to act. Moses explained His love to the generation about to cross into the Promised Land this way:

   > "The Lord did not set his heart on you and choose you because you were more numerous than other nations, for you were the smallest of all nations! Rather, it was simply that the

> Lord loves you, and he was keeping the oath he had sworn to your ancestors. That is why the Lord rescued you with such a strong hand from your slavery and the oppressive hand of Pharaoh, king of Egypt."

Unlike our expressions of love, which almost always seem to have strings attached, God's love is an exercise of His divine will. He chooses to love without cause or without an expectation of what He will receive in return.

God's love says, "I love you. No matter what you do or don't do; I love you."

God's love says, "I love you, even when you hurt Me; I will remain faithful and love you."

God's love says, "I love you so much I sent My Son to die for you."

God's love is the glue that holds His plan together. This bonding agent is stronger than any Super Glue and lasts for eternity.

Paul defines the strength of this "glue" when he writes:

> "Love is patient, love is kind, and is not jealous; love does not brag and is not arrogant, does not act unbecomingly; it does not seek its own, is not provoked, does not take into account a wrong suffered, does not rejoice in unrighteousness, but rejoices with the truth; bears all things, believes all things, hopes all things, endures all things" (1 Corinthians 13:4–7, NASB).

This **agape** love operates independently of circumstances. God **wills** to focus His love on us. It is His love, then, that is the motivating force behind His plan. And He wants us to reflect His giving spirit. He wants to have a personal love-focused relationship with you and me.

5. **God's plan produces peace.** I believe a spirit of peace characterized the seventh day of creation. God created a harmonious environment each day during the days of creation. Because of peace and harmony, He was able to say, "That's good," to each day's creation.

   Mankind lived surrounded by God's peace until the atmosphere drastically shifted, as recorded in Genesis 3. Since then, mankind has desperately tried to recreate a lasting environment of peace, but his efforts have been futile. The greater the attempt, the greater the failure.

Even we believers often get caught up in unhealthy competition and experience chaos in relationships and attempts to achieve peace. Rather than reflecting the inner peace that God promises His children, we become agitators that are preoccupied with our circumstances. The end result is a mess: strife, deceitfulness, disharmony, confusion, loneliness, emptiness, conflict, polarization—and death. In our sinful state, we believe somehow we can produce peace—but we fail miserably.

The world cries for peace daily. Watch tonight's newscast. You will probably hear the reference to "peace and harmony" as a goal mentioned at least once. But the majority of the news broadcast will demonstrate we are good at just the opposite. All of our attempts are a counterfeit of what we are seeking.

Over the centuries, since Adam and Eve were expelled from their perfect home, man has striven to create peace on his own. But manmade programs, at best, offer only brief interludes from chaos and tension. At the United Nations, men and women talk about but are far from, their goal of finding common ground, unity, and peaceful co-existence. Summit talks may provide a platform for negotiations among leaders of major powers, but distrust and opposing ideologies prevent these meetings from producing what the world wants more than anything else.

Why can't man obtain peace? Because he is using the wrong process! He is trying to create peace apart from the God of peace.

GOD KNOWS!

God designed us to live abundant, victorious lives. Certainly, He is aware of our frailties. He knows we have trouble comprehending eternity when we live in a confusing time. He knows we have trouble defining truth in a world full of deception. He knows we experience conflict in a greedy environment and have difficulty freely giving ourselves away. He knows **agape** love is not often experienced in our relationships because of our human frailty in reflecting His love to others. He knows that the peace He gives is not what the world attempts to give.

Yes, God knows! He also knows that we can grow to understand **His** perfect perspective on these areas as we learn to live in the power of the Holy Spirit. If we choose, we can be more than conquerors through the One who loved us first. If we choose, we can tap the wisdom and understanding that can come only from Him. In Chapter 9, you will find out how to live in the power of the Holy Spirit. There is an answer to the mess we are in! Learning this changed my life. It will change yours as well IF you want His solution.

God is eager to see you find your place in His plan! He wants you to thrive by living as He intended!

Key To Abundant Living

UNLOCKING YOUR LIFE OF CONTENTMENT

1. Read 1 Corinthians 13 aloud. This reflects how God loves you. Identify three things that especially mean a lot to you. Thank Him for loving you this way.

2. Reflect a bit. Identify ways God has expressed His love to you in the last month. What has he done for you lately?

3. Visit John 3:16. According to what Jesus says here, what has he done for you? Why did God do this?

4. How does this reality help you face your circumstances today?

5. Identify three things that seem to be missing in your life right now.

Chapter 3 WINNING BIG!

Therefore, since we are surrounded by such a huge crowd of witnesses to the life of faith, let us strip off every weight that slows us down, especially the sin that so easily trips us up.
—HEBREWS 12:1

Dad pulled the old 1948 Dodge panel truck into our driveway. My brother and I ran to meet him, eager to see what he had brought us from Arizona. Dad had an outdoor advertising business that supplemented the small salary the church paid him as church planter and pastor. He had been on a sign painting and repair trip for five days. A trip like this always meant something special for his two boys!

As Dad climbed out of his van, he had a special twinkle in his eyes. "Wait till you see what I've got for you," he said as he walked to the back and opened the doors of the van. Much to our amazement and shock, there stood a thirty-eight-inch-high full-grown miniature horse!

Prince was born and raised at the bottom of the Grand Canyon. His most recent home was an Arizona trading post in the Navajo Indian reservation. The owners decided to sell their miniature horse due to the high cost of feeding him. Dad showed up at the right time.

Prince was an unusual horse. While exceptionally small, he had a history. The little black and white fellow had been professionally trained to do tricks. He had been in at least two Hollywood western movies. Prince acted as though he was something special. His neigh from inside the van seemed to proclaim proudly, "Your star has arrived!"

The little rascal was untied and bounded out of the van like a spirited toy poodle. Surrounded by Colorado sunshine and fresh green grass, Prince was in horse heaven!

Soon after Prince arrived, I learned that pony races would be included in the upcoming horse show. The winner would take home a shiny pair of genuine leather cowboy boots. I decided I would enter that race and win the prize.

As Prince and I prepared together, I found that his thirty-eight-inch height did not limit his drive and speed. How he loved to run!

Finally, the day of the big race arrived at the county fairgrounds. Because the facility was seldom used, much of the property was in disrepair. The one profitable venture on the property was the huge alfalfa field inside the big oval track. The proceeds from the sale of hay to ranchers kept the facility from total financial collapse.

After some other events, the loudspeaker announced, "It is time for the big event of the day! Would the ponies and their owners prepare for the next race!" Prince and I took off for the starting gate. I was confident I would win this race. After all, I was racing against Shetland Ponies and I was riding a pedigree miniature horse!

As I arrived at the starting gate, I looked up and realized for the first time that there were over 2,000 people in the stands, watching. Then I realized that there were two other ponies running the race.

We lined up. Only minutes separated me from that shiny new pair of genuine leather boots. The starter gun fired, and the spectators leaped to their feet and cheered as the steeds bolted from the gate . . .

Remember that big alfalfa field? Little clumps of alfalfa also grew along the edges of the race track—and that alfalfa immediately caught Prince's eye. No longer was he interested in racing—he was interested in eating! Like a boy with a cookie jar, he was letting his greed get the best of him.

Prince was oblivious to the other circumstances around him—including me on his back, tugging at his reins, kicking his sides, and swatting his rump. I had lost control; Prince was giving in to the lure of alfalfa—and in front of 2,000 spectators!

Prince lost focus on the goal. He ran from clump to clump down the track as the laughing crowd cheered us on. What seemed to me like an eternity later,

Prince crossed the finish line, content with the green alfalfa salad he had just enjoyed to my disgrace. The two of us took third place that day.

What went wrong that day? Simply this: circumstances did not permit me to fulfill my plan. I was full of good intentions; I had practiced with Prince for days; I knew he had the ability to win, and I wanted those cowboy boots. But I soon discovered that good intentions and sincerity—or even ability—do not guarantee the results we expect. Prince was distracted and I had lost control.

Nevertheless, I believe there is a reason that things don't always turn out as we plan: our plans are often not **God's** plans for us. But when we understand more about His plan and realize that He always has our best interests at heart, we can respond better to unexpected circumstances.

Let unpack this by defining three words. These words are often used interchangeably, but I believe it is important to understand the subtle differences in meaning. The three words are **needs, wants,** and **desires.**

NEEDS!

A **need** is a lack of something required by life. A **need** is an essential item that must be obtained in order to survive. Food, clothing, and shelter fall within this definition. And **needs** may differ, depending on one's circumstances.

WANTS!

A **want** is a craving for something that often makes us focus our total attention on that object. A **want** has become extreme when obsession and impulsiveness have taken control over wisdom, understanding, and waiting for God's timing.

NEEDS AND WANTS!

If your friend announces, "I **want** a pizza for lunch," you understand that pizza is a preference for a type of food. Nourishment is the **need;** pizza is a **want.** Lunch could just as well be a glass of milk and a whole wheat sandwich.

God has promised to supply our **needs.** He has not promised to supply all our **wants.** As a loving Father, however, He often makes provision for our **wants,** too. I've thought about the subtle difference between these two words, and I've concluded that a **need** is based on God's promised provision, while a **want** is based more on one's own self-centeredness.

Early one Saturday morning, there was a knock on our front door. As I responded, I found an energetic young lady on our porch. Before I was able to say, "Good morning," she started in:

> "Hi, I'm Jennifer. I **want** to win $1,000, and I **want** your help. I **want** to go to Bermuda on a five-day cruise, but to get to that 'love boat,' I **need** 20,000 points. I've already got 19,000. I am lacking 1,000 points to make it. I **want** you to buy one of these magazines from me. You buy this one. It's worth 1,000 points. You can get what you **want** and I will get what I **want**."

I began to explain that I was not interested in a magazine subscription. Before I even completed my sentence, she turned and headed for my next-door neighbors without even saying thanks or goodbye. When she learned I was not planning to help meet her **wants,** I was no longer of value to her. Her obsession was turning an attractive woman into an offensive snoot.

Aren't we all faced daily with the various enticements of life that can turn us toward total self-centeredness? Are you allowing your **wants** to dictate your attitudes on life, or are you recognizing them and turning them over to your heavenly Father to supply in His timing as He sees fit?

DESIRES!

Now we come to the word **desire.** A desire is a deeply rooted longing in the heart for something. Typically, a **desire** is something that you cannot easily free your mind from thinking about.

I believe that God plants **desires** in His children's hearts. Many times He may give you a specific **desire**—with the expectation that you will take the actions necessary to see that **desire** become a reality.

Sometimes a **desire** can be something of significant spiritual value. God may have planted the **desire** for a loved one to find Jesus Christ as his Savior. This **desire** of your heart may cause you to pray, to share the **desire** with others, to share your testimony with the person, or to invite the person to church or other settings to hear the Gospel. Although you may stimulate others to pray, you carry the primary **desire** (or burden) for the person's salvation.

Not all **desires** need to be of a highly spiritual nature. Even so, the **desires** that God plants always will bring glory and praise to Him when fulfilled.

Helma Weber was available for a God-planted **desire** when she heard of the **need** for a bell in the little church's steeple. I believe God chose Mrs. Weber to be the one who would carry that **desire** in her heart until it became a reality. Because she responded to the **desire,** many thousands of people across America became involved.

God's message of love and forgiveness ultimately went forth across the nation via radio, newspapers, and magazines. God knew Mrs. Weber was capable of giving Him the glory. She was simply an instrument that He chose to use to bring attention to His Kingdom business! Many thousands heard that God loves them, and they could know him through this national campaign for a church bell. The Heart of America Bell still hangs in a giant cross outside of Living Hope Church in Grand Junction, Colorado today. It is still a testimony of a **desire** that grew to maturity and ultimate reality.

THE UNTOLD STORY!

There is another part to the Heart of America Bell story that is never told. I was in attendance as a three-year-old on that cold and snowy Thanksgiving in 1947. My Dad was the pastor of this new and growing church plant.

The night before the dedication of the bell, the "Heart's Desire" radio team presented my father with a giant gold-edged, pulpit Bible; the best money could buy. Uncle Ben asked Dad to select a Scripture verse from the enormous Bible that could be read over the radio just prior to the dedication and ringing of America's bell.

My father is not known as a "random access" verse finder; but not knowing for sure what to read, he stood the giant Bible on its spine and gently let the book fall open. He then pointed randomly to a spot on the open page before him and read aloud to the radio team:

> "Thou hast given him his heart's desire, And Thou has not withheld the request of his lips" (Psalm 21:2, KJV).

No one spoke. Each was momentarily stunned by what he had heard from God's timeless Word. It seemed that God had personally selected the same verse that He gave to his servant, King David, over 3,000 years earlier.

The silence was broken as a member of the radio team said, "If you read that verse on the air as the first verse ever read from this Bible, our listening audience will think we rigged the Bible. You must pick something else to read." My father chose an alternative verse: John 3:16. However, he and the radio team knew that God had kept His promise to the little new church that day.

In our materialistic society, so crammed full of self-gratification, it is often easy to forget that God's Word is packed full of promises and instructions that point us to God's desires for us. Even when we find a promise, too many of us snatch it up as a "good-luck charm," but never take time in prayer to see that promise become the fulfilled desire of our heart. I don't know if Helma Weber claimed the promise of Psalm 21:2. As a godly woman, she may well have—with her letter to Uncle Ben as the first step in claiming that promise.

Test this promise that David recorded in Psalm 37:4: "Delight yourself in the Lord, And He will give you the desires of your heart."

If you understand what God's Word says and claim His promises through demonstrated action and faithful prayer, God will do as He says. Because you are important to your heavenly Father, His desire is to fulfill those desires that He has planted in your heart.

Your responsibility is to **delight** yourself in the Lord—to focus with a joyful expectation on Him. His provision is more than adequate to meet your every need and to flavor your day-to-day experience with the seasoning of His love and peace. You need no longer be confused about needs, wants, and desires. You can relax and respond to His direction and provision.

Many of us have a tendency to sail through life by impulse. All too often, we live only for the moment. Like my horse, Prince, we run from one clump of grass to the next, satiating our immediate wants with no thought of the finish line. When we do so, there is no genuine sense of accomplishment.

This inclination to act without conscious thought is a by-product of our sinful nature; and if allowed to control our lives, it produces an **imbalance, selfishness, greed,** and **fear.** Let's look at each of these traits.

IMBALANCE!

God did not design the world to experience a shortage of anything. His creation was designed to provide all needs of all living things. What He created was sustainable and perfect. Yet today, we see a great disparity between rich and poor, between abundance and dire need. Something is terribly wrong.

The great plains of the United States have been blessed with abundant harvests of amber waves of grain for many years. Yet our abundance has created warehousing problems to the extent that the government now pays farmers

NOT to produce some crops because of oversupply. We don't know what to do with our plenty.

However, while we warehouse food, much of the world is close to starvation today!

We live with an abundance of food—plenty of hamburgers and fresh fruits and vegetables, usually with enough left over at the end of our meal to feed the family dog. Yet in Africa, food shortages threaten over 150 million lives. Prolonged drought has produced an environment where men, women, and children are starving to death. Entire villages have been abandoned as their residents forage the countryside for food.

There's no getting around it, there is a tremendous imbalance in our world today.

SELFISHNESS!

There is within each of us a selfish nature that holds onto things that have little real value to us. We act like the old dog in a manger of hay—he couldn't eat the stuff, but he wasn't about to let any animal that **could** even get close to it.

Just think what would happen to the needs of the poor, or to the proclamation of the Gospel, if we were not so selfish! Selfishness keeps us from reaching out to meet the needs that exist around us. Are we so concerned for our own welfare that we deliberately turn our backs on the needs and concerns of others?

GREED!

Greed also keeps us from reaching out to others. Greed prevents us from ever being fully satisfied. Haven't we all been through a Thanksgiving or Christmas when the entire family got together for a sumptuous feast? An abundance of food was spread before us, piping hot and tantalizing. The longer we sat around the table and visited, the more we continued to eat—and eat and eat! If you're like me, you probably ate three times more than you should have. When we are greedily focusing on our own stomachs, it's pretty hard to think of others.

Greed keeps us fighting for "our rights." When my daughters were in elementary school I recall a new doll arrived on the scene—the Cabbage Patch Kid! National news reports featured adults physically **fighting** in the stores to claim possession of that ugly coveted doll.

One woman was rushed to the hospital after she was thrown to the floor and trampled by a mob of other adults who greedily bolted to the Cabbage

Patch Doll display as soon as the store opened for business. I wonder how the little girls who received those dolls will one day look back on their parents' appalling behavior.

FEAR!

Today we live in a world fraught with fear, strife, and confusion. We're reaping the results of life characterized by man doing his own thing. One of the fastest-growing businesses today is the security business. The rise in crime and lawlessness today creates great anxiety in our hearts. We now go to great expenses to buy a degree of peace and security. Many cannot sleep at night because of the anxiety that fear has created.

During a nationwide media initiative called the "I found it" campaign some years ago, I assigned one of my associates to help raise needed funds in one of the largest historical cities in the eastern U.S. He identified a number of influential families who had exceptional financial influence and made appointments to ask for their participation in this city-wide initiative as financial sponsors.

One of his appointments was with an elderly man. On the day of their meeting, my friend and his partner drove to a very exclusive part of the city and pulled into the circular driveway of a beautiful three-story brownstone house. They soon learned, however, that the house was not the man's home but only his offices and security headquarters. They were instructed to drive around behind the brownstone and through guarded electronic gates.

Soon they climbed to the top of the hill to an enormous mansion overlooking the lush green hills and valleys below. At the door, they were met again by armed security guards and servants. They were ushered into the front marble hall, where alabaster walls were decorated with original Rembrandt paintings.

They visited with the elderly man in his private library. This gentleman was the heir of one of our nation's most popular food companies, and his affluence spoke out boldly from his secured surroundings. He now lived alone—the last of the "old guard."

As two men explained the purpose and strategy and the old gentleman was intrigued by the plan but refused to become involved. He told them that he no longer participated in any city affairs; in fact, he had not even left his residence to go into the city in over two years. He shared that he was afraid that someone would try to kill him.

Imagine living the life of a multi-million-dollar recluse. Afraid of the world. Afraid of living. Afraid of losing his life and his possessions. He lived in continual defeat and fear—a result of imbalance, selfishness, and greed! All the material riches he possessed could not buy him inner freedom and personal peace.

WHERE ARE YOU?

Are you one who has a clear focus on the finish line of your life, or are you currently wandering from one clump of grass to the next, hoping to get by somehow?

Before you can understand and fulfill God's purpose for your life, you must be sure of your personal relationship with your Creator. It's possible to put on a religious act and even be a really nice person; but you know, and your heavenly Father knows, what's really going on inside.

If you know that inside, you are actually in bondage to sin (falling short of God's standard), why not settle that issue right now? Admit to God that you have been living in rebellion against Him, intent on doing things **your** way. Ask Him to forgive your sins and thank Him that He sent His own Son, Jesus Christ, to pay the required penalty for your sins—your shortcomings. Then, as an act of your will, express that you want to trust in Jesus Christ as your Savior and Lord.

He is waiting for you to make that decision. And the moment you do, His Holy Spirit will come into your life, cleanse you from your sin, and give you the assurance that you are now God's child for all eternity!

The decision to become a part of God's family is the most important decision you will ever make. If you have not already made that decision, make it now!

Remember: *Wandering from clump to clump with no purpose is not necessary!*

Key To Abundant Living

UNLOCKING YOUR LIFE OF CONTENTMENT

Here is your next assignment: *Write down everything that God brings to your mind that has limited His ability to work his life through you. This is called sin. This will enable you to see more clearly what has separated you from His plan for you. This will prepare you for what he planned for you.*

When you have completed your listing write the following across the page: **"If I confess my sin he is faithful and just to forgive me of my sin and to cleanse me from all wrong)" (1 John 1:9)**

This is His promise to you. Claim it! At the bottom of the page sign and date this. This will help provide you a point of reference for what you are about to experience.

My Agreement with You

Father in Heaven:

As I examine my life I recognize that I have been preoccupied with what is in life for me. I have been focusing on what I want rather than what you know is best for me. I confess to you the following sins (my short-comings). Forgive me. I invite you into my life and begin to help me see what you have planned for me.

Chapter 4

UNLIMITED RESOURCES

You will be enriched in every way to be generous in every way, which through us will produce thanksgiving to God.

—2 CORINTHIANS 9:11 (ESV)

In 1867 a couple and their two-year-old son went camping. They chose a spot with a magnificent view of the Pacific Ocean a thousand feet below. Their campsite was just one of many hills on the father's Piedra Blanca Ranch. It covered over 270,000 acres and stretched along some fifty miles of the California coastline.

To provide some of the comforts of home, the boy's mother made sure that Persian rugs were placed on the tent floor and that appropriate antique furniture was included. Meals were always served on china with appropriate silver and crystal. Camping to this family was far cry from the adventure of "roughing it" most of us experience on camping trips today.

The boy's father had traveled to California in the mid-1800s to seek his fortune. In his search, he found something of value—the famous Comstock Silver Lode outside of Reno, Nevada! Overnight he turned his rags into riches. His son—William Randolph Hearst—was born with a "silver spoon" in his mouth.

William developed a special love for the outdoors and especially for Camp Hill, the isolated site of the family's unusual camping experiences on the Pacific coast of central California. He often returned to his favorite hill for solitude and reflection.

In 1919, he decided that he wanted something more permanent on Camp Hill so that his friends could enjoy what he so often had enjoyed as a boy. He named the hill La Cuesta Encantada—the Enchanted Hill—and set out to turn a dream into reality. At age fifty he began building his home on his hill to serve as a place of retreat and refreshment, and to house his massive art and history collections.

The first buildings to be constructed were three "small bungalows" for guests—one overlooking the ocean, with fourteen rooms; another overlooking the mountains, with ten rooms; and a third facing the setting sun, with eighteen rooms.

The main house came next, La Casa Grande. It grew to castle-like proportions, containing 100 rooms, including thirty-eight bedrooms, thirty-one bathrooms, fourteen sitting rooms, a kitchen, a movie theater, two libraries, a game room, a dining hall, and a massive assembly hall.

La Casa Grande was built for the furniture it was to house. The height of the ceilings and dimensions of the rooms were built around furniture, fireplaces, and ceilings—all collections William had found on his travels and dating back hundreds of years. He was addicted to collecting priceless objects. Many of the walls were home for priceless Persian tapestries and rugs or beautifully carved paneling from castles or monasteries of another century.

The Enchanted Hill became a sprawling complex and a pleasure palace for many of the world's rich and famous. Most of the "who's who" of the world eventually had to make a pilgrimage to La Casa Grande. Recreation was in abundance. There was the 345,000-gallon, outdoor Neptune Pool. It was heated year-round for swimming pleasure and watched over by white marble statues. There were miles of horseback-riding trails, protected by more than a mile of vine-covered pergola so that riders would not have to be exposed to the hot summer sun as they enjoyed the breathtaking panoramic view. Two tennis courts topped the roof of the heated indoor Roman swimming pool, which was lined with blue Venetian glass and twenty-two-carat gold tiles.

The Enchanted Hill also housed the world's largest private zoo. On the hills around La Casa Grande roamed sixty species of grazing stock, selected from around the world.

An invitation to the ranch was a ticket to "Never Never Land." Twenty-five servants were always available to meet each guest's every need. Guests knew an invitation meant they were now someone of importance in society. No invitation to The Enchanted Hill clearly signaled the person was a nobody.

Over 200 telephones were installed, but hidden away, on the rocks, in trees, camouflaged in stumps. No matter where one was on the grounds, a phone to the world was only a short distance away.

Delicious chef-prepared meals were offered to guests daily, and, between meals, refreshments and snacks were available on the many terraces.

In the 831-foot-long assembly room, guests could relax, dance, or play ping-pong under a 400-year-old ceiling. New swimming suits were available for the athletic guests, and once used, could be taken home as souvenirs. Lush fur coats were available for the cool evenings, but these remained at La Casa Grande when the guest left for home.

When one of the twentieth century's most important businessmen and newspaper tycoons died in 1951 at the age of 81, what did Randolph Hearst leave behind? Yes, he left it all. He was worth an estimated $360 million at his death, despite the fact that in the early 1930s, he was almost bankrupt and had to borrow money from friends to survive. An aggressive businessman that was known to be selfish and ruthless, he left behind ninety-four enterprises and a 125-page will with specific instructions as to how to disperse his personal estate of $200 million when he died in 1951—equal to $2.2 billion in today's dollars.[3]

Today San Simeon, California—Hearst Castle—is visited by over 750,000 people a year. La Cuesta Encantada is a costly reminder of a man who seemed to have it all—and in abundance!

But did he? Was William Randolph Hearst wealthy? No doubt about it, he was a *rich* man. To finance the purchase of thousands of treasures and the building of his ostentatious San Simeon took more than spare change! He was able to *buy* whatever he wanted. Money to him was not a concern.

But was he prosperous?

The world saw his wealth. What did Hearst see? For years Hearst and his wife lived two very separate lives—she on the East Coast and he on the West. Separation also meant he had limited time with his five sons. Poor health, selfishness, addiction to work, and less-than-happy family are not marks of prosperity. Prosperity is a condition of life, not a balance sheet. Prosperity is defined as having all of one's needs met and the freedom to *enjoy* that condition in abundance. Prosperity cannot be totaled on a calculator.

From God's point of view, I believe Mr. Hearst was a man of definitely limited resources. He may have appeared content and successful on the outside but was in pain, emptiness, and turmoil on the inside.

God our Father is the genuinely wealthy one. He has an unlimited supply of resources. He has an abundance of everything. He chooses to entrust His wealth to His children. This is His plan! As we learned in the previous chapter, we have a fiduciary responsibility to manage His wealth in a way that will bring glory and honor to Him. God expects His abundance to be managed well by His stewards. He expected his wealth to be in constant circulation.

During an Easter vacation when our, girls were in grade school, Pat and I took our two daughters to tour San Simeon. The experience was surreal and almost overwhelming. Talk about sensory overload! As we departed from the Enchanted Hill under the brilliant glow of the setting sun over the Pacific, I thought, *A man once lived here who had gained the whole world—power, influence, prestige, fame, riches. But was he all he could have been? Was he a wise steward for the King of kings?* That's something to think about . . .

WISE AND WEALTHY

Many years ago a wise and wealthy steward acted on with a God-given desire. He envisioned the construction of a temple that would be a physical reminder of God's presence with His people. Although he never saw the temple built, King David envisioned the idea, prepared the blueprints, raised the funds, and then gave extensive instructions to another wise and wealthy steward—his son, Solomon—to build what God had led David to design.

The task before Solomon was enormous! As a steward, he was responsible for building the temple of God. David instructed Solomon:

> "Be strong and courageous and do the work. Don't be afraid or discouraged, for the Lord God, my God, is with you; He will not fail you or forsake you. He will see to it that all the work related to the Temple of the Lord is finished correctly" (1 Chronicles 28:20).

The temple David planned for God would make San Simeon look like low-class government housing. David said this about his involvement:

> "Using every resource at my command, I have gathered as much as I could for building the Temple of my God ... I am giving all of my own private treasures of gold and silver to help in the construction. This is in addition to the building materi-

> als I have already collected for his holy Temple. I am donating more than 112 tons of gold from Ophir and 262 tons of refined silver to be used for overlaying the walls of the buildings and for the other gold and silver work to be done by the craftsmen. Now then, who will follow my example and give offerings to the Lord today?" (1 Chronicles 29:2–5).

Talk about a pace-setting gift to kick-start a funding campaign! David's example of wealth distribution stimulated more giving! The leaders of Israel took the obedient steward's challenge and followed his example seriously. Look at 1 Chronicles 29: 6–8 in your favorite translation. You will see what they give in response to David's challenge to them.

Talk about generosity! David's wise distribution of the wealth God had entrusted him to manage stimulated a multiplied harvest of obedient stewardship. This led to the people excited about giving. God's Word records: "The people rejoiced over the offerings, for they had given freely and wholeheartedly to the Lord, and King David was filled with joy" (1 Chronicles 29:9).

David by no means lived a perfect life. His shortcomings are in print! His adulterous affair with Bathsheba and the murder of her husband, Uriah, were serious crimes. But even though David's life was scarred by sin, his heart longed to be obedient to God. Notice what he prayed after the prophet Nathan proclaimed God's judgment on David for these sins:

> "Have mercy on me, O God, because of your unfailing love, Because of your great compassion, blot out the stain of my sins. Wash me clean from my guilt. Purify me from my sin. For I recognize my rebellion; it haunts me day and night. Against you, and you alone have I sinned; I have done what is evil in your sight" (Psalm 51:1–6).

Yes, he sinned tragically, but he was able to admit wrong. His life focus was on his God. There is no record of David worshipping other gods. His heart was desirous of serving God and obeying His principles. He was a man after God's own heart. Take a look at 1 Samuel 13:14 and Acts 13:22.

GOD'S DESIRE FOR YOU

God desires your life to be prosperous. He desires you to be faithful to him. He longs to see you trusting His sufficiency to meet all you needs. Remember, being prosperous from God's view includes far more than having a lot of money. His plan for you includes having all of your needs met, the freedom to enjoy where He has placed you, and contentment in your current condition, so that you can freely give what is not yours to serve the needs of others.

He wants you to live your life in reliance upon His unlimited supply of resources. Are you living this way now?

As I study God's Word, I see five basic principles which govern God's wealth distribution to His children. As a Christian, you have the privilege of writing checks from God's prosperity account. However, to use this privilege, you need to understand and choose to live by the principles of His distribution network.

GOD'S FIVE PRINCIPLES OF WEALTH DISTRIBUTION

1. GOD, OUR FATHER, OWNS AN INFINITE SUPPLY OF EVERYTHING THAT WE, OR ANYONE ELSE, COULD EVER NEED, WANT, OR DESIRE.
2. GOD HAS A HILARIOUS TIME CIRCULATING HIS WEALTH AND RESOURCES AND WANTS HIS CHILDREN TO SHARE IN THIS PLEASURE.
3. IT PLEASES GOD WHEN HIS CHILDREN ASK FOR, THEN DILIGENTLY SEEK, SOME OF THEIR INHERITANCE SO THEY CAN GIVE IT TO OTHERS.
4. IF I SOW ACCORDING TO GOD'S PRINCIPLES, I WILL REAP, AND I WILL ALWAYS HAVE AN ABUNDANCE TO HELP OTHERS AS WELL AS TO MEET MY OWN NEEDS.
5. MY GIVING CAN BEGIN TO REFLECT THE RESOURCES OF MY HEAVENLY FATHER'S HOUSEHOLD, NOT MERELY MY LIMITED EARTHLY RESOURCES.

The steward who is making daily application of these five principles will live life of prosperity that exceeds circumstances. Rather than focusing on getting, one can focus on giving. Choosing to live according to these principles is the key to abundant freedom.

Because each principle is so important, we are going to take a careful look at each principle individually. As we unpack each principle ask yourself, "How can I, as a steward, apply this principle to my life right now?"

As you study, claim Joshua 1:8: "This book of the law shall not depart from your mouth, but you shall meditate on it day and night, so that you may be careful to do according to all that is written in it; for then you will make your way *prosperous*, and then you will have *success*."

Remember those days in grade school when your teacher put a big gold, red, green, or silver star or some other happy face emoji sticker on your paper as a reward for your excellent work? As you apply these five principles, your life can become a "star" that radiates hope to a dark world. Your life as an intentional steward will become a model to others.

You will note that in our discussion of these principal statements, each one is illustrated by a five-pointed star. Each point corresponds to one principle and an abbreviated version of the appropriate principle is added to the star each time it appears. As you learn and follow God's five principles of wealth distribution, you will tap His inventory and be able to live a prosperous life that is characterized by success as one of His stewards.

PRINCIPLE 1

GOD, OUR FATHER, OWNS AN INFINITE SUPPLY OF EVERYTHING THAT WE, OR ANYONE ELSE, COULD EVER NEED, WANT, OR DESIRE.

This statement could make an excellent sermon theme. What does this mean to you? I have turned this power-packed, formal theological statement into a short, personal sentence by writing next to one of the five points of the start below: **My Father owns it all!**

My Father owns it all.

Think about it—*God is the owner.* God never has and never will give up His rights of ownership on anything!. King David understood this and declared God's ownership when he proclaimed, " The earth is the Lord's, and everything in it. The world and all its people belong to him" (Psalm 24:1).

Remember all that was given to build the temple, as recorded in 1 Chronicles 29? David and the leadership of Israel were not surprising God by bringing Him their hidden possessions. None of what they gave was new to God. All was His in the first place. They were returning to Him what was already His. As stewards, they were presenting to the owner well-managed investments.

When the initial temple offering was collected, David exclaimed to God, "Yours, O Lord, is the greatness, the power, the glory, the victory, and the majesty. Everything in the heavens and on earth is yours, O Lord, and this is your kingdom. We adore you as the one who is over all things. Wealth and honor come from you alone, for you rule over everything" (1 Chronicles 29:11).

Doesn't that stretch your imagination? It sure does mine! Our world system has subtly introduced us to the "mine and yours" way of thinking about everything. This kind of thinking is a ploy from Satan to delude our subconscious mind. As wise stewards, we must reprogram the way we think about things. *Everything belongs to our heavenly Father.*

Take a moment right now and look around you. What do you see from where you are reading this book? Who owns all that your eyes can see?

According to the laws of the state of California, I own a home, an SUV, a vacation timeshare, and an A-frame camping trailer. I am responsible for caring for and managing these items legally, but are they mine? No. My home, my vehicles, my clothes, the furniture in my house, and the money in my bank account are **not** mine. My Father owns it all. I am simply a steward to whom God has delegated the authority to manage these possessions on His behalf.

EVERYTHING

The apostle Paul summed up God's authority and ownership when he wrote to the Romans, "For everything comes from him and exists by his power and is intended for his glory. All glory to him forever! Amen" (Romans 11:36).

God's supply is unlimited. There is absolutely no way to take anything from Him, for it's all forever in His inventory. If every one of the eight billion people on earth today had all of everything they could possibly manage, we would not begin to make a dent in God's unlimited supply. What mankind needs is already here on earth.

God also has the ability and authority to gather His possessions whenever He chooses. This decision rests totally in His power. In God's amazing plan, He has chosen to delegate distribution authority to His Son. In turn, His Son willfully chooses to delegate His authority to those who are called children of God. Very simply put, *it is God to people and people to people.*

Amazing, isn't it? God's plan has always been to entrust His possessions to be managed by us. Nothing belongs to us but we get to use all that He entrusts to us. He never planned for us to be failures in managing His possessions. He expected wise stewardship from Adam and Even. He continues to expect wise management from us that will have multiplied impact.

I'll never forget the day I obtained my driver's license the day I turned sixteen. To demonstrate trust in me, my father and mother *chose* to allow me to have use of an old 1953, navy blue, four-door Chrysler sedan. I had wheels! I could go anywhere I wanted to go and do what I wanted to do. My folks delegate the authority to me, making me responsible for the car's upkeep and for the gas that I used. I thought of that car as "my" car.

Yet I was not the owner. The title belonged to my parents. They could take possession of my wheels whenever they wished to do so. They continued to maintain ultimate authority over my car. As their son, I had a sense of ownership because I was entrusted to be the steward of this car.

How do you and I, as believers, fit into God's plan of ownership? Remember what Jesus said just before He ascended into heaven? You can find His words to his twelve stewards-in-training in Matthew 28:18–20:

> "Jesus came and told his disciples, "I have been given all authority in heaven and on earth. Therefore, go and make disciples in all the nations, baptizing them into the name of the Father and the Son and of the Holy Spirit. Teach these new disciples to obey all the commands I have given you; and be sure of this: that I am with you always, even to the end of the age."

Jesus has been given *all* authority from God the Father. He chose to delegate that authority to His disciples—to you and me! He took this action with a specific purpose in mind: so that we would carry out our job description of making more disciples through intentional stewardship. We are to take what He's given to us and use it for His purposes. We are expediters, assigned to carry out His plan. *Everything* we have been given is to be used to this end.

MORE THAN JUST ENOUGH.

God never intended you or any other steward to have just enough to get by. He intends for you to live a life of abundance. The wealth God transfers to His kids to be distributed here on earth is but a minute part of the total wealth in His possession. God is not limited in His ability to supply abundantly.

Paul refers to God's ability to supply in Philippians 4:19 (NASB) when he writes, "And my God shall supply all your needs according to His riches in glory in Christ Jesus."

Note two things: First, this is a guarantee—*He shall.* Second, God supplies *according to* His riches, not *out of* His riches. Do you understand the importance of this for us as stewards? The supply itself is an unlimited inventory. As we use what He's given to us, He has the resources to give us much more without ever diminishing His total supply!

ONLY PART OF THE STORY

Paul further explains God's provision to the Corinthians in this way: "And God is able to make all grace abound to you, that always having all sufficiency in everything, you may have an abundance for every good deed" (2 Corinthians 9:8, NASB). God plans for you to have an abundance so you can carry out every good deed.

Although God has infinite resources, He doesn't want any waste. He, therefore, chooses to supply according to how His children demonstrate faithfulness in carrying out their job description through meeting the needs of others. The trustworthy steward has sufficiency in everything—yes, everything.

We have trouble at times relating to how much is available to us. We often think of wealth in terms of supply and demand. Thus, we put greater value on items that appear to be limited in quantity rather than on those that are in great abundance. Often the perceived value is set by our culture and our circumstances.

There is an abundance of dirt on this earth. In fact, most of us try to get rid of it because we have far more around us than we need. Yet dirt becomes of great value if you have a limited supply. I am told that people moving to some South Sea coral reefs often take dirt as a part of their prized possessions so that they can enjoy living plants that only good dirt produces.

I'm afraid we often have in our possession things that are of great value to God, but due to our immaturity or lack of perspective, we fail to recognize what God has entrusted to us.

FOOLED

Remember Esau and Jacob, the twin sons of Isaac and Rebekah?

Esau was minutes older than his brother. He had a beautiful bronze tan and a toned body that would make any weightlifter jealous. He loved the outdoors and was a skillful hunter. Today he would no doubt serve as president of the National Wildlife Federation or be a male model in a fashion magazine. He had confidence in himself—maybe more than he deserved. He knew how to please his father. He never failed to bring in the best from his hunting adventures. As the firstborn, he had a definite advantage over his twin brother: He held the right to a precious inheritance that his brother, Jacob, could not have.

Jacob, on the other hand, was Mr. Average. He was not a hunter and didn't seem to care too much for the outdoors. He loved to manage things around the home, and he loved to cook. But he was also very conniving!

Can you imagine the evening Esau returned home, exhausted and famished after a day or two of hunting? When you're tired and hungry, even stew looks like a feast. Lets listen in on a conversation they had:

"Man, what a day! Jacob, I'm exhausted. The heat is killing me, and my feet hurt. What's for dinner? Boy, am I starved! What's the red stuff there? Give me a bite."

"So you're hungry, huh, Esau? I'll make you a deal. I'll trade you a bowl of this delicious homemade stew, cornbread, and honey for your birthright. How about it, brother?"

"Look, Jacob, when a guy is about to starve to death, what good is a birthright?"

"Is it a deal, then? If it is, make your vow to God that what is yours is now mine."

"OK, Jacob, you've got a deal. I vow to God my birthright is yours in exchange for a square meal tonight. Now hurry up and get the food on the table."

Without thinking about the implications, Esau had made an unwise, foolish, and immature stewardship decision. Yes, at that moment, the decision seemed reasonable. Esau never once considered the consequences of this rash decision. He got an all-you-can-eat dinner and a drink along with it. He then went about his business, as usual, never giving a thought as to what he had done. But decisions always have consequences. It was not until many years later that he realized he had foolishly squandered the fiduciary responsibility that came with his position as the eldest son.

Are you guilty of making decisions without much thought of the implications? Many stewards today are living with the consequences of emotional spur-of-the-moment decisions. Yes, decisions ALWAYS have consequences!

YOUU NAME IT—HE'S GOT IT

Your heavenly Father, the great Jehovah, has an infinite supply of all you need, want, or desire. He is capable and willing to give to you. He is waiting for you to make a withdraw from His account. You need not fear that you will overdraw. The check will not bounce. The supply is far greater than your demand. He is capable of redeeming even bad decisions if He sees you are ready for redemption.

Are you aware that God's names mentioned in the Old Testament reflect His ability to supply?

> Jehovah Nissi: I am your banner.
> Jehovah Shalom: I am your peace.
> Jehovah Tsidkenu: I am your righteousness.
> Jehovah Jireh: I am the one who provides.
> Jehovah Rapha: I am the one who heals.
> Jehovah Raah: I am your shepherd.
> Jehovah Shammah: I am the one who is present.

Have you been living unwittingly on the corner of Poverty Street and Uncertainty Circle? Have you thought that your requests might overtax God's supply? Have you been living as if you owned it all, and you feel you don't have enough?

Why not decide now that you will begin to tap His infinite resources and start writing faith checks on His account? Rather than watching the parade of faithful stewards march by, you can join in and be in the parade.

God's wealth and riches are available upon request. All He is expecting from you is that you ask and then be obedient and faithful to distribute what He provides to you. He is ready to supply if you are ready to respond. If you are serious about being what He designed you to be? He is ready. The first step is to begin redistributing what He has given to you. He cannot give you more until you distribute what He's already provided to you. It's up to you. God to you; you to others.

A popular praise song by songwriter David Ingles sums up this first principle. The song is called "He's More Than Enough." Go take a listen and be blessed with this reminder.

Remember: *Your Father owns it all!*

Key To Abundant Living

UNLOCKING YOUR LIFE OF CONTENTMENT

My Father owns it all! Sometimes it's easy to forget this important truth. To help you focus on God's ownership, spend a few minutes listing everything you can think of that you view as being yours. Be specific. List both tangible and intangible items. Can you list 25 to 30 things in less than two minutes? When you have created your list review the following covenant:

MY TRANSFER OF OWNERSHIP COVENANT

To: My Father, who owns it all

From: ______________________________(your name)

Date: ______________________________(today's date)

Father, I recognize that You are the owner of EVERYTHING. All I have belongs to You. Nothing is mine. As an act of faith and obedience, I choose to assign everything I have in my possession back to You. Thank you for reminding me that you owe it all!

____

Signature

"For everything comes from God alone. Everything lives by his power, and everything is for his glory. To Him be glory evermore" (Romans 11:36, TLB).

Chapter 5
JOYFUL ABANDON

Remember this—a farmer who plants only a few seeds will get a small crop. But the one who plants generously will get a generous crop. You must each decide in your heart how much to give. And don't give reluctantly or in response to pressure. For God loves a person who gives cheerfully.

—2 CORINTHIANS 9: 6–7

I had made up my mind to fall into the fad and fashion of the day in men's hairstyling. After seeing numerous ads and a number of my friends sporting the new look, I knew I had to have a perm! I called a hairdresser friend of ours. A few days later, I left her beauty shop with the new curly style that was the rage in the '80s.

This new casual style was easy to manage. Even my friends said, "It looks so natural on you, Larry." Little did they know that this "new look" was very similar to the photos taken of me at the 1947 Heart of America Bell dedication when I was blond and had curly hair as three years old!

About a month later, an associate and I made a business trip to the Midwest. On our return to California, we were to change planes in Denver, close to where my mother lived. I called her and suggested that she drive out to the airport for a visit during my two-hour layover—this was back in the days before intense airport security.

As I stepped into the Denver terminal from the jetway, I saw mom, her face aglow with her famous big smile. But the minute she saw me, her mouth dropped open in shock and disbelief.

Her surprised reaction made me laugh. I had failed to tell her of my hair transformation. In an instant, I knew we were in real trouble. Surrounded by hundreds of travelers in one of the most congested airports in the world, we quickly lost control of ourselves in peals of laughter.

My associate saw what was happening and decided to lose himself in the crowd to avoid being identified with this odd couple. Mom and I laughed until we cried. We could not even speak. Passengers walking by assuredly thought us mentally off balance.

Every time Mom thought she had regained her composure, she would look at me and burst into hilarious laughter again.

You may chuckle at this incident, but no doubt you can think of a time when you were caught up in hilarity—a time you seemed to lose control of yourself in laughter because of unexpected humorous circumstances.

PRINCIPLE 2

Have you ever thought of God caught up in hilarity? Principle #2 states:

GOD HAS A HILARIOUS TIME CIRCULATING HIS WEALTH AND RESOURCES AND WANTS HIS CHILDREN TO SHARE IN THIS PLEASURE.

I have simplified this principle by writing on the second point of the star: My Father wants me to give hilariously.

What does God do with His time? There are some who believe God spends His eternal hours wandering around a cold, stained-glass cathedral, wearing a chocolate brown monk's habit, listening to Bach, Beethoven and occasionally an angelic choir singing the Hallelujah Chorus!

Others picture Him spending countless hours at some high-tech celestial switchboard, taking hundreds of thousands of calls a minute from His global family, and no doubt getting frustrated with all the pink reminder notes of requests that still require an answer. Perhaps He spends time on an advanced high-tech smartphone.

There is no way to visualize how God works. Our finite minds cannot comprehend His greatness. Yet, through my study of Scripture, I have come to believe that God actively *enjoys* life. He is not a recluse. He loves His creation and His children. More than anything, He wants mankind to respond willingly to His gift of love.

He longs to see those who accept His Son as their Savior grow into mature believers, capable of spiritual reproduction. We please Him when we trust Him and obey Him. He has invested a lot in us. We are His inheritance. I often picture God jumping for joy when He sees His children step out in faith to carry out their responsibilities as good stewards.

To grasp the importance of this second principle, we need to better understand two words: *hilarious* and *circulation.*

As a preacher's kid, I was a regular Sunday school attendee. I first enrolled at the age of three weeks and faithfully attended almost every Sunday thereafter. The theme verse for the nursery department, even though it was taken somewhat out of context, was: We shall not all sleep, but we shall all be changed.

GIVING WITH A GRIN

I started memorizing Scripture verses about the time I graduated to the mature age of three. One of the earliest verses I ever memorized was the last phrase of 2 Corinthians 9:7, "God loves a cheerful giver." For years I thought God wanted me to have a grin on my face when I put my pennies into the offering plate. The idea of being happy each time I gave money seemed logical and reasonable.

Over the years, however, I noticed that the time of giving in many churches is the low point of worship or almost an afterthought. It seems that most people have anything but a grin on their faces when the offering is taken. More often, offerings remind me of a funeral. It's almost as if each person is losing his best friend (and to some, maybe that's what their money is). There is no joy, no excitement, no expression of appreciation, no intentionality, and no laughter.

Even to many pastors, encouraging giving is viewed an interruption to ministry rather than ministry. I have found most pastors hate to talk to their congregations about money. Avoidance, rather than encouraging generosity, is more the norm rather than the exception.

BE CHEERFUL

When someone says to you, "Be cheerful," how do you respond? If you're honest, you will admit that cheerfulness at most is a smile. When the King James translation of the Bible was completed in 1611, I'm sure 2 Corinthians 9:7 was a problem to the translators. In their Greek text, they found the word *hilarious*. Because they were dealing with "holy writ," they must have decided to use a word that toned down the dynamics of what Paul was writing to the young Corinthian believers.

Hilaros is the Greek root for the English word "hilarious." A more accurate translation of the phrase found in 2 Corinthians 9:7 is: *God loves a hilarious giver.* God loves a steward who chooses to reflect God's very character. When we give we should reflect God's character and His love. If God loves a hilarious giver, it stands to reason that He too is a hilarious giver. He wants us to follow His example. He is our model for giving.

We are to be hilarious ambassadors of His kingdom.

The word *hilarious* means "to cause to shine like the sun." Does this definition confuse you? I can understand why. It seems that the Greek definition has nothing to do with what we think of as being hilarious.

But when we think about it, it's easy to see the analogy. The sun basically has a very simple task that God assigned to it on the day He created it: to give out heat and light. The sun was designed for a specific radiant purpose.

We too, are created with a purpose. We are created to give, just as the sun is created to give light and warmth to the earth. It is no mistake that Paul used the word *hilarious* when writing to the Corinthians about the kind of giver God loves.

One who gives hilariously is one who gives freely as a natural response to needs and the opportunity to meet those needs. Hilarious giving is a steward's spontaneous response to do what God has called him to do. In one sense, the response is "out of control." I can almost hear God saying, "I love the steward who freely gives in response to circumstances, just as the sun freely gives light and heat to the earth."

This principle far exceeds the giving of money, although you can easily test your hilarious giving spirit by seeing how easy or difficult it is for you to give money freely. Later we will examine the vast variety of ways you can give hilariously.

Effective hilarious giving stimulates continued circulation of that which is given and always has an impact on others.

HILARITY SPREADS

Imagine yourself at a social gathering with twenty-five of your friends. After a period of visiting, your host announces:

"Tonight, we have a group game to play. Each of you are to lie on the floor and look at the ceiling. To be comfortable, you each will need a pillow. We have twenty-five available for your use. Your pillow will be someone else's stomach! There is only one rule to the game: No matter what happens, no one is to laugh—absolutely *no laughing!*"

The events that follow the strange game's instructions are more fun to watch than an old "I Love Lucy" show on TV. Everyone feels awkward. Getting on the floor is an embarrassment. Once each person finds his "pillow," everyone seems to be at peace for about fifteen seconds. Then dear little Susy, somewhere in the middle of the mass of bodies, looks at Joe's head of hair laying on her stomach. She thinks, *This is crazy, what if someone walks in here and finds us all on the floor like this?*

The thought brings a smile, but then she remembers she's not to laugh. She bites her lip to suppress the chuckle. But then she notices how tense she has become. She may not be laughing on the outside, but she's dying with laughter and is in turmoil on the inside. Her diaphragm and stomach muscles begin to tighten and quiver.

As that happens, Joe's head, which is resting on her stomach, begins to bob up and down like an apple in a washtub at a Halloween party. Joe realizes his pillow is alive! Now he's biting *his* lip.

Susy looks down at Joe's bobbing head and realizes she can no longer suppress the giggles. Within seconds she bursts into laughter, and in a matter of moments, her laughter has infected the whole room of people. Despite the game's rules, twenty-five people are now rolling on the floor in hilarious laughter.

SPONTANEOUS MULTIPLICATION

What happened at our little party game?

First, spontaneous response resulted in hilarious giving. Susy did what any normal person in such a circumstance would do! She laughed! Although she tried desperately to suppress it, her very nature eventually forced her to burst out with laughter. She lost control. She had to laugh.

Second, hilarity spreads. In the game just played, laughter moved like a chain reaction. You can't keep a spirit of hilarity to yourself. Others around you will personally be influenced and experience the results.

CIRCULATION

God's entire plan of creation is based on the circulation of resources. He never intended for His stewards to use simple addition. He planned for massive multiplication. His instruction was to be fruitful and multiply! God plays a very key role in the process of circulation, but He works through a simple network: God to people; people to people.

We don't need to go far to see the greatest model of circulation ever created. Our bodies are amazing illustrations of the creative handiwork of God. Within the human body is an intricate network of muscles, organs, tissues, blood vessels, etc.—all of which are interdependent on one another. This amazing network of interdependence is a model for us to understand how God expects us to function as believers.

God designed His creation to be a linked network; no one part is able to stand alone. He intends for this intricate network to meet every personal need of every one of us. But to do this the network must be functioning properly. System failure is not an option when God's plan is working.

The key to successfully operating this circulation network is to use sensitive stewards who willingly and hilariously keep circulating God's wealth and resources. We are not to function under the pressure of obligation. We are to be stimulated from the heart to meet the needs of others. We are made to function this way!

TWO LIMITATIONS

Are you aware that there are two limitations to hilarious giving? Paul instructs the Corinthian believers, "Let each one do just as he purposed in his heart; not grudgingly or under compulsion; for God loves a cheerful giver" (2 Corinthians 9:7, NASB).

Hilarious giving is giving because one wants to give. It cannot be done with a bad attitude. It cannot be done out of obligation. Sad to say, much of the giving done today is done under pressure. Those who feel obligated to give do not experience the joy and excitement that comes from a spirit of hilarity.

How many times have you broken down and bought a chocolate candy bar from a child in your neighborhood who is trying to raise money for a school project? My daughters, as students, were annually involved in such fund-raising projects. They were pressured by school leadership to go from house to house, contacting their friends and asking for participation. After all, what were a few bucks to help a worthy cause?

Were they successful in their goal to sell a box of bars, lightbulbs, or beef jerky? You bet! Did people really want to buy what they had to offer? Not usually!

Most of us give in these situations because of neighborhood pressure and a sense of obligation to help a kid that is out raising funds for their school project. There is little eagerness involved. One dear lady put it this way, "Because of my health, I'm not to eat chocolate. I really don't like those little kids coming around, but I don't want to hurt their feelings. I buy so that they don't feel bad and pay money for what I don't want."

A few years ago, an aggressive middle-aged executive trusted in Jesus Christ as his Savior and was encouraged to join a men's Bible study. This small group of peers helped him begin a journey for personal spiritual growth. He began to blossom as he realized how much his heavenly Father had given to him.

At one of the Bible study sessions, each member of the group was asked to share an attitude change that had occurred in his life as a result of trusting Jesus Christ as his personal Savior. The businessman shared:

> *About eighteen months ago, leaders from my church asked me to underwrite the cost of the church's new multipurpose education building. They knew my family was rich materially. My parents were charter members of the church. They pressured and appealed to me to donate the funds to build the building as a memorial to my parents.*
>
> *I honestly did not want to give. Because of the pressure I felt I agreed to give a million dollars as a pace-setting gift for the building. I did not feel led by God to give. I felt obligated to do so. The building is completed and dedicated. Because of my attitude I've experienced no genuine joy in giving.*
>
> *I've received a greater blessing and joy in giving my life to Jesus Christ than I felt in giving a million dollars. I had known Jesus Christ before I was*

challenged to give that gift to my church. I believe if I had, I would have had quite a different reason for giving the gift.

Whether it's buying a candy bar from the neighborhood kid or giving a million dollars to your church, if it's not done with an attitude of joy and hilarity, you are not going to experience God's intended blessing.

As a junior in college, all I could see was my own emptiness. Then, one night, during my search for meaning and purpose, I ended up at a student Bible study on the University of Colorado campus, I was reacquainted with a passage of Scripture that I had memorized many years earlier.

I was shocked to learn that God viewed me as somebody very important to Him. My life began to take in new meaning that night as I personalized Ephesians 1:3–8, 13–14. You can read this passage but here is a summary:

God was happy with me (verse 3).
God has blessed me (verse 3).
God gave me every spiritual blessing (verse 3).
God chose me (verse 4).
God made me holy and blameless (verse 4).
God lovingly adopted me as a son (verse 5).
God willed that I would be His (verse 5).
God gave me undeserved favor (verse 6).
God freely bestowed His grace on me (verse 6).
God redeemed me through Jesus' blood (verse 7).
God declared me forgiven from sin—my falling short of his plan (verse 7).
God has lavished the riches of His grace upon me (verse 8).
God sealed me (placed protective around me) by the Holy Spirit (verse 13).
God has promised me an eternal inheritance (verse 14).

I began to see that God had made a sacrificial investment in me. He had a plan for me! Even today when I look at this list I cannot help but say, "Thank You, Lord." I am an important part of God's distribution plan. I am not a mistake.

You are important to Him. He wants your willing participation in His plan.

YOU ARE SPECIAL

You are special because God made only one of you. What you bring to the table is also special—no one else has the exact inventory you have been given to give. The way you choose to distribute your inventory creatively to meet the needs of others will be different from the way I will distribute mine. We are a part of a worldwide distribution network. We are to be wise, alert, and sensitive stewards. God is holding you and me both accountable for the proper distribution of what he has entrusted to each us. He has given you all you need to be a hilarious giver.

TO RECEIVE, YOU MUST GIVE

There is only one way we are able to receive more from our heavenly Father: We must give away what He's already given to us. It makes sense, doesn't it? Have you ever tried to fill a glass of water that's already full of water?

You can't without first removing some of the water. As you distribute to others what God has given to you, He plans to refill you again to overflowing. Remember: God to people; people to people.

Why does God give you refills? Simply so that you can continue to give even more. The more you give, the more you will receive. My heart goes out to those who hoard their time, skills and abilities, and possessions of all kinds. They are missing out on the greatest joy God has for man. Every time I hold back from giving, I miss the joy of being what I call an Authorized Wealth Distributor for God. (We will talk more later about what it means to be an "Authorized Wealth Distributor" in Part 2 of this book.)

Do you see now why Paul quoted Jesus in Acts 20:35, "It is more blessed to give than to receive"? The hilarity comes through giving, not getting. It's fun. It's exciting. It's living on the edge of faith. It's trusting Him to supply. It's getting a taste of what is to come.

This process of distribution was modeled to us by Jesus Himself. He gave His life so that He would receive us as adopted children. We now can give so that we can receive a multiplied return—*not to keep this return, but to give it away again.*

The one who chooses to hoard will eventually lose what he has hoarded. The one who chooses to give will gain. "For whoever wishes to save his life shall lose it; but whoever loses his life for My sake shall find it" (Matthew 16:25, NASB).

Jesus summarized the results of giving: "Give, and it will be given to you; good measure, pressed down, shaken together, running over, they will pour into your lap. For by your standard of measure it will be measured to you in return" (Luke 6:38, NASB).

When I look at this verse, I think of an overflowing triple-dipper, old-fashioned, hand-packed ice cream cone. Imagine your three favorite flavors piled high on a cone, just waiting to satisfy your taste buds. Every lick is heavenly. Why? Because it's been distributed in good measure, pressed down, shaken together, and running over. There's no fluff, no fillers, and no air. It's concentrated, genuine, packed, and satisfying.

As we give hilariously, Jesus promises that the return we can expect will be rich, full, complete, filling—and more than we could ever imagine, ask, or think. What a way to live!

DISTRIBUTION PROPERTIES

Your highest priority as a steward is to ensure that the distribution network is running. You are representing the greatest wealth distributor of all time, therefore, everything you do should be a reflection of His plan of circulation. You accomplish this priority in three ways:

1. ***Personally giving.*** You have the privilege of being a model. People around you need to see a hilarious giving in action. Your actions will speak far more loudly than your words. The way in which you hilariously circulate what you have in your inventory will be a testimony to others. When others see you giving, they are stimulated to do what you are doing.

   You have countless items in your inventory that you can distribute. You have material possessions, of course, but this represents only a small part of the many gifts you have already that are ready for your distribution to others.

2. ***Stimulating others to give.*** Not only are you to give, but you are also to help others see that they, too, have much to give. Every person alive has exactly what someone else needs. Encourage by example!

3. ***Graciously receiving from others.*** One of the saddest things I've observed over the years is people refusing someone else's desire to give to them. I'm sure you've witnessed restaurant scenes like this one:

   Two couples are out to dinner. They enjoy each other's company—until the waitress brings the bill when each man decides he is going to pay for the meal. As they argue over who

> gets the check, their happy fellowship sours and becomes an emotional dogfight. Neither is willing to graciously defer to the other. Finally, the waitress must split the check just to restore some semblance of peace.
>
> Such an incident can be avoided if we are willing to graciously receive as well as give. When someone initiates giving to you, be gracious and warmly receive the gift. Giving to you is likely that person's way of participating in hilarious giving.
>
> Remember: God to people; people to people. Be gracious and accept what is given to you.

After you have received from someone giving, you will have numerous opportunities to multiply that which you have received. God will continue to add to your inventory as you are distributing what He's already given to you. Don't be concerned that you must pay back someone for a gift of time, talent or possessions given to you.

You should not be concerned with a direct return. God may allow you to give to that person when he has a need at a later time, but that may not be the plan. God may intend for you to give to meet another's need. Circulating God's wealth and resources can create a network of giving. Properly functioning, everyone—Christian and non-Christian alike—will feel the impact of God's distribution system.

As I receive from others, I continually pray, "Lord, I've received from Your circulation network. Now make me sensitive to others: What have You given to me today that I am to give to someone else? What do You want me to give that will keep Your wealth and resources in constant circulation?"

GOD'S VIEW OF HILARIOUSD GIVING

The two power-packed chapters in Scripture reflect God's view on giving and receiving. Go to 2 Corinthians 8 in your Bible. Paul's purpose for writing these chapters was to encourage the readers to fulfill a pledge that the readers had already made. While the specific need was to give what was committed, I believe we can learn a good deal about giving freely from all that we receive from our Father.

Chapter 8 is loaded with nuggets about hilarious giving. As we look at this chapter, ask God to give understanding so that you can begin to apply what you read.

What truth we learn from verse 1:
Hilarious giving comes from God.
Hilarious giving demands that one must first receive from God.
Hilarious giving circulates God's undeserved favor.

What truth we learn from verse 2:
Hilarious giving starts with an attitude.
Hilarious giving stimulates an abundance of joy.
What one gives or how much one gives is not the issue.
The attitude in giving makes all the difference in the world.

What truth we learn from verse 3:
Hilarious giving is free from pressure or coercion.
Hilarious giving is giving because you want to, not because you have to.

What truth we learn from verse 4:
Hilarious giving is a privilege that results in a bond of unity among believers.

What truth we learn from verse 5:
Hilarious giving begins by giving yourselves to the Lord.
Hilarious giving exceeds man's expectations.
Hilarious giving seeks for God's direction.
Hilarious giving responds to the needs of others.

What truth we learn from verse 6:
Hilarious giving is enthusiastic.
Hilarious giving is stimulated by Christian leadership.
Hilarious giving is ministry in action.

What truth we learn from verse 7:
Hilarious giving is an act of the will.
Hilarious giving is the mark of maturing believers.

Hilarious giving stimulates others to give.
Hilarious giving requires more from us than we often anticipate.

What truth we learn from verse 8:
Hilarious giving cannot occur when the giver is under pressure to give.
Hilarious giving is proof that Christian love is real.
Hilarious giving is actually love in action.

What truth we learn from verse 9:
Hilarious giving was modeled for us by the Lord Jesus.
Hilarious giving considers others' needs as a priority.
Hilarious giving produces results.

What truth we learn from verse 11:
Hilarious giving can be interrupted by the things of the world.
Hilarious giving relies on the decisive action of the giver.

What truth we learn from verse 12:
Hilarious giving does not rely on quantity to give.
Hilarious giving comes from what one has, not what one does not have.

Did Mrs. Weber see a return on her investment of a letter she wrote after church one evening? Yes! Her letter opened the floodgates of penny giving. Letters came from Heart's Desire radio listeners in by the thousands; each told its own story and enclosed in each was at least a penny. Mrs. Weber received a bonus for her hilarious giving via a letter to a stranger. She was blessed by seeing the Heart of America Bell become a reality on Thanksgiving Day, 1947.

Are you ready to be used by God as a hilarious giver? I know that God is ready. He's waiting for your availability. He wants your intentional involvement in His distribution network. Are you ready to go for it?

Remember: *God to people; people to people. God* wants you to give hilariously!

Key To Abundant Living

UNLOCKING YOUR LIFE OF CONTENTMENT

We have all experienced giving under pressure. Jot down three different occasions when you gave your time, talent, or treasure but were not excited about doing so. Express how you felt on those occasions.

1.

2.

3.

List out a few practical ways you can personally become proactive in intentional giving and begin to give hilariously.

When can you take the first step in this direction? Do you need to jot this on your calendar?

Jot down a couple of practical ways you can help stimulate others to give hilariously.

Chapter 6
JUST ASK

Ask and you will receive so that your joy will be made complete.
—JESUS (JOHN 16:24)

After a twenty-two-hour drive from Colorado to California in early June 1969, I finally arrived at my destination—the International Headquarters of Campus Crusade for Christ in Southern California.

Nine months earlier, I had left Arrowhead Springs in my new Oldsmobile Cutlass. I was on a special mission. My Cutlass and I traveled together throughout thirty-one states and logged over 35,000 miles as I set up college concerts for the New Folk, an evangelistic music group that was performing in hundreds of college campuses. Everything I owned was in the trunk of my car.

At last I had a place to call home for three months. Nine months alone on the road can drain anyone. I was looking forward to living in an apartment for the summer, sleeping in the same bed for three months, renewing old friendships, and having a few dates like a normal person.

Soon after I arrived, I headed for the president's office, hoping to find a student from the East Coast who was assigned to work as a secretary for the summer. Maybe she would like to go out for coffee.

She wasn't in. Only the full-time secretary for Dr. Bright's office was there—a cute girl named Pat Menghini. I immediately recognized from the summer before. I had tried to get to know her then, but she was "booked." I never made it to first base.

As we talked, we exchanged friendly greetings. I was about to be late for another appointment, so I excused myself. But as I left I made a mental note that Pat was still around. Perhaps she might have some time for me *this* summer.

It wasn't long before we had our first date when I asked Pat to join me for the day at Disneyland. She accepted, and I was ecstatic!

We were on Tom Sawyer Island when it happened. Somehow I had to take her hand to steady her, but we never let go! I liked her laugh, her personality, and her way of doing things; something was happening... she was indeed special.

The more we spent time together over the next couple of weeks, the more we knew there was a special dimension to our relationship. I knew this was God's choice for my lifelong mate. I sensed she felt the same way.

HAVE YOU ASKED?

My summer assignment at Arrowhead Springs was briefly interrupted by a four-day trip to Colorado for a family reunion. While there, I confided in my brother, "Jerry, I'm going to marry a girl I met and began dating about two weeks ago. She's committed to the Lord. She is excited about serving in ministry. We really fit. She's the one."

Jerry had a simple but very direct question, "Have you asked her to marry you?"

"No, Jerry . . ."

"Well, you will never marry her unless you ask her to marry you." That was the end of the conversation.

Jerry was more right than I wanted my brother to be. For Pat to marry me, I had to ask her to do so.

Three days later, when Pat picked me up at the airport, she was as beautiful as ever. I had really missed her in those four days away. She seemed to have missed me, too.

That night, with my faithful trusty Cutlass as my witness, I asked Pat to be my wife. Her response hit me between the eyes, "You know I will; I love you, Larry."

Because I asked Pat to marry me on August 18, 1969, we spent forty-five wonderful years together. She is now with her Savior, but for years she was my dearest friend, best counsel, greatest lover, biblical advisor, and the best ever companion. To receive all of this and more, all I had to do was ask her to be my life partner. What a deal I got! My ask provided many rewards.

Pennies were given from across America in 1947 to help a little country church get a bell because Mrs. Weber *asked* Uncle Ben for a bell for the church. If Mrs. Weber had not asked, the Heart's Desire radio team would never have learned of the need. In turn if "Uncle Ben" had not asked his daily listeners to give a penny no one would have participated in meeting the need for the bell. To receive, one must ask. Asking a person to give is doing something **for** them, not **to** them!

PRINCIPLE 3

IT PLEASES GOD WHEN HIS CHILDREN ASK FOR, THEN DILIGENTLY SEEK, SOME OF THEIR INHERITANCE SO THEY CAN GIVE IT TO OTHERS.

Put more simply, this third principle becomes: My Father wants me to ask.

I've observed that most people view asking as hurting someone, rather than helping them. Have you ever felt this way?

Asking someone to do something is the greatest way to demonstrate confidence and trust in that person. Asking should be the natural result of a developing relationship. God wants us to ask. He desires that we express our concerns, needs, wants, and desires to Him. He wants our requests to be the overflow of our relationship with Him.

LOOK AT A FEW OF THE CHOICE PROMISES WE FIND FROM JESUS HIMSELF:

> "You can pray for anything, and if you have faith, you will receive it" (Matthew 21:22).

> "I tell you the truth, anyone who believes in me will do the same works I have done, and even greater works because I am going to be with the Father. You can ask for anything in my name, and I will do it, so that the Son can bring glory to the Father. Yes, ask me for anything in my name, and I will do it. (John 14:12–14).

> "But if you remain in me and my word remains in you, you may ask for anything you want and it will be granted! (John 15:7).

> "You haven't done this before. Ask, using my name, and you will receive, and you will have abundant" (John 16:24).

I don't know about you, but I get the feeling from reading these declarations from the Lord Jesus that He expects us to be expressing to Him what's on our hearts. He is ready to hear and respond to our requests. Jesus wants us to ask of Him. He models for us to ask from others.

RELATIONSHIP MATTERS

Is your relationship with God so close that you feel you're at His footstool, that you are free to express to Him all that's on your heart? You are His. He wants the same relationship with you that He had with heroes of our faith. He wants open and transparent communication with each of His stewards. He's waiting to hear you express your heart's desire to him. He wants you to ask so that He can respond to your request.

Are you beginning to see that our asking is key to triggering His response? He could do it differently, but he wants us to engage with the ask. He is prepared and ready to respond. He wants us to ask in faith first.

A good friend of mine serves in an unusual niche ministry that very few people are called to undertake. He is exceptional in this work. I admire him in many ways. To help him raise the support required to do this ministry full-time he needs to ask others to partner with him. I have expressed that I would be glad to support him as well if he would simply asks me to join him in partnership with him. For some reason, he cannot get the courage to ask me to help—even though he knows I will respond positively if he asks. I want to help—but I want him to ask.

Are you like my friend? Are you fearful of asking? Are you asking God and his stewards for what you need so you can redistribute the proceeds to help meet the needs of others? Have you resorted to hinting about a need but not coming out with a simple ask?

God's Word is full of classic testimonies of men whose relationship with God allowed them to ask without hesitation and to experience the power of God. He was an abundant supplier in response to the needs that faced them:

> ***Because of Noah's relationship with God,*** he received the grace of God. God entrusted to him the blueprint for a seagoing vessel that saved Noah's family from the flood. Noah faithfully took the steps necessary to construct a ship 450 feet long, seventy-five feet wide, and forty-five feet high, in the middle of the dry, desert ground. He gave to his sons what God gave to him. As a result, the animals of the earth and Noah's entire family were saved so that they could give again to a new generation.
>
> ***Because of Moses' relationship with God,*** an entire nation was set free from bondage. Moses' relationship with God was so honest that he even asked God to send another leader. God, however, chose Moses to be His chief steward - - the man to give leadership to the Exodus. God did answer his request by providing Aaron to speak for Moses. Moses gave as God instructed.
>
> ***Because of Gideon's relationship with God***, he could ask God to confirm His will when Gideon put out a fleece. Gideon then accepted God's direction and was appointed to give leadership to three hundred chosen men. Because of Gideon's obedience and faithfulness as a steward, the entire Midianite army was defeated.
>
> ***Because of Daniel's relationship with God,*** he was chosen to serve as a counselor to King Nebuchadnezzar. When the king experienced a terrifying nightmare one night, he summoned his wisest men to tell him the meaning of his dream. Daniel and his three friends—Shadrach, Meshack, and Abednego—all went to prayer, asking God to show them the secret of the dream. God responded to the request and gave Daniel the interpretation.
>
> While serving later under King Darius, Daniel was thrown into the lions' den because he refused to obey a law of the Medes and Persians—forbidding anyone in the kingdom to ask a favor of God or any

man except the king himself. Daniel was thrown to the lions for one reason: He continued to pray and ask God for His provision three times a day. God sent His angel to shut the lions' mouths because Daniel was demonstrating obedient stewardship by asking God for direction.

Because of Elijah's relationship with God, he was able to take on King Ahab and Queen Jezebel's sinful kingdom. On Mount Carmel, Elijah challenged the king and queen and their 450 pagan Baal prophets to a contest to determine the true God. After the prophets of Baal spent the entire day dancing, shouting, and cutting their bodies, trying to get Baal's attention to come and light the fire to the prepared sacrifice, they gave up. Elijah then laid out his sacrifice and to make it harder, poured five barrels of water on the altar. Then he prayed, "O Lord God of Abraham, Isaac, and Israel, prove today that you are the God of Israel and that I am your servant; prove that I have done all this at your command. O Lord, answer me! Answer me so these people will know that you are God and that you have brought them back to yourself." (1 Kings 18:36). Fire flashed from heaven, totally consuming the waterlogged sacrifice. Elijah asked, and God answered.

Because of David's relationship with God, he had the confidence to act with boldness in circumstances that would overwhelm most people. When David went to battle against nine-foot Goliath, he shouted to the giant, "You come to me with sword and spear, but I come to you in the name of the Lord... and Israel will learn that the Lord does not depend on weapons to fulfill his plans—he works without regard to human means! He will give you to us!" (1 Samuel 17:45, 47, TLB). David's confidence was based on his belief that God would answer his requests.

Because of Solomon's relationship with God, he reigned as king of Israel for forty years. As Solomon took the throne, God said to him, "Ask me for anything, and I will give it to you!" Solomon, as you know, asked God to give him wisdom and knowledge to rule his people properly. Then God replied, "Because your greatest desire is to help your people, and you haven't asked for personal wealth and honor, and you haven't asked me to curse your enemies, and you haven't asked for a long life, but for wisdom and knowledge to properly guide my people—yes, I am giving you the wisdom and knowledge you asked for! And I am also giving you such riches, wealth, and honor as no other king has ever had before you!" (2 Chronicles 1:7–12, TLB). Solomon was given an abundance because he asked God for what was really important.

JUST AN ORDINARY MAN

What comes to your mind when you are confronted with these heroes of the faith? I used to get a little frustrated as I read accounts of the outstanding men God chose to lead His people. I thought, *"God, that's great, but these men proved to be exceptional leaders. How about the average people—the ones who never make the front page—the ones like me?"*

God answered my question over thirty-five years ago by introducing me to an obscure ordinary man. I met him in 1 Chronicles 4:9–10. Jabez was a guy just like you and me. In fact, the meaning of his name gives you an idea of how typical he is to most of us who stand in awe of such spiritual giants as Daniel, David, and Solomon.

Jabez's name means "distress." His mother gave him this name because of the difficult labor that she experienced at the time of his birth. Know any kid today that is named Jabez?

His name is mentioned in only one place in Scripture—in the middle of one of those lively and dynamic "begot" sections!

Then I was introduced to Jabez through a friend who challenged me to pray the prayer that Jabez prayed. Jabez prayed a one-sentence prayer: "Oh that Thou wouldst bless me indeed, and enlarge my border, and that Thy hand might be with me, and that Thou wouldst keep me from harm, that it may not pain me" (1 Chronicles 4:10, NASB).

Do you know how God responded to Jabez's ask? Scripture says, "And God granted him what he requested.". How simple. How powerful. His four-part ask was received by God. God responded and did exactly what Jabez requested:

1. God's blessing poured out upon him.
2. God enlarged his border. No doubt this included the size of his land holdings, but very likely, it also included his influence and perspective.
3. God kept His hand on him. There is no better protection than to sense God's hand on your shoulder in a deceptive, confused, and polarized world.
4. God kept Satan from him. God was Jabez's bodyguard from the attacks of his enemy. Jabez experienced both protection and freedom from the power of sin.

Think about it: an ordinary person receiving all of this just because he asked! No other prayer in Scripture has impacted my life as much as this one has. I have experienced God's response just as He responded to ordinary Jabez over three thousand years ago. This is now my daily prayer for my six grandkids.

UNLOCKING YOUR LIMITATIONS

Probably nothing pleases God more than hearing His children ask Him for wisdom, direction, understanding, and other needs. Asking God for what you see as your need demonstrates to Him that you recognize His leadership and lordship. You demonstrate dependence on Him and confidence in Him when you ask for His divine intervention.

When you ask, you should be honest, transparent, and regular. There is no need to play games with God. No hinting! He already knows your heart. Remember, seeking Him for counsel and direction is not merely an activity. Asking Him is a testimony of your relationship with Him. He is your Father! He wants to hear from you.

One summer I was privileged to sit under the teaching of Dr. Jack Taylor. His insight into asking God made the profound so simple. He suggested that the key which unlocks the treasures of God's inventory to us, His children, is found in 1 John 5:14–15 (NASB):

> And this is the confidence which we have before Him, that, if we ask anything according to His will, He hears us. And if we know that He hears us in whatever we ask, we know that we have the requests which we have asked from Him.

Read the verse again. What do you see? I'm afraid many people these as just words to be memorized. These two little verses can strip away your perceived limitations—if you choose to *act* on their promise.

Do you have confidence that God can do anything? I'm afraid that all too often, we act as if God were limited in His ability to respond to our requests. Or we may view God as sitting at His computer, calling up our past failures to see if we deserve our current requests. But God does not keep a tally of our past sins. When He forgives us, He *removes* our shortcomings and sin from His memory bank and remembers them against us no more. All He needs from us is our confidence in Him to act.

The size of the request does not bother Him. He is capable of responding to a giant request just as easily as to a tiny one. So why ask for peanuts when God can give you a seven-course meal? He has absolutely no reason to withhold anything from His children unless it is truly harmful to us.

Do you have confidence that if you ask according to His will, He hears? Many times we have a tendency to think, *He's too busy to take my request*, or *I don't want to bother Him with such a petty problem.* There's good news! God hears! He's not preoccupied with heavenly activity. If you ask according to His will, He hears. It's that simple.

Do you have confidence that when He hears you, and you confess that He hears you and believe this, then He will grant your request of Him? If you have confidence in God, you need to demonstrate your faith in Him by acting as if it is so when it isn't so, so it *will* be so.

When you come right down to the bottom line, the issue is not a matter of God answering, but of your having *confidence* in Him to answer. If you have confidence, why not ask and then begin telling others that God *has* answered your request? Begin thanking Him for the answer and praising Him for His response. True, you may not have the tangible results of the answer in hand, but that need not stop you from demonstrating your confidence in God by faith.

Are you going to trust God by faith, or are you going to trust in some tangible result?

Do you have confidence in God's faithfulness? No doubt you have experienced a time delay in seeing the tangible result of your prayer to God. The reason we experience such apparent delays is not that God hasn't answered. It is that, from our limited perspective, our needs must be met within a particular time frame. But remember this: God always delivers on time—not one second too early or one second too late.

When you ask, don't get hung up with the timing. You may think you have new insights on a matter that God needs to know about—as if He were unaware of a detail. He knows already. He will respond in His perfect timing. Remember, He is not on your clock!

LEARNING TO RIDE!

Have you ever asked God for something, yet felt that He ignored your request? I'm sure we've all experienced the time delay crisis. But this delay in no way implies that God is on vacation or is ignoring you.

Delays in delivery are in your best interest. God knows the best timing for you. Even when things might look hopeless to you, God sees things differently and knows just the right timing.

Parents experience this with their children. Many years ago, my younger daughter, Jessica, came to me and asked me to allow her to ride her bicycle in the street in front of our home. At the time, she was almost five years old. She still had training wheels on her bicycle.

"Can you ride your bike without the training wheels, Jessica? I want you to be able to ride in the street, too; but in order for me to say yes, I need to see how well you can ride without the training wheels."

Jessica responded, "Oh sure, Dad, that's easy." I removed the training wheels, and she confidently got on her bike. But she had ridden only one foot when she fell. Even my help didn't seem to benefit her much that day. She just couldn't get the hang of steering, peddling, and balancing herself all at the same time.

After watching her do her best to ride without the training wheels, I decided she wasn't ready for the street. I did not tell her she could *never* ride in the street; however, I did explain that before she went into the street, she first had to conquer the two wheels on the sidewalk. I wanted to deliver her request; but because of her lack of balance, maturity and ability, she would have to wait.

Some months passed, and Jessica was still riding on the sidewalk with the training wheels. She occasionally asked me about the street, but I reminded her what had to happen first. There were times when the two of us would go for a check out, but each time she proved not to be ready.

On Easter Sunday, when Jessica was six, she came to me and said, "Dad, let's go take off my training wheels. I'm ready to ride my bike without them."

We took the bike without the training wheels to a park area near our home. I gave her a good push, and she was off. First ten feet, then twenty-five feet, then fifty feet, then half a block. Within thirty minutes, she was riding very well on a nearby school playground. She was ready for new challenges.

What changed? It was Jessica who changed. She was no longer interested in looking backward. Her focus was on looking ahead. She demonstrated balance, boldness, and greater maturity. She got even better as a rider as she learned bike safety rules. My answer changed from no to yes because she was now ready for her request to be fulfilled. I waited to say yes for her benefit. My no for months was for her protection.

I see God responding to us much as I had to respond to Jessica. Just as it took time for her to be ready to receive her request, so it often takes us time to grow spiritually before God is able to deliver our request to us.

He knows when we are ready to handle what we have asked for.

During the time she could not ride in the street, Jessica never complained about not riding in the street—even though she asked often and even though her older sister, Cari, had permission to ride in the street. Jessica understood that my response was not based on my ability but on hers.

As you grow in your walk of faith, God does not mind your asking as often as you want. It is okay to be persistent. In the process of asking, you no doubt will learn much about yourself and, I hope, much about your heavenly Father. Keep in mind, however, that your persistent asking is of greater benefit to you than it is to him. He has already answered your request and will not fail to deliver it at just the right time.

The next time you find yourself repeating the same request, you don't plead or beg. Rather, ask God to allow you to grow and mature as you wait for the arrival of His timed delivery. It's OK to remind him occasionally. He loves to hear you express your faith.

We are very limited in our perspective of things. We don't see things as God does. If He were to act and deliver on our demand, He would not be stimulating our spiritual growth. It is important, therefore, that we maintain an attitude of gratitude.

We must continue to express gratitude to God for His wisdom, understanding, insight, and concern for our best interests. Thanking Him continually frees our spirit to learn from our times of waiting. Let praise be on your lips at all times; despite the circumstances, giving praise and thanksgiving to Him.

Don't allow the spirit of ingratitude to creep in like a thief in the night. The side effects of ingratitude are painful. Ingratitude leads to poor health, a loss of hope, a bitter spirit, depression, and negative thoughts. Social relationships crumble, and soon irresponsibility becomes the hallmark of one's life. Greed and selfishness eat away at the soul.

There are times when you need to be still and let God speak to you. I'm sure there are many times God wants to answer you, but He has to wait for you to stop running or talking. He will wait until you are ready to listen.

As you ask from God, don't forget why He wants you to ask. He wants to give to you so that you can give to others. Whatever you ask of God should be something that can in some way be given to someone else. Whatever God gives to you becomes a part of your working inventory as a steward. What you ask for and then receive may change form before it is passed on to benefit someone else, but it is to be used to meet someone else's needs as well as yours.

Keep in mind also that God will use you as a steward to make deliveries for Him. Wouldn't it be embarrassing to learn that a friend's request never got answered because you failed to make a Spirit-directed transfer from your inventory to his (so someone else received that pleasure)?

EXPRESS THANKS

There are so many ways to say thanks to God for providing for us. Be creative in expressing thanks. Do things that cause you to focus on all that He's done for you. One wonderful way to say thanks to God is through generous financial giving to His work around the world or helping meet a specific need in your community.

Remember: *Your Father wants you to ask.*

Key To Abundant Living

UNLOCKING YOUR LIFE OF CONTENTMENT

As you reflect on asking, meditate on 1 John 5:14–15 (NASB). Here is what it says:

> And this is the confidence which we have before him, that, if we ask anything according to His will, He hears us. And if we know that hears us in whatever we ask, we know that we have the requests which we have asked from Him.

Based on this promise, write a prayer to your heavenly Father, asking Him for something that is on your heart. Close your written prayer with thanksgiving and confidence in Him and His timing.

My prayer:

Now date and sign your prayer letter of request.
Date ______________________________
Signature ______________________

From now on you need not ask for this request again, based on 1 John 5:14–15. He knows your request and he will not forget it. However, you are sure free to remind Him of the request as often as you want. He is your Father!

And whenever you mention this request, remember to thank Him for His answer. Thank Him that you know that your answer is on the way and that you are choosing to trust Him with the timing, rather than trusting your circumstances for the outcome. He is faithful. He will accomplish His will.

Chapter 7
EVERYTHING YOU NEED

Sow a thought, reap an action; sow an action reap a habit; sow a habit, reap a character; sow a character, reap a destiny.
—STEVEN COVEY, *THE 7 HABITS OF HIGHLY EFFECTIVE PEOPLE*

One Saturday morning in early April, I decided to stop procrastinating and go for it; I was going to become a gardener.

Raised in western Colorado, I was familiar with the gardening process. I had never planted a garden but many relatives and many of church members from Dad's little church were always eager to provide us with sacks of their fresh garden vegetables. Every sack they provided was a tribute to their labors—as well as to the law of the harvest.

Nothing whets my palate more than fresh garden and orchard produce. Childhood summers were filled with fresh green beans, beets, sweet corn, peas, carrots, peaches, pears, plums, apricots, grapes, and myriad other mouth-watering delights. With those memories in mind, I thought planting a backyard garden would be a simple task. I knew one gardening principle: Whatever a man sows, this he will reap. Based on what I knew I anticipated an abundant harvest.

As the sun was coming up in the eastern sky on Saturday morning, I headed for the backyard with my garden tools. I felt like a pioneer about to conquer the great frontier! Because my backyard had never had a garden plot, I had to start by digging out the grass in my selected garden plot. In no time I would be ready to plant.

But as the sun was sinking in the West many hours later, I finally cleared out the last of the creeping grassroots. What I had anticipated would take only an hour or two, took an entire day. My hands were sore; my back ached; I was sunburned; I was exhausted. As I climbed into bed that night, I thought to myself, *Is this going to be worth it?* I wanted the outcome but was beginning to wonder if the process was worth it.

But I continued to prepare the ground over the next few days. I added fertilizer and other minerals to the soil. Over a week of backbreaking labor later I was ready to plant. I followed the instructions on each package of seeds—to a point. On a few packages, the instructions were specific: When the little shoots sprouted, I was to thin the plants by pulling some of them out.

Here I rebelled. No way was I going to throw away the little seedlings. After all, I wanted a big crop. It simply did not make sense to me at the time to pull up half of the new garden! Without further counsel, I decided not to thin the seedlings.

Then we had a hot spell. Despite my watering, the heat began to hurt the young crop. The lettuce wilted long before the season was over. The peas and beans died on the vine. I never even saw a beet. The sweet corn? Beautiful plants but no ears of corn. As for the tomatoes, the blossoms wouldn't even set.

And the carrots? I got carrots all right, but because of my wise judgment in refusing to thin them as instructed, they were the scrawniest things I'd ever seen! The one redeeming crop was our zucchini and crookneck squash. My friends were right, these plants would go anywhere!

As the summer wore on and the heat soared to over 100 degrees for days at a time, I decided that city farming was not worth my effort. No matter what I tried, I was unable to redeem anything but the squash. But I learned through my gardening experience that there are both principles and procedures to follow if one wants to experience an abundant harvest.

PRINCIPLE 4

IF I SOW ACCORDING TO GOD'S PRINCIPLES, I WILL REAP, AND I WILL ALWAYS HAVE AN ABUNDANCE TO HELP OTHERS AS WELL AS TO MEET MY OWN NEEDS.

To put it in simple personal terms: What I sow, I will reap.

To see the practical reality of this principle work in your life, you need to recognize certain conditions which govern a bountiful harvest.

As I look back to my summer gardening venture, I realize now that although I followed *some* of the procedures listed in the instructions, I also took the liberty to ignore some of the others and do as I pleased.

Do you know what my two main problems were? My selfishness and my greed!

For example, the instructions said to thin; I said, "No way!" The instructions said not to plant after a certain time of year (due to California heat). I went ahead and planted anyway. I was advised to water my garden in the evening or early morning; I chose to do it when it was convenient—occasionally forgetting to water at all.

I planted a garden, but I failed to tend to my garden according to rules related to a productive harvest. I did enough of the right things to give the appearance of a potential harvest, but I fell short. I failed to recognize that you have to obey certain farming principles to be successful.

In contrast, a friend of mine who lived a few miles away had the proverbial green thumb. Anything he planted grew. Consequently, he was able to enjoy home-grown fruit, fresh garden veggies, and beautiful flowers almost year-round. He had learned to operate according to the laws of the harvest. The result of his efforts was a bountiful yield.

SIX KEYS TO A SUCCESSFUL OUTCOME

As I've compared my garden failure to successful farming endeavors, I've come up with six critical elements that are necessary to produce a bountiful harvest. I believe these six elements relate not only to farming but also to the heart of stewardship and to our fourth principle.

1. **Focus on the harvest.**

I've never met a farmer yet who worked for months only to say, "I wasn't expecting a harvest—my effort this year was only for fun." A farmer plants in anticipation of the yield that he expects to reap at harvest time. He follows directions!

Likewise, you should know what to expect as a result of your labor. Keep a mental picture in your mind of what you will actually see at the end of the process. The anticipated outcome must be in focus.

Each of us determines how much God will be able to bless us. If you want a little, give a little. If you want a lot, give a lot. God uses what we sow to provide our return on the harvest. Although we are to focus on the harvest, Jesus admonishes us not to **worry** about the return:

> "That is why I tell you not to worry about everyday life—whether you have enough food and drink, or enough clothes to wear. Isn't life more than food, and your body more than clothing? Look at the birds. They don't plant or harvest or store food in barns, for your heavenly Father feeds them. And aren't you far more valuable to him than they are?" (Matthew 6:25–26).

Jesus promises to be our total sufficiency. Our responsibility is to plant intentionally, manage wisely, plan toward the return, and allow Him to produce the harvest.

2. **Remain committed to the end.**

The farmer knows that planting is only one step in the process that produces an abundant harvest. He must be committed to following through on each step of the entire process. Achieving the expected results requires attention to following the laws of the harvest.

No farmer in his right mind would decide to take a four-week vacation during the growing months of his crops. Similarly, you must not change direction halfway through a time of spiritual growth if you wish to have a maximum return on your investment.

3. **Sow the right seed with generosity.**

The farmer who properly plants corn expects corn. If he properly plants a crop of grain, he expects a harvest of grain. That which is planted is the basis of the return.

In Genesis, God gives specific instructions to the seed-bearing plants:

"Let the land sprout with vegetation—every sort of seed-bearing plant, and trees that go seed-bearing fruit. These seeds will then produce the kinds of plants and trees from which they came. (Genesis 1:11).

Around sixty years ago, the first owner of our second home planted an avocado tree in the backyard. What started out as a little tree eventually covered over half of our backyard. It was a giant in the neighborhood. This mature tree faithfully produced an enormous delicate-skinned avocado crop each year. In a good year, we would get at least fifteen bushels of avocados.

Never once did I find an apple, a peach, or a banana growing in that massive tree. God made that tree to produce only one type of fruit—avocados.

If you sow seeds of love, expect a harvest of love. If you sow a seed of joy, peace, or concern, expect a multiplied harvest of the seed you have sown. If you sow money, what can you expect to receive in return? According to the law of the harvest, you can anticipate receiving what is planted.

Keep in mind that God controls the time and quantity of the return. Everything you have to sow is His anyway. Be careful not to get caught up in a self-serving live-for-the-moment scheme to try to trick God into giving you something you want. You cannot play games with His harvest or manipulate Him into creating a return so that you can hoard or gain earthly wealth, influence, or gain.

What you sow, God returns to you in overflowing measure **so that you can give far more.** The more you receive, the more you are to give. You should never give to get. Rather you should give to get to give to get to give to . . . you get the idea. You give to receive so that you can give again. Your task is to keep His possessions in circulation. Don't shortcut the process.

Doesn't it stand to reason that we should sow with generosity? A wise farmer is never stingy with his seed. He knows he must plant his seed with abandon in order to receive an anticipated harvest. The more generously you sow, the more bountiful your harvest will be.

A word of caution: The principle of sowing and reaping is not limited only to positive, good things that can be planted. Be careful not to sow seeds of discord, hate, bickering, grumbling, criticism, gossip, disrespect, division, and discontent. God's Word warns us:

> "Don't be misled—you cannot mock the justice of God. You will always harvest what you plant. Those that live only to satisfy their own sinful nature will harvest decay and death from that sinful nature. But those who live to please the Spirit will harvest everlasting life from the Spirit" (Galatians 6:7–8).

During my time on the staff of Cru, I came to deeply appreciate president Bill Bright's example and insight on living the Christian life in the power of the Holy Spirit. He was especially concerned about believers who do not take their stewardship responsibilities seriously. Dr. Bright once stated:

> *I am amazed at the lifestyle of the average Christian, a lifestyle that differs little from that of nonbelievers in terms of attitudes, actions, motives, desires, and words. Many Christians are experiencing financial difficulty, emotional turmoil, and even physical illness as a result of the kind of seed they are sowing. Unlike Job, who suffered for the glory of God, they are being disciplined for sowing unrighteously, as was King David after he committed adultery and murder.*
>
> *If every Christian fully understood the law of sowing and reaping, his lifestyle would change dramatically. If I know that I will reap what I sow and more than I sow, I am more like to sow love than hate, harmony than discord, compliments than criticism, generosity than stinginess and selfishness.*[4]

It is God who returns a harvest of blessings. At His choosing, He will also limit the return if He sees us selfishly profiting from the return rather than extending the work of His kingdom.

God's Word clearly indicates that misuse of His resources can result in a substantial shortfall in returns. Two passages from the Old Testament teach us about this through the experiences of the children of Israel.

In Micah, we find that when God's chosen people decided no longer to trust and obey Him, they soon learned that their sowing of crops was in vain. God chose to withhold His blessing because of their sin. God communicated His displeasure through His prophet:

> "You will plant crops but not harvest them. You will press your olives but not get enough oil to anoint yourselves. You

> will trample the grapes but get no juice to make your wine" (Micah 6:15).

Two hundred years later, following the captivity of the children of Israel in Babylon, God's people again neglected the Lord. They chose to focus on their selfish needs in Jerusalem, ignoring the fact that the temple lay in ruin. They were preoccupied with self-gratification and personal pleasure and filled with greed. The first chapter of Haggai records the Lord's admonishment:

> "Why are you living in luxurious homes while my house lies in ruin? This is what the Lord of Heaven's Armies says: Look at what is happening to you! You have planted much but harvested little. You eat but are not satisfied, You drink but are still thirsty. You put on clothes but cannot keep warm. Your wages disappear as though you were putting them in pockets filled with holes. . . . You hoped for rich harvests, but they were poor. And when you brought your harvest home I blew it away. . . . It's because of you that the heavens withhold the dew and the earth produces no crops" (Haggai 1:4–6, 9a, 10).

Many stewards are missing the special blessing of the Lord because they are not in sync with the Lord's commands. Rather than generously distributing what God has given to His priorities, they hoard their harvest and misuse it for their pleasure. They fail to remember what Jesus said:

> "Don't store up treasures here on earth where moths eat them and rust destroys them, and where thieves break in and steal. Store your treasures in heaven, where moths and rust cannot destroy, and thieves do not break in and steal. Wherever your treasure is, there the desire of your heart will also be" (Matthew 6:19–21).

This directive is given for our good, not for our harm. The one who hoards treasure of any kind soon begins to take on a self-centered view of the world. When this happens, the steward's impact on his world is lost.

The farmer who sows seed must give up a treasure with the anticipation of multiplying what is given up. Sometimes we feel emotional pain when we are called to give up something. But Jesus makes us a fantastic promise:

> "I assure you that everyone who has given up houses or brothers or sisters or mother or father or children or property, for my sake and for the Good News, will receive now in return a hundred times as many houses, brothers, sisters, mothers, children, and property—along with persecution. And in the world to come that person will have eternal life" (Mark 10:29–30, NASB).

4. **Keep alert to growing conditions.**

An alert farmer knows the seasons. Unlike my home gardening endeavor that summer, he is aware that the present environment has a great deal of influence on the harvest that is yet months away. He understands the effects of the temperature, the intensity of the sun, the wind, and the rain—all of which have a significant impact on his crop.

By being sensitive to how environmental conditions can affect his crop, he is able to make compensatory decisions. You, too, need to be alert to the world's influence on that which you sow.

If you are extending love and concern to a hurting friend, watch for others who are not concerned for your friend and who may discourage rather than encourage him. You may have to go the extra mile to protect your investment of love and concern as it takes root in your friend's life. Stay alert! Protect the investment you are making.

5. **Focus on details.**

An experienced farmer has an eye for detail. He is concerned about insects, weeds, water levels, weather conditions, crop diseases, and chemical balance. Every day he examines the crop and decides when it needs water, fertilizer, or insecticide. He is continually taking appropriate action to create and produce the maximum yield.

The farmer gives tender, loving care to what he has sown. He does whatever is necessary to guard against conditions that could thwart growth or eventually kill the harvest.

Using God's Word as your garden manual, learn to identify those conditions that can stunt the growth of what you sow—such as a negative attitude or a self-serving spirit. Make corrections as needed so you can realize a bountiful harvest.

6. **Reap the harvest.**

The farmer's reward for sowing is reaping the harvest. An abundant harvest should never be stored. Except for a small amount that is used to sustain the farmer and his family and to provide the seed for the next planting season, the harvest should be put into circulation. As other people are affected, their joy is also made full.

In God's timing, you will be privileged to gather in what you have sown, and you too will be rejoicing. You will then have the privilege of circulating the harvest into the hands of others; and perhaps without knowing it, you will have sown again.

INSIGHTS FROM PAUL

Paul gives us greater insight into the process and benefits of sowing and reaping in his second letter to the Corinthians. We've examined the principle of giving hilariously, which is covered in 2 Corinthians 8.

In Chapter 5 we looked at 2 Corinthians 8 about hilarious giving. Grab your Bible and lets now look at Chapter 9 for more nuggets of wisdom and insight regarding the principals of the harvest:

What truths we learn from verse 1:
What one sows and then reaps is a means of direct ministry.
The harvest is given for one reason: to help others.

What truths we learn from verse 2:
An abundant harvest produces eagerness to sow again
An abundant harvest creates enthusiasm and hope in the hearts of others.
An abundant harvest stimulates others to sow and watch for their harvest.
An abundant harvest provides the ability to meet needs immediately.

What truths we learn from verse 6:
An abundant harvest is determined by how much is planted.
An abundant harvest is based on the farmer's willingness to sow freely.
An abundant harvest circulated guarantees a bountiful return.

What truths we learn from verse 7:
The disbursement of an abundant harvest rests in the hands of the steward.
The abundant harvest is to be administered by hilarious stewards.
God is pleased when a harvest is distributed to meet the need of others.

What truths we learn from verse 8:
The circulated harvest has a high yield to the farmer.
God guarantees a bountiful return on whatever is given.
The circulated harvest produces a joyful experience for the giver.
The one who sows and gives has more than enough to meet his own needs.

What truths we learn from verse 10:
God supplies the seed for the farmer in the first place.
God produces the harvest.
God will give more see and make it grow.
God gives so that the farmer can give away more and more of the harvest.

What truths we learn from verse 11:
God supplies abundantly so you can give abundantly.
God often supplies agents for his steward to help ensure that the giving is meeting genuine needs.
Those who benefit from our harvest sow thanksgiving and praise to God.
An abundant harvest properly circulated reaps an additional harvest of thanksgiving and praise.

What truths we learn from verse 12:
A distributed harvest always results in needs being met.
A distributed harvest always results in abundant thanks to God.

What truths we learn from verse 13:
A distributed harvest stimulates praise to God.
A distributed harvest is testimony that one's actions reflect one's beliefs.
A distributed harvest is the testimony of God's salvation for mankind.

What truths we learn from verse 14:
A distributed harvest will stimulate prayer on behalf of the distributor.
A distributed harvest demonstrates God's grace at work through his stewards.

ECHO PRINCIPLE

As a young lad of six, I was introduced to what is known as the echo principle. I remember the first time I experienced the return of my voice.

My family had joined other members of our church for a picnic at the inspiring Colorado National Monument. At dusk, as the sun was setting into the west, Dad took me over to the edge of the cliff.

Enormous, dramatic sandstone monoliths reached from the valley floor to the darkening sky. Their shadows made them look even larger than their actual size.

Dad said, "Listen, Larry." Then he yelled toward the canyons and cliffs across the valley, "Hello, friend."

In seconds, the canyons called back, "Hello, friend; hello, friend; hello, friend." Never in my life had I heard canyons talk before, but these did!

Dad then yelled, "How are you?"

Again, the canyons responded, "How are you? How are you? How are you?"

Then Dad encouraged me to try it. I boldly yelled a six-year-old, "Hello," and listened excitedly.

"Hello, hello, hello," the canyons called back.

Whatever I said came back to me. Furthermore, what I sowed with my lips returned to me multiplied.

Everything we do—every word we say, every feeling we express, every dollar we give—will echo back to us multiplied. It is a law of the harvest. Therefore, how important it is to sow positive words, deeds, and actions. Only as we sow seeds of righteousness can we expect God's blessings and a bountiful harvest.

It is important that we continue to give abundantly from what we have. Don't stop. There is never a time to quit sowing and reaping. To stop is to short-circuit the circulation process. As long as God provides you with seed to sow, you should sow cheerfully, systematically, and unto the Lord. You will experience an abundant return.

Remember: *What you sow, you will reap!*

Key To Abundant Living

UNLOCKING YOUR LIFE OF CONTENTMENT

What do you want to plant? You have a wide variety of seeds available to you—financial resources, encouragement, wise advice, love, grace, time etc. What would you like to plant today from your seed collection? Pick just a couple of seeds for this exercise.

Now think about a year from now. Dream a bit. Pray. Visualize what you would like to see as a result of this planting. Describe what you believe this harvest could look like:

As the farmer for this planting, what do you now need to do to ensure a productive harvest? Jot down some things you will need to do to see the results you anticipate.

Chapter 8 ENJOYING ABUNDANCE

Now to him who is able to do immeasurably more than all we ask or imagine, according to his power that is at work within us . . .
—EPHESIANS 3:20, NIV

While on a trip to the Northwest many years ago, before the technology of smartphones, mobile banking, and credit card readers of today, Pat and I needed to replenish our cash supply. We had the latest in technology at our disposal: an automatic bank withdrawal card. Back then, we simply found our bank's local branch, inserted our card in the automatic teller, entered a pin, pushed a few other buttons, and instantly we had the cash we needed. You know the routine.

Our daughter, Jessica, thought this was a great game. She believed that all I had to do was push some buttons and, like magic, crisp new bills were delivered into my hands. During our trip, we made several more stops at various branch banks in various cities. Each time I allowed Jessica to help me obtain the money. What a fun game to play—or so she thought.

Several months later, as our family was driving across our hometown, Pat and I were discussing the pros and cons of making a particular purchase that afternoon. "Larry," Pat said, "we would benefit from the purchase; but as I see it, we don't have the money right now. I believe we should wait."

Before I had a chance to respond, Jessica piped up, "Daddy, you can get all the money you need. Just go over to the bank and use that machine. All you have to do is press the right buttons."

From Jessica's view, there was an unlimited supply of money available to me. Although she knew very little about how banking works, she did understand one simple truth—the person who knew what buttons to push one could receive ready cash.

PRINCIPLE 5

MY GIVING CAN BEGIN TO REFLECT THE RESOURCES OF MY HEAVENLY FATHER'S HOUSEHOLD, NOT MERELY MY LIMITED RESOURCES.

Beside the fifth point of the star I have written: I can give from my Father's abundant supply.

As stewards, you and I have been given free access to God's unlimited resources. What He has is available to those who have the access code to His supply.

A few months following our trip to the Northwest, I learned a valuable lesson concerning my bank access code at my bank. This lesson also gave me some insight into accessing God's resources.

CARD NOT VALID

One Saturday afternoon, we needed some cash. I went to the automatic teller machine, inserted my bank card in the appropriate slot, pushed the correct buttons, and waited. Instead of money this time, I received a message: "Card not valid." I made a half dozen attempts, but each time the machine gave me the same short, not-so-sweet answer. Baffled, I went home that day without the money I needed.

On Monday I paid a visit to the bank to investigate my invalid card problem.

The friendly bank representative checked my number. She looked up my account and saw that everything was in order. She examined the card. It appeared to be OK. Now she, too, was perplexed. She contacted the business administrator of the bank with the dilemma.

"Do you work at the Campus Crusade for Christ administration center?" she asked me.

"Why, yes, I do," I replied.

"Then I'm sure I know the answer to your problem," she replied. "You have an electronic card key system that permits you to enter your building, rather than using a traditional key, don't you?"

"Yes," I replied.

"Do you carry your card key in your wallet?" she asked.

"Yes, it's right here." I took my billfold out and showed her my office building card key.

She explained that a magnetic field was built into the plastic card that identified me as one who was authorized to enter my office building when I placed the card in the appropriate slot.

My bank card was also magnetically coded to show that I was authorized to receive the bank's services. Under normal conditions, the bank card performed faithfully for me. However, when the magnetic field of my bank card came in contact with the magnetic field of my office access card, the bank code was scrambled or erased.

Without my knowing it, my bank card had lost its authority to access my account. It looked and felt the same, but could no longer perform with the authority that it once had. Therefore, I had to obtain a new card.

As I walked out of the bank that day, I had a new insight into banking security—and into the importance of a steward living in the power of the Holy Spirit, with every known sin confessed.

CODE TO GOD'S RESOURCES

To tap into the resources of your heavenly Father effectively, it is necessary for you to choose to live your life in the power of the Holy Spirit. It is only the Spirit-filled steward who has unlimited access to God's abundant resources.

The vast majority of Christian stewards today live lives of defeat and frustration. They try hard but seem to get nowhere. They are powerless. Many today are living like a person that has lost all his computer passwords or bank access code. Under these conditions they are not capable of performing as they should. They may look as though they have it all together; but on the inside, they know that their access code has been scrambled. They are virtually worthless as far as Kingdom business is concerned. It is time for a reset!

A steward in this condition may still show up at all the right places. He can pray when called upon to do so. He may teach a Sunday school class. He may even give a little when asked to do so. He *appears* to be living a dynamic life.

It's only when he seeks to access God's unlimited resources that he painfully realizes he doesn't have the password needed to withdraw from God's account. Something has short-circuited the system.

SHORT-CIRCUITED POWER

One of my hobbies as a kid was an elaborate and complex model train setup. My brother and I used to spend hours running five engines and their cars around a giant 6' x 12' train table. On occasion, however, the entire train operation abruptly halted. Even though it had access to the Colorado Public Service Power Company, nothing worked.

When this occurred, I knew that somewhere on that intricate table layout, something was wrong. One time when it happened, I checked everything, but nothing seemed out of place. All the cars were on the tracks. From all appearances, my trains should have worked.

After many hours of frustration, I decided to run a small magnet over every inch of the 200 track layout. Eventually, I found the problem—a tiny nail that was used to hold the track in place had worked its way out of its position and became lodged between the outer rail and the center track.

This insignificant nail had caused a complete shutdown of my entire railroad for over two days. Once I removed the nail and turned on the transformer, the entire table came to life again. Power was once again flowing freely through the system.

In a similar way, sin in our lives can short-circuit our power supply from the Holy Spirit. The concept of spiritual breathing—exhaling and inhaling—can keep you free from obstructions and give you unlimited power to carry out your stewardship responsibilities.

POWER FOR A PURPOSE

Shortly before His crucifixion, Jesus told His disciples:

> "I tell you the truth, anyone who believes in me will do the same works I have done, and even greater works because I am going to be with the Father. . . . And I will ask the Father, and we will give you another Advocate, who will never leave you. He is the Holy Spirit, who leads you into all truth. The world cannot receive him, because it isn't looking for him and doesn't recognize him. But you know him because he lives with you now and later will be in you. No, I will not abandon you as orphans—I will come to you soon" (John 14:12, 16–18).

Jesus then explained to them:

> "You didn't choose me. I chose you. I appointed you to go and produce lasting fruit, so that the Father will give you whatever you ask for, using my name" (John 15:16).

Think of it! You were chosen by God Himself as one of His stewards. You have been appointed to be productive in carrying out your tasks. You are given the authority to ask of the Father whatever you wish to carry out your tasks. *You are given the power to be all that God wants you to be.*

Jesus promised He would send the Comforter. The Comforter is the Holy Spirit—the Spirit of Jesus Christ Himself. Jesus was willing to die on the cross and then break the bonds of death because He was not satisfied merely to *walk with* His disciples. He wanted to *live through* His disciples! But because He could not take residence in sinful lives, He chose to pay the price of our sin. Once our sin was covered by His blood, He could move in.

AUTHORIZED WEALTH DISTRIBUTOR

Do you see now why you are an Authorized Wealth Distributor of God's unlimited riches? He has chosen to distribute all He is and has through His stewards to others. He seeks those who will allow Him to work His life freely through them. He does not force Himself on any steward; but when He has an available, Spirit-controlled steward, He freely gives Himself through that steward.

You are the only view of God's character that many people will ever see. How you act, what you say, and how you respond to circumstances will either draw people to Him or cause people to turn from Him. As you are filled with the Holy Spirit, you reflect the very nature of God to those you touch. When you are not you are not very attractive to those that don't know who you know!

As a Spirit-filled steward, you are responsible to see that every resource He distributes through you gains maximum returns in bringing about His will.

The authority you have at present is part of your on-the-job training to prepare you to exercise additional authority with Him in eternity. He is training you to think as He thinks, love as He loves, and give as He gives. How privileged you are to have a Teacher like the Holy Spirit. He is eager to work through you. You are His agent—His Authorized Wealth Distributor.

TWO APPROACHES TO GIVING

Your responsibility is to distribute God's resources to others. There are two ways to give:

1. **Selective, logical giving.**

This approach to giving is a counterfeit of the way God planned for His stewards to distribute His wealth and resources. Unfortunately, most stewards today are greatly limiting their access and distribution through this form of giving.

Selective, logical giving is based on the premise that there is a limited supply that can be given. Therefore, it's important *not* to give—or at least give sparingly. If you give freely, you very well might run out. Selective thinking borders on indifference to the needs you see around you. If you believe there are limits to giving and you already feel you don't have enough to meet your needs, you can easily ignore the needs of others.

The Mazatec Indians of southwestern Mexico have an interesting approach to life, based on their concept of limited good. These people believe there is only so much good, so much knowledge, and so much love to go around. Therefore, if one gives himself to teaching another person how to do something, there is a good possibility that the teacher will drain himself of knowledge. To love a second child means you have to love the first child less.

Many thousands of believers in our culture today seem to think the same way. Many today act as if God was helpless and had limited resources.

Selective, logical giving:

- Is based on what one can reasonably give. If giving something away will not greatly affect the inventory or disrupt a plan of action, then the giving may occur. If, on the other hand, it looks like giving will disrupt a plan of action, the response is usually, "Sorry, I just can't help."
- May cause the giver to feel abused by people making requests because he feels over-extended. Have you ever felt you were being taken advantage of? If so, you like giving from a selective, logical viewpoint.
- Meets needs, but the joy of giving is largely lost. Rather than experiencing excitement in helping meet a need, the selective, logical giver often feels empty or depressed after giving.
- Is often viewed as a pledge or debt that must be paid. A friend once confided in me, "I made a pledge a few years ago. I have since changed my mind on the worthiness of the organization, but I'm a man of my word. Next month will be my last payment. I'm sure glad to be free of this burden." Selective, logical giving fails to rely on God's insight in making commitments.
- Can be defined as giving without seeking God's direction. This is the only way the unbeliever can give, for he is not in communication with God. At best, he can rely on his and other people's knowledge and judgment, but he has no ability to tap God's wisdom and understanding.

2. **Supernatural, Spirit-directed giving.**

The believer who is filled with the Holy Spirit has the privilege of giving in the second way—a supernatural, Spirit-directed way. To be able to give in this way is one of the greatest blessings one can experience from God. All it takes is an act of faith to supercharge your giving.

The steward who chooses to exercise his authority in giving is relying on God's specific direction to give. You're authorized to meet the needs that God lays before you.

This form of Spirit-directed giving is based on several truths:

- God knows what is needed. He is aware of your every need. Read what Jesus himself promised in Matthew 6:25–33. Two verses summarize this passage of promise (vs 31,33):

> "So don't worry about these things, saying, 'What will we eat? What will we drink? What will we wear? These things dominate the thoughts of unbelievers, but your heavenly Father already knows all your needs. Seek the Kingdom of God above all else, and live righteously, and he will give you everything you need."

- God will enable and provide to each steward to give what He leads that person to give. Paul says this to another community of stewards and you can count on this promise:

  > "And God will generously provide all you need. Then you will always have everything you need and plenty left over to share with others….Yes, you will be enriched in every way so that you can always be generous. And when we take your gifts to those who need them, they will thank God" (2 Corinthians 9: 8, 11).

- Giving from God's resources does not limit the steward to the number or amount of one's earthly resources. Paul wrote the following about a poor community of stewards in Macedonia that was generous beyond their capacity to give:

  > "They are being tested by many troubles, and they are very poor. But they are also filled with abundant joy, which has overflowed in rich generosity. For I can testify that they gave not only what they could afford, but far more. And they did it on their own free will" (2 Corinthians 8:1–3).

When you give from God's resources and at His direction, you become the first to realize the benefit. Your needs are met and you grow in faith and obedience to the Lord. You experience firsthand His unlimited resources flowing through you to others. You will often be shocked at what happens when you freely give in this way.

Giving supernaturally does not rule out the use of thoughtful evaluation. When you give supernaturally as a steward, you do not put your brain on a shelf. God created you with a sound mind. He has given you the capacity to reason and to think and evaluate the need before you. He is expecting you to be wise and prudent as a steward. When needs are presented, you may be led to say no. You may see alternatives to addressing the need that don't involve you. Emotional high-pressure responses are not what God has in mind for you. Allow Him to be the motivator of your giving, not circumstances. Again, be prudent. You are not distributing what is yours—it is His.

Recently I left a meeting at a coffee shop. As I was getting into my SUV a guy approached me, begging for money. He looked desperate and in need. I could tell he needed to eat. As he stood at my car door with his hand out, I felt my response to his appeal should be to provide him with an alternative that would actually help him. I said I would not give him money, but I would purchase breakfast for him at the coffee shop if he was hungry. He turned me down on the offer. He wanted money to support his addiction, not a meal.

God is waiting to bless you supernaturally as you follow His leading. I pray that you will choose to apply this truth in your life and discover the dynamic life that God has prepared for you as one of His distributors.

THE BOTTOM LINE

Supernatural, Spirit-directed giving boils down to your choice to live by faith and dependence on Him. Faith and trust in Him unlocks your Father's fortune. Only as you exercise your faith in this area will you increase in understanding how this principle works. The only limit to your tapping all that God has for you to give away is your unwillingness to trust Him, obey Him, and act on His leading.

Start by claiming God's promises. If you have never asked God to cleanse you and fill you with the Holy Spirit, you need to start here. Yes, we need to clean up our act for his supernatural giving to flow freely through us.

Remember: *You can give from your Father's abundant supply!*

Key To Abundant Living

UNLOCKING YOUR LIFE OF CONTENTMENT

WHAT IS CURRENTLY SHORT-CIRCUITING YOUR EFFECTIVENESS AS A BELIEVER AND A STEWARD?

Identify a bit more specifically how this happened.

What do you need to do to get the power available to you back on?

When will you take the action you know you need to take?

WHEN WAS THE LAST TIME THAT YOU USED SELECTIVE LOGICAL GIVING IN YOUR DECISION TO MEET A NEED?

What was the circumstance?

At the time, what did you feel you were lacking?

REFLECT ON A TIME WHEN YOU TRULY SENSED GOD LEADING YOU TO GIVE SOMETHING.

With this in mind, what was your response?

Did you meet the need in a way that was different from the way it was requested?

Based on this experience, what have you learned . . .

About yourself?

About needs?

About God?

Chapter 9
PLUGGED INTO POWER

It is Christ Himself—living within us, in all of His resurrection power, walking around in our bodies, thinking with our minds, loving with our hearts, speaking with our lips—who will empower us with the Holy Spirit...It is not our wisdom, our eloquence, our logic, our good personalities, or our persuasiveness . . .

—BILL BRIGHT

Are you trying to live like a faithful steward on the outside while realizing that something is missing on the inside? Take heart. There is a solution ready for you. It is ready for you to implement now. God does not want to watch you "trying hard" to do what He has planned for you. He does not delight in mediocrity. He is not satisfied with your living an "average" Christian life.

He has unlimited power and provision available to you right now. God delights in seeing the supernatural expression of His power work in every facet of your life.

You can begin to live a dynamic life in the power of the Holy Spirit and freely tap God's unlimited resources. I know this is true. I'm a living example of radical transformation!

TRANSFORMED

As a college student majoring in theater arts at the University of Colorado in 1964, I was at a crossroads in life. I loved the theater. I had dreams of making a name for myself in the entertainment industry—either Hollywood or New York. I had already invested four years in high school and two years of college study in developing my acting and directing craft. I was experiencing success.

Yet deep inside I knew something was not right. I felt empty. The dream of my future seemed to be foggy and fading. I felt stuck. My future was now uncertain. I had no clue as to how to get my life on track.

I knew I was a true believer. Yet, for years my attempt to make the Christian life work for me was failing. As an actor I knew how to play the Christian role quite well. I was active in the right things. I was good at playing the role. But my Christian life had no genuine joy or peace. I was frankly miserable, defeated, empty, and lost. I knew something was wrong. But what was I missing?

Because of this sense of failure, I had concluded the Christian life was full of fake people living by man-made do's and don'ts. Nothing I saw in the lives of other believers I knew was attractive to me. With rare exceptions, they too were also empty, depressed, and despondent. I decided the best way out of my Christian misery was to give up trying.

The first step seemed logical. Stop going to church. Since I rarely got anything out of showing up to be with other depressed hypocrites, I decided regular attendance was not a priority. But one Sunday I woke up with an strange desire to try another church. It occurred to me that maybe I could find some new friends that were not looking to be famous on the stage. I was responding to direction but did not know it.

As I arrived at a new church, I almost immediately met two outgoing engineering students. We connected. They were welcoming and positive. It was evident that they had their spiritual act together. They expressed joy, talked about Jesus, and seemed eager to live the Christian life. They had something that I knew I did not have. These guys were refreshingly different.

A friendship developed. A few weeks later over coffee I asked them why they seemed so excited about their faith, Jesus, and living a Christian life at the University of Colorado—of all places. These guys shared they too were about to give up Christianity less than six months earlier. Then they explained that they had discovered the simple and yet profound solution to their frustrating attempts in trying to live a Christian life: They had learned how to live life controlled by the Holy Spirit. They proceeded to shared with me what they had learned.

A GAME-CHANGER!

What you are about to read literally transformed my life that semester. I had never heard about asking the Holy Spirit to clean me up and empower me. My Christian experience was to "gut it out" and try harder. What they shared had nothing to do with **trying** to live the Christian life. It was about allowing the Holy Spirit to **empower** and control their lives.

UNDERSTANDING HOW TO BE FILLED BY THE HOLY SPIRIT.

The following is the consolidated message that my friends shared with me over coffee. While this will help you, I encourage you to visit CruStore.org. Purchase your copy of the complete Transferable Concept 3: How You Can be Filled with the Holy Spirit by Bill Bright. Transferable Concepts are a time-tested Bible study series that teach the principles of the abundant Christian life.

Understanding the truth of what you are about to read will change your life forever. I guarantee it!

In his introduction to The Letter to the Young Churches, J.B. Phillips wrote: "The great difference between present-day Christianity and that of which we read in these letters (New Testament epistles) is that to us, it is primarily a performance; to them, it was a real experience. We are apt to reduce the Christian religion to a code, or, at best, a rule of heart and life. To these men, it was quite plainly the invasion of their lives by a new quality of life altogether. They do not hesitate to describe this as Christ living in them."

That same first-century power—the power of the indwelling Christ—is available to us today. To experience this power, however, it may be necessary to answer some important questions about the Holy Spirit.

1. **Who is the Holy Spirit?** The Holy Spirit is God. He is not an "it." He is not a divine influence. He is not a fleecy white cloud. He is not a ghost or a concept. He is God—with all the attributes of deity. He is the third person of the Trinity—co-equal with God the Father and God the Son.
2. **Why did the Holy Spirit come?** The Holy Spirit came to earth to glorify Christ and to lead believers into all truth. On the eve of His crucifixion the Lord Jesus said to the disciples, "It is to your advantage that I go away; for if I do not go away, the Helper shall

not come to you; but if I go, I will send Him to you. . . . But when He, the Spirit of truth, comes, He will guide you into all the truth. . . . and He will disclose to you what is to come. He shall glorify Me; for He shall take of Mine, and shall disclose it to you" (John 16:7, 13–14).

As we study the Bible, the Holy Spirit reveals to us the truths of the Word of God and makes it relevant and meaningful in our lives.

As we are empowered by the Holy Spirit, He also guides our prayer lives and gives us the power to witness to others of His love and forgiveness.

In fact, it is impossible for anyone to even know Christ apart from the regenerating ministry of the Spirit. Jesus told Nicodemus, "Unless one is born of the water and the Spirit, he cannot enter into the kingdom of God" (John 3:5).

3. **What does it mean to be filled with the Holy Spirit?** To be led by the Holy Spirit is to be filled with Christ and to be abiding in Him. The word filling means "to be controlled, not as a robot, but as one who is led and empowered by the Spirit of Christ.

   This amazing fact that Christ lives in us is one of the most important truths in the Word of God. The standards of the Christian life are so high and so impossible to achieve that only one person has been able to succeed—Jesus Christ. Through His indwelling presence, He wants to enable all who will place their trust in Him to live this same supernatural life.

   Being filled with the Holy Spirit has a twofold significance.

   First, the Christian will bear spiritual fruit. Jesus said in Mark 1:17, "Follow Me, and I will make you become fishers of men." It is our responsibility to follow Christ. It is His responsibility to make us fishers of men, to draw people to Himself through our lives and words. But if he is not bearing fruit in the sense that he is introducing others to Christ, as well as living a holy life, he is not filled and controlled by the Holy Spirit, according to the Word of God (John 15:8).

He has chosen and appointed us to share the good news of His love and forgiveness with everyone, everywhere (John 15:16). To fail to witness for Christ with your words is to disobey His command. Yet, as we are faithful to obey Him, the Holy Spirit gives us the supernatural power we need for witnessing.

Second, as we continue to walk in the control of the Holy Spirit, our personalities also change and the fruit of the Spirit becomes increasingly obvious in our lives. Galatians 5:22 and 23 states that "the fruit of the Spirit is love, joy, peace, patience, kindness, goodness, faithfulness, gentleness and self-control."

An important word of caution. The Christian life is a life of faith, not a life of works. We should not *strive* to live a holy life. Nor should we seek an emotional or mystical experience, The Word of God must be the basis of our spiritual growth.

It is important to recognize the relationship between the Word of God and the Spirit of God. The Bible has little meaning to us apart from the illumination given by the Holy Spirit, and the Holy Spirit is hindered in speaking clear and life-changing truth apart from the Word of God. Therefore, there must be an emphasis in our lives of *both*. As we allow the Holy Spirit to direct and empower us, and as we meditate upon the Word of God, our lives will glorify God and will manifest more and more of the attributes of the Lord Jesus Christ.

4. **Why is the average Christian not filled with the Holy Spirit?** The average Christian is not filled with the Spirit for two reasons: first, lack of knowledge; and second, unbelief.

   Many Christians continue to live frustrated, fruitless lives simply because they do not understand who the Holy Spirit is and what the rich, abundant Christian life is all about.

   They do not know that the Holy Spirit actually lives in them and is willing to give them all the power they need to live the Christian life—the same power that belongs to Jesus Christ Himself. Many do not realize that they can draw upon this power by faith, or if they do realize it, many do not know how to appropriate the fullness of the Holy Spirit by faith, enabling them to live consistently, maturing Christian lives.

Thus, many live by feelings rather than by faith. Consequently, they find themselves on a spiritual rollercoaster, living from one emotional experience to another.

Many Christians are not filled with the Holy Spirit because of unbelief: they do not trust God. May are afraid to surrender their lives to Christ. They believe that God will change their plans, require them to give away their wealth, take all the fun from their lives, or make them endure tragedies.

God has proven that He is a loving God worthy of our trust. Jesus assures us, "If you then, being evil, know how to give good gifts to your children, how much more shall your Father who is in heaven give what is good to those who ask Him" (Matthew 7:11).

It is true that God may change our plans or circumstances, but in return, He gives us more of His blessing than we could ever receive apart from His grace. We need not fear the one who loves us so perfectly that He gave His own Son for us.

5. **How can one be filled with the Holy Spirit?** We are filled with the Holy Spirit by faith, just as we became Christians by faith. "By grace, you have been saved through faith; and that now of yourselves, it is a gift of God; not as a result of works, that no one should boast" (Ephesians 2:8–9). "As you, therefore, have received Christ Jesus the Lord, so walk in Him" (Col. 2:6).

   You do not have to beg God to fill you with His Holy Spirit. You do not have to earn God's fullness. You receive the fullness of the Holy Spirit by faith.

   To understand this truth, consider this illustration: When you want to cash a check, you do not go to the bank where you have a deposit, place your check on the counter, get down on your knees, and say, "Oh please, Mr. Teller, cash my check." Of course not. You simply go in faith, place the check on the counter, and wait for the money which is already yours. Then you thank the teller and go on your way.

Although you are filled with the Holy Spirit by faith and faith alone, it is important to recognize that several factors contribute to preparing your heart for the filling of the Spirit.

First, you must hunger and thrust after God and desire to be filled with the Holy Spirit. We have the promise of our Savior, "Blessed are those who hunger and thirst after righteousness, for they shall be satisfied" (Matt. 5:6).

Second, surrender your life to Christ in accordance with Paul's admonition in Romans 12: 1–2: "I urge you, therefore, brethren, by the mercies of God, to present your bodies a living and holy sacrifice, acceptable to God, which is your spiritual service of worship. And do not be conformed to this world, but be transformed by the renewing of your mind, that you may prove what the will of God is, that which is good and acceptable and perfect."

Third, confess every known sin that the Holy Spirit brings to your remembrance and thank God for the cleansing and forgiveness which He promises in 1 John 1:9: If we confess our sins, He is faithful and righteous to forgive us our sins, and to cleanse us from all unrighteousness."

If you are a Christian, the Holy Spirit already dwells within you. The moment you received Christ, the Holy Spirit not only came to indwell you, but He also imparted to you spiritual life, causing you to be born anew as a child of God. The Holy Spirit also baptized you into the body of Christ. In 1 Corinthians 12:13, Paul explained, "By one Spirit we are baptized into one body."

There is just one indwelling of the Holy Spirit, one rebirth of the Holy Spirit, and one baptism of the Holy Spirit—all of which occur the moment you receive Christ. However, there are many fillings, which is made clear in Ephesians 5:8. The command of God means to be constantly and continually filled, directed by, and empowered with the Holy Spirit as a way of life."

If you wish to be technical, you do not need to pray to be filled with the Holy Spirit; no scripture in the Bible tells us we are to pray for the filling of the Holy Spirit. However, since the object of our faith in God and His Word, you can claim the fullness of the Holy Spirit as an expression of your faith in God's command and His promise. You can demonstrate your faith right now.

Have you met these conditions? If so, you bow and claim the fullness of the Holy Spirit by faith. Here is a suggested prayer:

Dear Father, I need you. I acknowledge that I have been in control of my life and that, as a result, I have sinned against You. I thank You for forgiving my sins through Christ's death on the cross for me. I now invite Christ to take control of my life. Fill me with the Holy Spirit as You have promised in Your Word that You would do If I asked in faith. As an expression of my faith, I now thank You for filling me with your Holy Spirit and for taking control of my life.

If this prayer expresses the desire of your heart and if you have met God's conditions of heart preparation, you can be sure that God has answered you. You are now filled with the Holy Spirit whether you "feel" like it or not. Do not depend on emotions; we are to live by faith, not by feelings. You can begin this moment by drawing upon the vast, inexhaustible resources of the Holy Spirit to enable you to live a holy life and share Christ's love and forgiveness with men and women everywhere.

Remember, being filled with the Holy Spirit is a way of life. Thank Him for the fullness of His Spirit as you begin each day. Continue to invite Him to direct and empower your life moment by moment. This is your heritage as a child of God. [5]

Over coffee that day I began to realize it was the Holy Spirit's power that was missing in my life. This power is central to being an effective steward.

Being controlled and empowered by the Holy Spirit is key to tapping the unlimited resources of God's power. As you submit to the power of the Holy Spirit, you become an empowered Authorized Wealth Distributor. The one who is filled with and walks by faith in the power of the Holy Spirit is the one who can give freely without limitation. You can experience fruitfulness and the power of God working through you.

When I decided to take a step of faith and I asked God to empower me, fill me, and control my life, I was transformed. I simply acted on a command and a promise. I began a new adventure of being set free and be all that God planned for me to be—not by acting, trying harder, by guilt or obligation, or by how I felt. All I had to do is ask God to do what He promised He would do.

SPIRITUAL BREATHING

As I began to apply the truths you just read, my life took on an entirely new dimension. I was no longer living in a life from frustration and failure in my own strength. I was beginning to understand my role as follower of Jesue and a steward of all He offered me.

My life was transformed. I learned that I need not look for "feel good" mountaintop experiences. I did not need "more of Jesus." All I needed to do was to tap into His power and apply the principle of spiritual breathing. Applying this principle daily continue to give me an unlimited moment-by-moment supply of God's resources. I learned how to "breath spiritually."

> *Spiritual breathing is simply exhaling the impure and inhaling the pure by faith so one can continually experience God's love, power, and forgiveness.*

- Exhale is to confess your sin.

  To confess means simply to agree with God concerning your sin. He is not surprised when you sin, for He was aware of your sin the moment it was committed. When confessing sin, or exhaling, name the sin, agree that it is sin, and thank Him for His forgiveness of that sin. It is OK to list them if you need to.

  Claim this promise: "But if we confess our sins to him, he is faithful and just to forgive us our sin and to cleanse us from all wickedness" (1 John 1:9).

  Confession involves repentance, or a change in attitude or action. This is exhaling. This is when you get rid of those things that will limit the Holy Spirit from working in your life.

- Inhale is to surrender the control of your life anew to the Holy Spirit.

  When you do this, you are allowing His Spirit to work freely in and through your as a steward. Your feelings are not a prerequisite to being filled with the Holy Spirit.

> **This is a command to you, not an suggestion.** Just as you received Christ by faith, claim His power and resources also by faith. Here is your directive: "Don't be drunk with wine, because that will ruin your life. Instead, be filled with the Holy Spirit." Ephesians 5:18
>
> **Claim this promise:** "And we are confident that he hears us whenever we ask for anything that pleases him. And since we know he hears us when we make our requests, we also know that he will give us what we ask for" 1 John 5: 14, 15.

You can breathe spiritually as many times as is necessary every day. Exhale the junk and inhale the power of the Holy Spirit. Spiritual breathing is your access code to keep God's power and resources flowing through your life to transform your life and help you meet the needs of others. The Holy spirit sets you free to experience His power and tap His unlimited resources.

Are you now plugged into His power?

Key To Abundant Living

UNLOCKING YOUR LIFE OF CONTENTMENT

Reflect on what you have learned in this chapter. What did you find most helpful? Jot down five game-changers for you.

Express in your words why is it important for you to be empowered by the Holy Spirit.

Exhale sin; confess it!

Inhale His power; claim His promise to fill and work through you.

This act allows you to walk in the Spirit with freedom beyond all human comprehension. When you are living this way you will truly sense His spirit working through you.

As a demonstration of your faith, thank Him for filling and controlling you and for giving through you—whether you feel it or not! Put your faith in God and His Word.

PART TWO

YOUR INTENTIONAL NEXT STEPS

You can't go back and change the beginning,
but you can start where you are and change the ending.
C. S. LEWIS

Chapter 10
FINDING YOUR WAY

Remember how far you've come, not just how far you have to go. You are not where you want to be, but neither are you where you used to be.
—RICK WARREN

My wife and I were scheduled to attend a leadership retreat in the mountains of Southern California. We awoke that morning to a beautiful blue-sky day. Rain the day before had lasted into the night, and the early morning sun shining on the wet green foliage in our yard was a sight to behold!

As we headed toward the mountains, we realized that the storm of the night had left the San Bernardino valley but not the mountains. Black, forbidding clouds loomed ahead of us.

As we drove we soon caught up with the storm. Within minutes we had left the blue skies of an April spring day and were engulfed by thick mountain fog.

While in the sunlight, we had visibility, and clear direction as to where we were going. Our way was bright and peaceful.

But when we entered the fog we encountered a totally different dimension. We faced a tremendous potential for danger as we drove into the white, thick, and murky shroud. We could barely see the front of our car, much less the winding narrow road that hugged the mountainside with no guardrails.

No longer was our focus on the retreat where I was scheduled to speak. The foggy conditions that surrounded us created feelings of tension, fear, helplessness, disorientation, and confusion.

To creep ahead we had to open both car doors and watch for the white lines that marked our path. As Pat watched for the continuous line on her right, I watched for the center line on my left. We drove at a snail's pace, trusting that no cars had stopped ahead of us—the only way we would know would be by impact!

While we can often get distracted by our immediate conditions, you can be assured that God isn't caught in the fog. Knowing His view of things gives us confidence in our heavenly Father's plan, even though we understand very little of the big picture.

Wouldn't it be great to travel through life without the restrictions of earthly circumstances and human frailties? Adam and Eve had a good thing going in Eden until the gray, dark cloud of sin moved in over their balmy paradise.

It is important to remember that, regardless of the circumstances, God is still working out His plan for us. He has not changed His mind, even though we may have to slow down to a snail's pace at times because the fog of our circumstances makes us blind to what's ahead.

WHY ALL THE FOG?

To understand better what causes the fog around us, come with me back to the Garden of Eden. Adam, as the receiver, was happy with all that God had given, including his beautiful helpmate, Eve. Their days were full of clear azure skies as they were learning to give back to God, their Creator. Every moment of every day, they experienced contentment. It was rewarding to be stewards of what God had created.

God's creation lived in total harmony. No strife. No discord. No pain. No sorrow. No distrust. And the result of God's giving plan was total, perfect peace.

Every evening Adam and Eve had company. The Bible tells us that God personally came to be with them—to instruct them and to have close fellowship with them. They had open, free conversations with their Creator. The love relationship they had with God gave them a freedom that man has never experienced since.

In Genesis 3, we are introduced to a new deceptive plan that would result in emptiness and disorientation. Little did Adam and Eve realize that the decisions they were about to make on a balmy afternoon in Eden would throw the world into confusion and despair. The fog was about to overtake them!

A LESSON IN GARDENING!

Remember the story? Eve was out enjoying their garden paradise. Everything was perfect. Adam may have been taking a nap, or he may have gone "skinny dipping" in the nearby Euphrates River. We know by the account that he was not far from Eve.

Then the craftiest of all God's creatures slid over to Eve and initiated a conversation. In their brief dialog, we are introduced to Satan's plan of **getting.** He was out to steal two stewards.

Satan looked upon all of God's magnificent creation and found only one possible place where he could gain a toehold: man's will. He went for it with all he had and put a full-court press attack on man's will to choose. Let's listen, from behind a bush, to an expanded version of what that conversation might have sounded like:

> "Good afternoon, Eve. My, what a beautiful day! Looks like you're enjoying yourself."
>
> "Oh, yes, Mr. Serpent, We love my new home. Adam's out for a few minutes, and I thought I would do a little stewarding this afternoon."
>
> "Really? Eve, I'm taking a garden survey today. Do you have a few minutes? Good. I have a couple of questions for you. I hear you're not allowed to eat any of the fruit in this garden—direct orders from God. Is that right?"
>
> "Of course, we may eat, Mr. Serpent. It's only from the tree in the center of the garden that we are not to eat. God says we are not to eat it or even touch it, or we will die."
>
> "You can't be serious! That's not true! Look, Eve, I've known God much longer than you have. Let me assure you, you won't die. You see, God knows very well that the instant you eat of that tree, you will become like Him, for your eyes will be opened. If you eat the beautiful fruit of that tree, you will be able to distinguish good from evil. When did He tell you that anyway?"

> "Why, just last week as we walked by there on our evening stroll—He reminded us to not eat the fruit from that specific tree."
>
> "Last week? Well, now I understand what he meant. Eve, the fruit wasn't quite ripe then. Things are different now. I was by there earlier today, and that fruit is ripe now. It's ready for picking! Come on, let's take a look."
>
> As they approach the center of the garden, Eve says, "Yes, Mr. Serpent, it does look ripe. I can't remember if it looked this beautiful last week."
>
> "Eve," says the Serpent, "you need to understand: things change—conditions change. Help yourself to the best fruit basket in Eden. It's yours! Trust me. Get it. If you don't, that one—right there—is going to spoil. I had a bite earlier today. Absolutely wonderful—best fruit in this garden."
>
> "But, God said—"
>
> "Eve, come on . . . reach out and touch that soft texture and smell that aroma. It tastes as good as it looks and feels. You will simply love the flavor—out of this world!."
>
> "I really shouldn't—"
>
> "Oh, go ahead—try it; you will love it, and you'll have one up on Adam. He's always showing you new things. Now's your chance to show him a thing or two. Take the lead this time and surprise him!"

You know what Scripture records. Eve was deceived. The fruit did look lovely. Now she knew what God was not telling her: This would make her wise. She tried it just as Adam showed up. She gave some to Adam, and he, too ate. Both were now biting into deception! Satan had achieved his objective. Sin now controlled them.

FOGGED IN!

And as they ate the fruit that day, they suddenly became aware of the difference between good and evil. They now saw their nakedness as something bad. They knew they had blown it. By not trusting in God's word in one bite, they experienced separation from God, their Creator. They got lost in the fog. They became consumed about themselves. This separation from their Creator was worse than physical death. Their seemingly innocent act of disobedience began to create havoc in their lives. What was good was now bad. What was bad seemed to actually be good.

Just what did crafty Mr. Serpent pull on Eve? Satan used his famous four-point whammy to get their focus off of trusting God and onto their circumstances:

1. Satan insisted that everything is relative.
2. Satan emphasized getting.
3. Satan appealed to sensual responses.
4. Satan fostered covetousness.

It's important that we understand each of Satan's primary ploys, for this same plan is used just a successfully today.

SATAN INSISTS THAT EVERYTHING IS RELATIVE!

Satan insists that judgment is relative. Depending on the circumstances and the condition, you can make different decisions. His plan has no room for absolutes, for there is no right or wrong in relativism.

A number of years ago, I was skimming the *Wall Street Journal*. In the midst of the business news, I found my old friend Mickey Mouse. I learned that Mickey was having some trouble keeping up with our changing times.

Remember the old evergreen favorite Disney films: *Peter Pan, Mary Poppins, Cinderella, Lady and the Tramp, Snow White,* and the great cartoons of Donald Duck, Mickey and Minnie, and Pluto? Disney keeps the old favorites in "the vault" and only occasionally releases them. The industry calls these "evergreen classics."

What is Disney producing today? Movies that reflect a new social order with a new social agenda. The executives are proud of the changes that they have brought to their worldwide viewing audience. And many of their new products are failing financially!

You see, conditions have changed since Peter Pan and Tinker Bell took Wendy, Michael, and John to Never Never Land.

This is Disney's way of attempting to have its cake and eat it too. Ol' Mickey has decided to live a double standard. Everything now is relative. Mickey has decided to fully embrace the new God-free culture! The changes reflected at Disney are changes you now see throughout our society.

The moral revolution of the last 70 years has created a "new standard" that has removed God from the picture. Our new progressive world is characterized now by a redefinition of words, new thinking on sexual identity, acceptances of profanity, a pandemic of drug addiction, and out-of-control suicide. What was once considered as wrong is now accepted as normal behavior. When boundaries are removed there is no right or wrong.

SATAN EMPHASIZES GETTING!

On that afternoon in Eden, Satan found that Eve's self-centeredness could be manipulated. Remember what Satan said? "You won't die!" the serpent replied to the woman. "God knows that your eyes will be opened as soon as you eat of it, and you will be like God, knowing both good and evil" (Genesis 3:4–5).

What a deal! Take it, Eve! This opportunity may pass. You cannot pass up this offer!

This is not a 50 percent off sale. This is a 100 percent giveaway! Get it now!

As Eve's greed reached for the ripe fruit, Adam also was stimulated to take part and get in on the deal. Their greed was exposed. In a single act, Satan derailed their wills, which were designed to respond freely to God.

Rather than giving attention to God's plan for them, now they could see only their immediate wants. They forgot who they were and why God had created them. Here. They became self-centered as they changed their focus from giving to getting.

The world's system has a masterful marketing scheme working today. It is out to focus our attention on things around us and destroy our commitment to biblical values and virtues. In the fog, we forget why we are here and live only for the present. With our focus on the present, we become fearful of the future.

A cartoon in *Time* magazine once caught my attention. Mr. and Mrs. Average American were enjoying a quiet evening at home. As he read his favorite book, she was reviewing the sales ads in their local paper. The silence was broken as she looked up at him and said, "I wonder if we shouldn't start hoarding things before it becomes unpatriotic again."

That was way back in 1979, but only recently did I discover that cartoonist Chan Day had created this essay on the American attitude for the *New Yorker* magazine in 1948! Strange, isn't it, that the commentary is still relevant today?

We are preoccupied with wanting more and more. We hoard and store our possessions. The more we get, the more we want.

Jesus had an encounter with a young man who was obsessed with things. The young man came to Jesus to ask a question: "What must I do to get into heaven?" In Mark 10:19–22, we find their conversation:

> "Jesus said: 'But to answer your question, you know the commandments: you must not murder. You must not commit adultery. You must not steal. You must not testify falsely. You must not cheat anyone. Honor your father and your mother."
>
> 'Teacher,' the man replied, 'I've obeyed all these commandments since I was young.'
>
> Looking at the man, Jesus felt genuine love for him. 'There is still one thing you haven't done,' he told him. 'Go and sell all your possessions and give the money to the poor, and you will have treasure in heaven, then come and follow me.'
>
> At this the man's face fell, and he went away sad, for he had many possessions."

This young man was so obsessed with his possessions that he was in bondage to them. By the world's standard, he lived a righteous life. He apparently gained his possessions through honest business practices. Such a nice guy!

No doubt, he was an outstanding young upper-class business executive in Judea. He had acquired all the nice things, but his possessions controlled him. When Jesus told him what to do, he left in dismay. He could not give up what he was hoarding.

Often, we look back on conversations of this type and say with a pious attitude, "Poor guy, he wasn't willing to pay the cost of following Jesus." Are we forgetting that we too often decide how we will follow Christ by what we possess?

Are there things you have today that stand in your way of following Christ all the way? Is there a habit or a relationship that has first priority? Is there a status in your community that you enjoy, a dream house you now own, a summer home on the lake, or a hobby that is keeping you from being maximized in the Kingdom business? How about a inappropriate sexual relationship or an addiction that you enjoy? What is holding you back?

Don't get me wrong, things that you have are not bad—but the issue is, "Who controls who?" Have you relinquished to God your rights to the many possessions He has already given you? Are you willing to give up temporal possessions for eternal gains?

Today we are caught up in a whirlwind of materialism. We simply can't seem to get enough stuff! Like drug addicts, we must continually support our habit by getting more. We seem to be on a continual buying spree.

In the last few years, a new business enterprise has come onto the scene, which enables us to enjoy getting even more. Have you noticed the phenomenal growth of the mini-storage business? Because we have outgrown our place to store the things we collect, we can now rent space! No longer are we limited to our home storage.

Doesn't storage-mania remind you of the illustration Jesus gave in Luke 12:16? The farmer was growing so much that he created a storage problem for himself. He decided to tear down the old, small, inadequate barns and build bigger ones.

That in itself might not have been wrong, but what was his motivation? He wanted to store more. His motivation was self-centered. He expected that all he had would be there for his personal pleasure for years to come. Are we not also guilty of storing up for a time of self-centered pleasure?

The craving for more has led even to an increase in gambling. Today, Americans throw away **tens of billions** of dollars in hopes of getting more "the easy way." A few years back, only a few states permitted gambling. Now it is aggressively encouraged by many state and local governments. The jackpots are now in excess of a billion dollars!

To be with it today, you have to have at least one lottery ticket stashed away as you "pray" that your number will be the winner. Daily we hear of the big winners and hope that our number will be next. On numerous occasions, I have heard even believers comment, "When I win, I will be helping the church and the missions I support."

Satan uses other subtle ways to get us focused on our needs and on getting. As we grow in affluence, many of us become preoccupied with success and ease of getting. Technology and COVID-19 have helped make hoarding even easier and faster. Today I can order my "wants" without leaving my home via Amazon—and have my wants delivered to my door within twenty-four hours. My "want-of-the-day" is satisfied.

Being successful in itself is not bad. God made us with a mind to excel as faithful stewards, but often the drive for success becomes a means to stomp on others in the pursuit of self-satisfaction. When pursued to the extreme, success leaves in its wake all forms of sickness, broken families, neglected children, and career disappointments.

SATAN APPEALS TO SENSUAL RESPONSES!

The enemy of our soul is a master at using our senses of hearing, taste, sight, smell, and feeling to advance his personal agenda of self-centeredness and greed.

God gave us five senses so we could fully appreciate God's creation. He still desires that we experience every aspect of creation as it lives out its continuous cycles of giving and receiving. However, Satan knows that through the senses, he can misdirect man into thinking only of himself and his passion for pleasure.

Eve had enjoyed the privileges of living in Eden through the senses. She **saw** the beauty. She **smelled** the fresh air and the fragrance of each flower. She enjoyed the fruit of the garden as she **tasted** the lush ripe produce. She could **hear** nature singing and could also communicate with Adam and with God. And as Adam and Eve walked arm in arm and occasionally stopped to pet an animal, they **felt** the closeness that reflected their oneness with each other, nature, and God.

Once Satan saw this was his means to turning our hearts from givers to getters, he was able to capture our self-interested hearts. Today, his subtle persuasion keeps us reaching out for fulfillment through sensual satisfaction.

While driving home from work one day, I came face to face with a beautiful woman clad in a skimpy white bikini. There she was in broad daylight, stretched out in all her bronze glory, smiling at me. She called her home a giant billboard—least thirty feet tall and eighty feet long. Her smile, beauty and tan body were impossible to ignore.

Her image topped a building at the corner of a busy intersection. No one could miss seeing her—and no man wanted to. It was only after her beauty caught my eye that I noticed a commercial statement accompanying this dream girl: "Things go better with milk."

The medium of advertising has proved an effective accomplice for Satan in carrying out his schemes. In fact, the people in the advertising business have become masters of manipulating our senses. In order to stimulate our buying and hoarding impulse. Advertising specialists work overtime to make things as attractive as possible.

As long as the world system can keep your attention focused on pleasure and comfort, you're not likely to be effective in your Christian walk. Every form of sensual response possible is used to misdirect you and get you to think about yourself. Beware! If you're not careful, you could walk quite innocently into your enemy's web and be trapped.

SATAN FOSTERS COVETOUSNESS!

Satan's plan results in an unhealthy passion for self-gratification. He knows that our craving for pleasures can result in negative competition, envy and strife. No matter where you look today, you can't help but see the result of the plan to satisfy your passions.

The result of our self-gratification is discord, disunity, distrust, broken family relationships, community strife, economic turmoil, and political fighting. Even within our churches today, we have cliques, gossip parties, backbiting, and excessive materialism.

Covetousness breeds unhealthy competition that creates an accelerated spiral of greed.

On a number of occasions, I flew in a low-flying commuter jet from Los Angeles International Airport to Ontario, California. On these short flights, I noticed that sections of greater Los Angeles seem to have a passion for backyard pleasure. In some areas, every single home has a pool in the backyard.

The fad probably started when one family decided that a pool would be good for the kids and their friends, so they build a basic rectangular pool. No more. Today the investments in backyard pleasures now exceeds the cost of the home on the property. What is even more amazing to me is that seldom is anyone **in** any of these lavish pools!

Let's admit it: we believers often get caught up in the game of getting as much as the non-believers do. Because we live in a world full of wants and greed, we tend to adapt to the culture around us. We end up thinking just as the world thinks.

During the Here's Life America campaign in 1976, when 185 cities were involved in special evangelistic outreaches, I attended a local city funding committee meeting in a major city.

I proposed to these leaders that to raise the funding that was needed a majority of the needed funds should be secured from influencers in the city, with each of the leaders giving by $5,000 or more to help set the needed momentum. I invited the leadership to each give $5,000 or more. I explained that this would quickly create needed financial momentum, give credibility to the unified city-wide efforts, and help to stimulate more giving from within the community.

One influential person in attendance balked at my invitation to help set the pace, saying, "There isn't anyone in this city who can give $5,000. That kind of money simply is not available here!"

Regardless of his emotional retort, the funding proposal was adopted by the committee. Commitments made that day helped launch a successful funding plan. Those present left excited and encouraged—that is, all but the first person who spoke up. He still was convinced that getting the needed finances in their city would be an uphill battle. And he was still "praying" about what he might commit.

As we walked out of the restaurant where we met, the conversation changed to business deals and other investment opportunities. Suddenly the vocal, cautious member of the group came alive as he excitedly told us about the good deal he had found that morning.

His wife's birthday was in just a few days, and for a present, he had bought her a dream car—a new luxury model with a plush interior and loaded with all the modern extras, for a fraction of the dealer's cost. Our business friend then boasted that he had made considerable savings in the deal by paying cash.

I'm not sure what went through the other committee member's minds that noon in the restaurant parking lot, but I couldn't help but remember the man's comment just 45 minutes earlier: "There's no one in this city who can give $5,000." His passion for material possessions would likely prevent him from experiencing all the blessings that his Heavenly Father desired to give to him. He was caught up in pleasure and greed.

Do you find yourself living in a fog of confusion and focusing on yourself? Every day of our lives, the subtle appeals of the world call us, and we can easily respond without realizing that we have been trapped in a web of deceit.

Have you ever bought a product simply because it was on sale and then three months later realized that you'd never used the purchase? Is the item you are currently thinking of still in the box that it came in? This has happened to me

Satan is doing his best to create in us an unhealthy passion for self-gratification, but he is a defeated foe. You need not be afraid. If you are a believer, he has no power over you—greater is He who is in you than he who is in the world. Being aware of Satan's schemes can enhance your ability to counter his hassles. He may even win a battle or two, but he has already lost the war.

Before moving on to the next chapter, complete the KEY TO ABUNDANT LIVING, on the following page. It is important for you to identify ways that you get caught in the trap of covetousness. Now that you know the game being played you can be ready to counter the attack! There is no reason for us to play his games of deceit. We can be winners, not losers!

Key To Abundant Living

UNLOCKING YOUR LIFE OF CONTENTMENT

Describe in your own words how you unknowingly have been caught by Satan's plan of getting. Write down three examples from your own experience.

1.

2.

3.

We all have a tendency to be impulsive at times. Jot down examples that come to your mind in the following categories—be specific:
While shopping:

While enjoying leisure time:

While going about your daily tasks:

When you learn of a need in your church or in your community:

Chapter 11
MAXIMUM IMPACT

The two most important days in life are the day you were born and the day you discover the reason why.
—MARK TWAIN

Biblical principles are great to know, but what good are they if you can't apply them to your life in practical ways? Many stewards are sitting before excellent Bible teachers, soaking up the Word of God, but souring because they are doing nothing with what they are learning except hoarding it for themselves.

The real test of stewardship comes when you are called upon to take action. If you are not breathing spiritually and walking in the Spirit, you could easily miss the opportunity to demonstrate effective stewardship.

In the following pages, I want to help you begin making practical applications of the five principles of God's wealth distribution system that you learned in Part One. Just reading about the principles will not make you what you want to be. I pray that this chapter will begin to help you begin to live the life of a wise, thoughtful and intentional steward.

THERE ARE SEVEN STEPS YOU CAN TAKE TO BEGIN APPLYING WHAT YOU HAVE LEARNED:

1. **Give yourself and your possessions to God.** Have you, as an act of your will, turned your life over to Him? Have you said, "Lord, I relinquish all rights to my life. Put me to work as a steward for Your king-

dom." God is able to work only through the one who chooses to turn the control of one's life over to Him.

Have you given your possessions to Him? Yes, I know, He already owns everything; but as an act of your will, have you intentionally turned everything over to Him? How about your health? Your job? Your family? Your hobbies? Your material accumulations? Your home? Your dreams? Your future? God can do a lot with a little if He has all of you.

2. **Recognize that God is your total and final supply of all you need.** The post-Christian philosophy of today wants you to believe that you are the controller of your life. The world yells to you, "Work harder and you will experience success. Your job is your source of provision. Your leisure time is your source of rest and relaxation." God is marginalized until you choose to recognize His role and your purpose.

   It is because of God's generosity to us that we live, breathe and have our being. Your income cannot make you happy. Your family and friends cannot provide you with contentment and joy. God, and only God, is your total and final supply of all you need.

3. **Count on Him by faith to empower you with the Holy Spirit.** There is no one more miserable than a believer trying and striving to live the life of a steward in his own strength. God provided us the Holy Spirit so that we could be all that He planned for us to be. He planned for you to live a victorious Christian life. He planned for you to be an Authorized Wealth Distributor. He planned for you to have His power plugged into your life.

   Soon after Pat and I were married, we decided to purchase our first home. It was a small two-bedroom starter home built over ninety years ago. Six years later, we found a historic Spanish-style house. It was also over eighty years old, but we loved its quaint Spanish charm. One issue faced us: each room had only two electrical outlets and an old 15-amp electrical system. A few years after we moved in, we decided to remodel our kitchen and make some deferred maintenance upgrades. High on our list was an electrical upgrade to 110 amps. With this power upgrade, we could now use modern conveniences that previously were not available to us.

Wouldn't it be ridiculous for Pat and me to continue in our upgraded home, living as if the power upgrade were not there? We now had an abundance of power. The power company was eager to supply our power needs. All we have to do is plug into the power source. Likewise, the power to live a victorious life as a steward is at your disposal right now. All you need to do is plug into the power. The Holy Spirit is eager to supply.

4. **Begin to give according to His directions**. He has already provided you with hundreds of things that you can give. Now it's a matter of you distributing what you have. God cannot provide you with more until you give away what you already have. As you give what you have, you are ready to receive more. God is then able to make a compensating deposit into your stewardship inventory.

   Be alert for opportunities to give. Chapter 14 will whet your appetite and stimulate your mind to consider creative ways to give. There is no limit. To reap a harvest, however, you must consciously sow, and care for what you have planted. The harvest you are expecting will be the result of your care and intentionality.

5. **Thank and praise God for the privilege you have of distributing His wealth and resources.** I am convinced that thanksgiving and praise unlock the gates of His storehouse more than anything else. Thanksgiving demonstrates our humility and gratitude for all He does for us. Thanksgiving is an act of worship that demonstrates we are walking by faith. Even when, from our vantage point, the situation may seem bleak, we are told: "Be thankful in all circumstances, for this is God's will for you who belong to Christ Jesus." (1 Thessalonians 5:18).

   Praise and thanksgiving is the language of heaven. Since we are a part of His kingdom, it is only reasonable that we communicate in the official language. Consider two reasons:

   First, our heavenly Father is worthy of praise. Look at all He has done for us. He is the omnipotent Creator and Giver of everything. The psalmist put it to music with these words:

> "Let all that I am praise the Lord. I will praise the Lord as long as I live. I will sing praises to my God with my dying breath" (Psalm 146:1–2).

Second, we are to praise God for the many benefits and privileges He lavishes upon us. If you're having trouble remembering His benefits, take a look at Psalm 136 and Psalms 145 through 150. There is no way we could ever begin to acknowledge all the privileges and benefits He has extended to us, His children.

God also takes action when we praise Him. In 2 Chronicles 20:12, King Jehoshaphat found himself up against incredible circumstances. The armies of Ammon, Moab and Mount Seir had declared war on Judah. King Jehoshaphat called the people of Judah together and prayed:

> "O our God, won't you stop them? We are powerless against this mighty army that is about to attack us. We do not know what to do, but we are looking to you for help."

The Lord answered the request of His people. He instructed them not to be afraid. He promised deliverance without fighting. God had an incredible rescue operation planned for His people.

King Jehoshaphat decided to appoint a choir to sing and to lead the army into battle. They were dressed in sanctified garments and instructed to sing a song of praise, "His Loving Kindness is Forever."

What happened? Praise unleashed God's power and provision for His people:

> "And at the moment they began to sing praises, the Lord caused the armies of Ammon, Moab, and Mount Seir to begin fighting among themselves, and they destroyed each other!" (2 Chronicles 20:22).

If you are facing a problem, don't fret—praise God. The greater your challenge and the more difficult your circumstances, the more important it is to praise God and express your thanks to Him for His provision for you. Every time you praise and thank God, you are demonstrating faith in His ability to supply.

6. **Expect results.** You demonstrate faith when you watch with expectancy for the multiplied harvest of what you sow. And be assured that God will return to you what you have given at the point of your need. You will also receive a multiplied return. Remember, Jesus promises:

> "Give and you will receive. Your gift will return to you in full—pressed down, shaken together to make room for more, running over, and poured into your lap. The amount you give will determine the amount you get back" (Luke 6:38).

God controls the return. He determines when your giving is to return to you. He may choose to be very creative in how your return is delivered. He will deliver when he knows you are ready.

A few years ago, I had a major project due. It was a rather complex report that involved interviews, analysis, and considerable creative planning, and writing. I had good intentions but other responsibilities had kept me from giving it the attention it needed.

The deadline had crept up on me—it was now due within a day. The only way I saw to finish the task was to cancel everything else and focus on only one thing. I directed my team not to interrupt me.

I was less than fifteen minutes into my focus and my intercom buzzed. At first, I thought I'd ignore it, but I reluctantly picked up the phone.

"Larry, there is an urgent matter that I really believe you would want to take," my secretary told me. She assured me it would take only a few minutes.

Before I picked up the phone I paused and prayed, "Lord, I'll give time to this matter now, but I'm counting on You to multiply back to me the time I give to this matter."

I picked up the phone. An hour later, we finished dealing with a delicate matter and we closed the conversation with prayer. As I hung up, I wondered how I was going to make up the time when in only a few hours the project had to be finished. I started to panic!

I told my secretary, "Please, no more calls, not even from Pat! I've got to get going, or you and I will be here all night." As I hung up, I prayed, "OK, Lord, let's see You pull this one together. Thank you that You know more about this matter than I do."

Yes, I expected to see God give me a quick course in Spirit-powered writing. Amidst my anxiety and near desperation, the intercom buzzed again. "Oh, no, not again . . . I said no more calls!" I answered with some disgust in my voice, "What's the problem?"

"It's Rick, and he's calling concerning your project. I told him you asked not to be interrupted, but he said it was important to talk to you personally," my secretary told me.

With some hesitancy I took the call. "Hi, what's going on?" I asked Rick.

"Larry, I've been doing some evaluation this afternoon and the deadline we are under. We need to push pause and rethink our options on this one. I'm not ready. I'm moving the deadline up by at least two weeks. Relax. I'll get back to you tomorrow so we can meet and get things rescheduled."

There never was a follow-up meeting. Other priorities pushed the urgent project to a low priority. God didn't just extend my few hours that afternoon; He gave me multiplied hours to invest in others that I never thought I would see.

7. **Give again and again and again.** Don't play games with giving. Although there will always be a multiplied harvest, please, **never** give to get. Rather, give to receive to give to receive to give. God is not pleased with manipulators!

   Think of giving and receiving as a continuous cycle. Never stop. What God gives to you is just what someone else needs. You have an unlimited inventory to draw upon. Use it freely. Your continuous giving will change your life as well as meet many specific needs. Be creative in your giving. Have fun distributing what God has given to you.

As you choose to take these steps, you are joining a special association of believers whom I have been referring to as Authorized Wealth Distributors. This is a network of Spirit-filled believers who choose, as an act of their will, to give freely to help meet the needs of others.

How about signing on as one of God's Authorized Wealth Distributors? Are *you* ready right to take the step of faith and "sign on"?

Here is your covenant agreement:

AUTHORIZED WEALTH DISTRIBUTOR COMMITMENT

BY FAITH, I HAVE GIVEN MYSELF AND MY POSSESSIONS TO GOD AND RECOGNIZE HIM AS MY TOTAL AND FINAL PROVIDER OF ALL THAT I NEED. I HEREBY COUNT ON HIM, BY FAITH, TO EMPOWER AND CONTROL ME WITH HIS HOLY SPIRIT. I DECLARE THAT I SHALL GIVE ACCORDING TO HIS DIRECTION, EXPECTING OBVIOUS RESULTS THAT WILL STRENGTHEN MY WALK OF FAITH.

SIGNED **DATE**

Authorized Wealth Distributors have been active in every culture since Adam and Eve had to move out of their garden retreat. As you study God's Word, you will find hundreds of examples of men and women who choose to trust, obey, and give what they had to meet the needs of others. Some were famous. Most were average people like you and me. Take the woman in 2 Kings 4:1–7, for example.

AN AVERAGE WOMAN

In 2 Kings 4:1–7, you will meet a single parent with two young boys. Her husband died while attending seminary. He apparently left his wife with some outstanding debts. Because she was not able to pay the creditors, she was in jeopardy of losing her sons to slavery as compensation for the debt.

In desperation, she turned to God's prophet, Elisha. She explained her dilemma and asked him what to do. Elisha responded by asking her what food she had in her house—a rather strange question considering her circumstances.

She explained that all she had left was one jar of olive oil. Not very much—but God took what she had and multiplied it. Elisha told her to gather all the pots and jars she could borrow from everyone in her neighborhood, take them into her home and close the door. She obeyed.

Elisha told her then to pour one jar of her olive oil into another jar and set the filled jar aside. She was to continue filling the other containers until they were all filled. As she gave from the one jar she had, God took care of the multiplication. One container after another was filled. The more she gave, the more she had. Only when the last jar was filled did the oil from the original container stop flowing.

From the abundant return of God's unlimited inventory, she was able to sell the oil, pay her debt and protect her boys from the threat of slavery. As an act of her will, through faith and obedience, she became an Authorized Wealth Distributor for the Lord.

The issue is not what you have or how much you have; the issue is, what are you going to do with what God has given to you?

Keep your priorities in order:

1. **Give to God.** Keep your eyes on Jesus. He's the best example you have. The more you focus on Him, the more effective you will be.

- *Keep walking in the Spirit.* Yes, you will stumble. You will fall. But you can exhale and inhale and keep your heart and mind free from the distractions of the world. The Holy Spirit can work only through a clean vessel.

- *Keep saturating your mind with God's Word.* The Bible is full of examples of giving and contains thousands of promises. The effective Authorized Wealth Distributor knows his procedures manual.
- *Keep asking God for direction.* Ask Him what you should ask for. Ask Him for wisdom and insight in how to respond to needs. There will be times when He will tell you that someone else will meet the need. Be sensitive in asking and in listening.
- *Keep living a life of integrity.* As a child of God, and as His steward, you should reflect the mindset of the Kingdom at all times—even when no one is watching you!
- *Keep walking in reverence and obedience to the Lord.* Your desire should be to please the One who has called you to be a faithful steward. God is a holy God. Give Him reverence and obedience. Your life will be full of peace and joy as you respect His authority.

2. **Give to your family.** Nothing is sadder to me than seeing a steward stuck on the sidelines of life's greatest adventure because he hasn't given attention to his family.

   Your family needs you to give to them. But please don't fall into the trap of giving them only money and material possessions. You cannot "buy them off." Your family needs YOU.

   Focus attention on giving your family many of the items listed in Chapter 14. Be creative in giving yourself to them. Don't allow Satan the joy of messing up your model of effective stewardship to the world. Make your family your first priority.

   A special note to the husband: There is no way you can hire or delegate your responsibility to your family to someone else.

   God has placed you as the senior vice president of your home and family. You cannot be an effective Authorized Wealth Distributor to a world in need if your wife and children are starving for what you have to give to them.

   Remember, those closest to you spell love: *T-I-M-E.* Kids want a father, not simply a financial officer who shows up periodically to hand out the allowances. And your wife would much rather have a companion than an exhausting business success.

   It's not just the amount of hours spent that makes the difference, but also the quality of the time spent. Ask God to give you balance in this area of life. When the family is a priority the other demands of life will fall into order.

3. **Give to yourself.** Don't misinterpret what I'm saying. I'm not saying you should look out for number one or see how much you can hoard. By now, you know this way of thinking is contrary to God's design of effective stewardship. Soul care is important for the marathon of life.

   Make sure to allocate quality personal time for getting ones batteries recharged. In order to give from your inventory, you need to have God's perspective. You need to be renewed. You need time to be alone so that God can talk to you through His Word. Read. Reflect. Be still. He needs your attention in order to give calibrate your direction. By giving to yourself, you will be enriched and refreshed to give more to others.

   And be creative in giving to yourself. Read at least one book each month that can help you in your work, your worship, and your walk with God. Take walks in a quiet park or on a mountain trail. Soak in God's presence. Read a psalm a day or other passages that lift your spirit. Take a nap in a hammock or lie in the sun for an hour with your eyes closed.

   What you do is not the issue. The objective is taking time to be alone to think, to pray, and to listen. Giving to yourself will multiply your impact on the lives of others. As a steward, you need rest and relaxation on a regular basis.

4. **Give to the body of believers.** You won't have trouble finding people to give to. In fact, your challenge will be focusing on areas of greatest need. Determine where is the best place for you to focus your attention. Consider how you can use your strengths. Major in your strengths and minor in your weaknesses.

   Just as a farmer focuses his seed sowing on a specific plot of land, you too will be more productive if you focus your giving. God touches each of our hearts in a different way. Sometimes our motivation is stimulated by a spiritual gift and or strengths.

   Although there are many ways I can give, I often choose to focus my giving to gain the maximum impact possible. As you look at the body of believers that you know, don't forget the poor. Sometimes a gift of money is helpful. However, often you have other items in your inventory that can be equally helpful to them.

Don't get caught in the old trap of buying your way out of genuinely getting involved in the lives of believers.

As a believer, you have a responsibility to give toward helping to advance the cause of Jesus Christ through your church. Find ways to stimulate growth in your church through your systematic, regular giving of time, talent, and treasure to your church body.

God will no doubt lead you to give to other Christian causes as well. Again, evaluate how you can accomplish the most through a focused approach. Select causes that reflect your heart's motivation. What is not important to you will be important to another steward. You are not called to give to everyone or everything.

You have much to offer by giving your talents, abilities, insight, and experience. Giving a financial donation is only one of many ways you can give to most Christian causes. Remember these guidelines in your involvement in civic responsibilities also. Give your expertise to help the needs of your community.

5. **Give to people whose lives you touch each day.** The vast majority of God's stewards don't live and work in a protected Christian environment. God has placed us in the dark and confusing world to be salt and light. We are to stimulate the growth of God's kingdom, and this means rubbing shoulders with the one who is not a steward of God's kingdom.

   The ways to give are unlimited. The interest we show, the listening ear, the freshly baked loaf of bread, the bouquet of home-grown flowers or the skill to unlock the car door when the keys are left in the ignition are all ways to share God's love with a person.

   But to stop at just doing nice things is to short-circuit genuine stewardship responsibility. You have the answer to life eternal! You have tasted heaven! You know the Savior! You have the privilege of giving living bread to a hungry world!

   You should be equipped in how to personally share your faith with people and then look for opportunities to share how you found Jesus Christ with those God brings to you. Nothing is more rewarding than to be an agent for the kingdom of God by helping another person come to know Jesus Christ as his Savior and Lord!

Do you feel hesitant in sharing your faith? If you do, seek out some helpful training through your church or a parachurch organization. Learn how to informally communicate your faith with others by telling your personal story. Knowing how to communicate your faith story will open new doors of opportunity for you

CULTIVATE POSITIVE ATTITUDES TOWARD GIVING

The attitude you choose to have concerning giving will have a direct correlation with your effectiveness in giving.

Surrounded by so much greed and desire for materialistic benefits, you will want to cultivate a positive attitude. The attitude you have determines your success as a steward. To have and maintain a positive attitude about giving, I encourage you to follow the six guidelines listed below.

1. **Cast all your cares on the Lord.**

   If you find yourself preoccupied with worry, fear, loneliness or other things that drain you or your strength and positive view on life, give those cares to the Lord in prayer. He wants to take your burdens.

   When you get discouraged, you cannot concentrate on meeting the needs of others. Give up your concerns by giving them to the Lord in prayer and trusting Him for the answers.

   Dr. Henrietta Mears—who discipled such godly leaders as Bill Bright and Billy Graham—once encouraged some of her students to prepare a gift for God. In the package, they were to put all those things that caused frustration and concern. She instructed them to wrap up the package and symbolically give it to Him. Then she said, "Once you've given it to Him, stop stealing His property!"

   Let God have all those cares that limit you from having a positive attitude. Cultivate casting your cares upon Him and live freely in His Spirit.

2. **Rejoice in the Lord.**

   Paul instructed the church at Philippi, "Always be full of joy in the Lord. I say it again—rejoice!" (Philippians 4:4). It often takes an act of our will to say thanks, to give praise, and to rejoice. Sometimes circumstances seem so bad that the last thing we want to do is to rejoice. Yet God's Word simply says, REJOICE! You will miss His plan if you are not rejoicing.

The rejoicing steward is able to see opportunities for ministry. He sees the need. He's in touch with God's view of things. He is able to discern how God would have him respond. He's free to be salt and light.

3. **Give with others' needs in mind.**

As a student in college, I attended a student conference where the late Dr. Raymond Edmond, then president of Wheaton College, was the keynote speaker.

One night he leaned over the lectern and said, "Men and women, I would never have made it through school without claiming Philippians 2:4." And then he read out of his King James Bible: "Look not every man on his own things, but every man also on the things of others."

He then continued, "I justified cheating on my exams by using this verse until I learned that this verse had nothing to do with cheating and everything to do with caring. We are to look to others, find their need, and step in and meet that need."

A more accurate translation of this verse reads, "Do not MERELY look out for your own personal interests, but also for the interests of others" (Philippians 2:4, NASB).

Watch. Look. Listen. Respond. Don't let opportunities slip through your hands. Cultivate watching for opportunities to give, and then give.

4. **Give your best.**

I once heard a story of a wheat farmer in the Midwest who always supplied his friends on adjoining farms with all the seeds they needed to plant each spring. Year after year, he insisted that they come to him and get their seed. He would not accept payment. All he asked was that they plant the seed he provided. After several years his fellow farmers were at last able to get him to explain why he insisted on giving them seed every year to plant.

With reluctance, he explained, "I give you my best seed every year because I know that what you plant will affect my harvest. You see, my farm is in between the rolling hills. Your farms are on those hills. When our grain begins to grow, pollination occurs. If you don't have the highest quality of grain planted, it will affect my quality of return, too. I give my best so I can harvest the best."

To give less than your best when you give is a reflection on your heavenly Father's inventory. Cultivate the habit of always giving the best you can give.

5. **Give systematically and regularly.**

   Developing a positive attitude is like forming a good habit. It takes practice to be good at a skill. To be a good steward takes a commitment of your will, and it takes practice. Giving only occasionally does not sharpen the skill.

   What would your life be if you were not systematic in other areas of life? Try not eating for a few days. Try not paying your bills regularly. Try showing up at your job only when you feel like it—an hour here, an hour there. Systematic living gives us purpose, focus, and freedom as a steward.

   Just as a musician must practice daily in order to be successful, so too your expertise in giving will develop only with daily practice.

6. **Give willingly.**

   Our old sinful nature would want to hold back. We all have a tendency to let someone else do it. Although God may direct you not to do something because He has another method in mind, I believe this is the exception rather than the rule.

   When God instructed Moses to build the first mobile worship center (the tabernacle), He told Moses to invite the people to give whatever they had. In Exodus 35, God provides us with a record of what the people gave. The tabernacle was constructed because of the time, talent, and treasure of God's stewards responding to meet a need.

   When Moses extended the invitation to give, the people willingly responded. Scripture records this for us:

   > "So the people of Israel—every man and woman who wanted to assist in the work given to them by the Lord's command to Moses—brought their freewill offerings to him" (Exodus 35:29).

The King James version uses the expression, "whose heart made them willing." There was no sales program, no begging, and no pressure tactics; they gave freely and because they wanted to!

CULTIVATE GIVING FROM A WILLING HEART

As you cultivate your attitude as an Authorized Wealth Distributor by distributing God's resources, you will realize benefits that far exceed the investment you made:

- You will be doing what God planned for you to do.
- You will be meeting the needs of people.
- Your needs will be met.
- People who receive from you will be praising God.
- People will be drawn to pray for you.
- People will be giving glory to God—hilariously!

It is a privilege for me to extend a cordial welcome to you as a member of the Authorized Wealth Distributor Network on behalf of its Founder, the King of kings, and Lord of lords!

Key To Abundant Living

UNLOCKING YOUR LIFE OF CONTENTMENT

Return to the Authorized Wealth Distributor's Commitment a few pages back. Have you signed and dated your copy yet? If not, are you ready to do so?

If not, what is holding you back?

Now make a copy of this commitment so you can have it with you over the next seven days. Perhaps you prefer to scan it or take a picture of it so you can store it on your phone.

At the beginning of each of the next seven days, read this commitment. This is your commitment to your Supplier.

Focus your reflection on how God wants to use you each day to meet a need that He provides to you. As you do this over a week, you are helping develop a habit of being intentional in your giving.

Chapter 12
MONEY MAGIC

Tell them to use their money to do good. They should be rich in good works and generous to those in need, always being ready to share with others. By doing this they will be storing up their treasure as a good foundation for the future so that they may experience true life.

—1 TIMOTHY 6:18–19

Paring words together is a common experience. Here are a few typical responses:

- When I say "bacon," most people respond "eggs."
- When I say "fire," many will say "hot."
- When I say "autumn," most will say "leaves."
- When I say "pool," most say "swim" or "table."
- When I say "thirsty," most will respond and say "water."
- When I say "give," most say or at least think "MONEY."

Many today think of giving to be synonymous with money. Church bulletins often announce the weekly offering as "worship by giving." The United Fund drive uses a catchy phrase: "Give the United Way."

If someone says, "I need to ask some people to give to meet this need," don't we automatically assume that he means he will ask people to make financial donations?

Hopefully, you are beginning to see that there are many ways to give that don't include money—but giving money is indeed a part of being a good steward. God does provide us funds that we are to give to meet the needs we see. In fact, your generosity with money says a lot about about your values and your view on life.

If you really want to know what someone is like on the inside, watch how he utilizes his money on the outside! Does he hoard it? Does he spend it on impulse? Does he use his money to buy items of lasting value? Does he freely give his money to meet the needs of others? Does he have a defined plan for his money, or is it "here today and gone tomorrow?" Spending and saving patterns speak loudly about our character and personality.

MONEY TALKS

Did you know that you can identify the health of a body of believers' by how much money is given to meet the ministry needs of that church body? If a church is meeting its budget and is giving to advance ministry, you are likely seeing a church of growing believers. If, on the other hand, the church is struggling financially, the church is likely made up of baby Christians or of self-centered, carnal believers.

The steward who walks consistently in the power of the Holy Spirit will be using his money to advance the cause of Christ. He is free from the obsession of selfishly hoarding his money. He is wise in circulating what he has been given.

Sadly, our society's materialistic self-centered focus has created a get-all-you-can-while-you-can mindset among non-believers and believers alike.

According to the Giving USA 2021 report, $471.44 billion was given away to charity in the United States—an increase of four percent over 2020. While this is a record high, and given in a year of a global pandemic, this represents less than 4 percent of individuals' total 2021 national income. Ninety-six percent of income is spend satisfying personal wants and desires.

When you look at the numbers, we as a people are driven by a desire for comfort and the good life. As a culture, we are lacking in generosity to others. Self-centeredness is robbing many stewards of the unlimited blessings that God has prepared for His Authorized Wealth Distributors. Thousands of believers have chosen to accept the limited rewards that the world offers, rather than tapping the abundance that God offers.

Without establishing wise boundaries, defining priorities, and applying some discipline, money will corrupt everything a person touches. Money in itself is not evil. Loving money is the problem. How stewards use this tool is the issue. If you don't manage money well, it will end up controlling everything you do. Are you managing the money given to you or is the money you have managing you?

EARN - SAVE - GIVE

The famous circuit-riding preacher, John Wesley, was asked for his advice on the use of money. His response sums up the wise steward's beliefs, "Earn all you can. . . . Save all you can . . . Give all you can." You, too, can follow this simple advice of money management.

> ***Earn all you can.*** Be creative. Work hard. Be wise. Be faithful in your work. Use the sound mind that God gave you to turn your time and talent into the maximum return possible.
>
> ***Save all you can.*** Wisely manage what you earn. Put your earnings to work so that they also will produce a multiplied return. You should make careful and prudent investment decisions. You want your earnings to gain the maximum return possible. Saving is not hoarding as old Mr. Scrooge did. A wise savings program keeps you from foolishly wasting what you earn and planning for a life of impact and effectiveness.
>
> If you are going to save all you can, you need to educate yourself in best practices as to where and how to save. A wise steward should also live his life based on balanced accounts and good budgeting processes. This is the way your earnings and savings are maximized.
>
> ***Give all you can.*** From the harvest of your earnings and savings, you can be generous in giving. Your goal as an Authorized Wealth Distributor is not to collect and store as a miser. Distribute all you can so that God get all the glory.

As a young boy, I learned of R. G. LeTourneau, the founder of the Caterpillar Tractor Company and LeTourneau College. As a steward he chose to live on 10 percent of his earnings and savings. He gave 90 percent to the work of God's kingdom.

ASK QUESTIONS; GET ANSWERS.

You should be concerned about how your giving will be used to further God's purposes here on earth. Investigate where you plan to give before you give. Do your homework.

To help you, here are ten questions that you should be asking. As you get answers, you can determine how God wants you to respond. Here are ten questions that you should consider as you wisely consider a response to a need:

1. **Who is asking for a contribution?** Do you know the person asking? What do you know about the reason for the ask? Is this person trusting in God or in your donation? What do you know about this person's integrity?
2. **Why is the gift being requested?** Do you understand the need? What caused the need? Was it a result of poor management or was it stimulated by a real step of faith and a conviction to be on mission?
3. **Who will benefit from the need being met?** Will your gift be used to cover bad debts, or will lives be directly touched as a result of your help? How much of your gift will be used for overhead expenses? How much of your gift will be used for direct ministry? How will reporting be done; outcomes and accountability are both a part of a steward's responsibility. Giving "on a wing and a prayer" should be the exception, not the rule.
4. **What do other prudent stewards think of the need?** What counsel can you receive in your investigation to confirm or question the validity of the need? Who else has endorsed the request? Would other stewards consider giving if asked to do so? If the answer is no, find out why!
5. **Will your gift go to a bona fide institution, church, or organization that is recognized for its service to people?** What do you know about the institution/organization? How long has it been in existence? What is its track record of ministry success? Is the purpose and the motivation of the organization/institution clearly defined? Is its purpose consistent with your biblical views and convictions? Can you have an accounting of expenses and income for the previous year or two?
6. **To whom does the one seeking the gift (individual, organization, or institution) focus its ministry?** Do you have a genuine interest in this type of need that is to be met? Would a contribution from you stimulate your faith and personal involvement? Do you connect spiritually

to the mission's purpose and goals? If you don't connect you likely are not the one to give.

7. **Is the appeal for help creating high pressure or emotional guilt?** Do you feel that the appeal is trying to put a burden on you; i.e., "It's going to be your fault if we don't meet this need"? Are you being treated as a donor, as an investor, or as a partner? How you are treated reflects a good deal about the leaders seeking financial help.
8. **What kind of reporting can you expect to receive?** Can you see the results of your gift? Will you receive regular written communication regarding progress in meeting the need? What will be the lasting benefits of your gift?
9. **In what ways other than giving money can you be involved?** Is there also a need for other ways you can give as a steward? Is the one seeking your help eager for your personal involvement or is he interested only in your money?
10. **Will your gift stimulate more giving?** Is there a way you can talk to other supporters of the cause? Can you help raise additional funds as a volunteer? Will your generosity to this cause help create an atmosphere for more generous giving?

You will likely not get an answer to every question, but asking probing questions should be welcomed. The one asking should be eager to provide you with answers. Some of the proposed questions require you to be a good listener and observer. Do your homework. Seek the insight of others. Do your homework. What you will be giving is His, not yours!

As an Authorized Wealth Distributor, you should not give blindly with no sense of stewardship accountability. You should give with the goal of seeking to advance the work of God's kingdom business here on earth. You are circulating His money. He has called you to reflect, reproduce, reign, and manage with His authority. You are His agent. Give wisely. Don't rush to judgment. Be prayerful as you consider a financial need presented to you.

A few years ago, I interviewed a man of exceptional wealth. He received great pleasure from using his resources to impact the world. As we visited, he confided to me, "Larry, I have found that the more God blesses me financially, the more responsibility He gives to me to ensure that what is given is properly used. It is not easy to give God's resources away. As a steward, I must trust God for more insight, wisdom, and understanding than ever before. My giving must result in lives being reached for my Savior."

THERMOMETER OR THERMOSTAT?

The way in which you manage and give your money tells the world more about you than your words can ever express. It tells, for example, whether you are a thermometer or a thermostat.

A thermometer provides only a report of the surrounding temperature. It has no ability to change the circumstances. It merely tells what's currently taking place. A thermostat, on the other hand, not only reports but also triggers action that *changes* circumstances. A thermostat regulates the environment.

The steward who is not actively distributing his money is missing out on the opportunity to help *change* his environment by changing people's lives. Christians today may give a lot of other things, but many of them hold on to their billfolds so tightly that they miss the joy of being totally free and effective for God.

MONEY IS A TEACHER

Giving money will teach you more about the principles we've learned in our study together than any other single thing you can give. Money is something tangible. You can see it, feel it and experience its power and influence. God has provided us with a medium of exchange so that we can give and receive more efficiently. Money is not evil; only the *love* of money is evil.

God uses money to teach us how to trust Him. As we see God works through our money management, we can understand how He works through our management of other items in our stewardship inventory.

It is sometimes difficult to see how giving intangible things, for example, returns in a multiplied harvest of more lives. However, when you give something as tangible as money, you can easily observe and calculate the return. Money is the Authorized Wealth Distributor's tutor. Through giving money you learn the dynamics of walking by faith, trusting Him on the return, and obeying His direction. Are you ready to learn from Him in this area of your stewardship?

God never promised to provide excessive material possessions to every steward. He promised to meet every steward's *needs*. The amount of money a person has does not determine his happiness and peace. What one does with what he has is the great determining factor in the test of stewardship.

Jesus says:

> "Don't store up treasures here on earth where moths eat them and rust destroys them, and where thieves break in and steal. Store your treasure in heaven, where moths and rust cannot destroy, and thieves do not break in and steal. Wherever your treasure is, there the desires of your heart will also be" (Matthew 6:19–21).

THE AMOUNT MAKES NO DIFFERENCE

Despite the dollar amount that we have in our personal portfolio, we are to be obedient in our use of what God has entrusted to each of us. God's Word admonishes:

> "Do not love this world or the things it offers you. for when you love the world, you do not have the love of the Father in you. For the world offers only a craving for physical pleasure, a craving for everything we see, and pride in our achievements and possessions. These are not from the Father but are from this world" (1 John 2:15–16).

Disobedience in this or any other area of stewardship may result in the chastening of the Lord. I have known believers who hoarded their money and lavished material possessions on their family members. They soon lost interest in the Lord and then began to reap conflicts with spouses, children, friends, and others as they too turned from the things of God. Disobedience under any circumstance is not worth the results.

The children of Israel who returned from captivity in Babylon to Jerusalem had a responsibility before the Lord to rebuild His temple. But rather than being obedient stewards, they became selfishly preoccupied with their own affairs. They reveled in their prosperity and forgot their responsibilities. We find God's chastening in the first chapter of Haggai:

> "Why are you living in luxurious houses while my house lies in ruin?" This is what the Lord of Heaven says: Look at what's happening to you! You have planted much but har-

> vested little, You eat but are not satisfied, You drink but are still thirsty. You put on clothes but cannot keep warm. Your wages disappear as though you were putting them in pockets filled with holes!" (Haggai 1:3–6).
>
> "You hoped for rich harvests, but they were poor. And when you brought your harvest home, I blew it away. Why? . . . It is because of you that the heavens withhold the dew and the earth produces no crops. I have called for a drought on your fields and hills—a drought to wither the grain and grapes and live trees and all your other crops, a drought to starve you and your livestock and ruin everything you have worked so hard to get" (Haggai 1:9–11).

The Lord chastens those who are disobedient in their stewardship. And those who are obedient reap the abundance of His provision. Guard yourself to use your money, possessions, time, and talent for His glory and according to His plan. You can count on God's blessing as you faithfully fulfill your responsibilities as a wise and sensitive steward.

WHAT ABOUT TITHING?

What is your opinion of the idea of tithing? Do you tithe? If so, why do you tithe? How much are you to tithe? Do you like to tithe? Are there any benefits to tithing?

I've found that the vast majority of Christians today know very little about the tithe—its history or its purpose. Unfortunately, even many churches today see tithing as simply a funding scheme to help the church meet its budget. Pastors seldom teach the biblical purpose of tithing. When it is addressed, it is taught to achieve a church funding objective. Getting people to tithe is viewed as an uphill battle that is rarely won. Many teach 10 percent as a goal, rather than as a place to begin.

Yet I have found that those individuals who do understand the concept of tithing are *excited* about giving in this way. They do not—as others often do—give grudgingly, out of a sense of obligation and pressure. Giving a tithe should not an obligation. It is a privilege.

Let's see what tithing is all about.

ONE-TENTH?

The word "tithe" means one-tenth. Tithing is simply giving 10 percent of your income to God. But the real question is, "Why do it?

An attorney friend of mine spoke at a Christian financial seminar in California many years ago. For some reason, the *Los Angeles Times* covered his lecture, then quoted him:

> *The good Lord has entrusted certain assets to you and made you an agent. . . . The Master has a duty to cooperate with you. He will indemnify you and compensate you. Real estate agents get 7% to 10%; attorneys, maybe 33% to 40%. God has said you can have 90% agency. With generosity like that, don't you feel bad about limiting your giving to 10%?*[26]

Think about it. As an Authorized Wealth Distributor, you are an agent for the King of kings. All you have belongs to Him. You are responsible for the distribution and sound management of everything that He has entrusted to you. His request is that you give only 10 percent back to Him. You manage and distribute the other 90 percent.

What a deal! What a tremendous privilege and honor! God trusts you so much that He allows you the responsibility and privilege of managing 90 percent and returning only 10 percent to Him. You are, of course, free to give much more, but your agency agreement as a steward calls for only 10 percent.

Let's see what God's Word has to say about this fantastic concept . . .

IT STARTED OVER 4,000 YEARS AGO

The first tithe recorded in Scripture was given over 4,000 years ago—over 425 years before God gave the law to Moses. Abraham returned from a successful battle to the city of Salem, the current location of Jerusalem. There he was met by Melchizedek, the king of Salem, who gave him nourishment to strengthen him after the battle.

According to Genesis 14, Melchizedek was a priest of the Most High God. Melchizedek blessed Abraham by saying, "And blessed be God Most High, who has defeated your enemies for you" (Genesis 14:20).

Abraham then gave Melchizedek a tenth of all he had won in the battle that day. Out of gratitude to God, he gave this gift freely and willingly. Melchizedek never asked for it. Abraham simply gave it as an expression of his thanks. As I see it, Abraham really gave *God*—by way of Melchizedek—an agency fee of 10 percent as an expression of his gratitude for God's divine leadership and intervention in the battle.

JACOB'S TITHE

The next example of giving a tithe is in Genesis 28. Jacob, as you may recall, eventually had to flee his home because he tricked Esau out of his birthright. As he slept one night during his journey, he dreamed of a staircase that reached from Earth to heaven. Angels of God went up and down the staircase.

In his dream, God appeared to him and promised him the land he was sleeping upon, many thousands of descendants, and protection wherever he went. When he awoke the next morning, Jacob built an altar and made this vow to God:

> "If God will indeed be with me and protect me on this journey, and if he will provide me with food and clothing, and if I return safely to my father's home, the Lord will certainly be my God . . . and I will present to God a tenth of everything he gives me" (Genesis 28:20, 22).

Jacob took the initiative to commit 10 percent of what God had promised to provide to him. God did not require this of him. Jacob willingly offered ten percent. He chose to put God first and demonstrated his commitment with his tithe.

THE LAW REQUIRED TITHING

Many years later, God gave His Law to His people. By now, God's promise to Jacob in Genesis 28 had become reality. When God gave His Law to the nation of Israel, He included the requirement of tithing:

> "You must set aside a tithe of your crops—one-tenth of all the crops you harvest each year. Bring the tithes to the designated palace of worship—the place the Lord your God chooses for his name to be honored—and eat there in his presence. This applies to your tithes of grain, new wine, olive oil, and the firstborn males of your flocks and herds. Doing this will teach you always to fear the Lord your God" (Deuteronomy 14:22–23).

> "One-tenth of the produce of the land, whether grain from the fields or fruit from the trees, belongs to the Lord and must be set apart to him as holy. If you want to buy back the Lord's tenth of the grain or fruit, you must pay its value, plus 20 percent. Count off every tenth animal from your herds and flocks and set them apart for the Lord as holy. You may not pick and choose between good and bad animals and you may not substitute one for another. But if you do exchange one animal for another, then both the original animal and its substitute will be considered holy and cannot be brought back" (Leviticus 27:30–33).

The Law was specific. The tithe was required by God from the people. This was the means of paying for the operational cost of their government—a theocracy. God appointed the Levites to be in charge of all matters pertaining to civil and religious government. With the tithes they collected, the Levites managed all the governmental affairs. This included maintaining the cities of refuge, supervising religious worship and education, and taking care of the needs of all widows and orphans. This was governmental taxation.

But this required tithe for the nation of Israel was not just 10 percent! The people were required to give 10 percent two times each year, plus a special one-third tithe each year. The annual required giving by the Israelites was now 23 percent per year!

And in addition to the required tithes—their income tax, if you will—the people also gave freewill offerings. On numerous occasions, people gave these special offerings, not because they had to, but because they wanted to. Tithing was required. Offerings given were given from a heart of gratitude.

THEY BLEW IT

About 400 years before Christ was born to redeem us from sin, the nation of Israel had once again forgotten God's commands. Their lives were no honor or reflection of God's holiness. They had badly blown it! God spoke to His people through the prophet Malachi:

> "For I am the Lord—I do not change. That is why you are not already utterly destroyed [for my mercy endures forever].

> "Though you have scorned my laws from the earliest time, yet you may still return to me,' says the Lord of Hosts. 'Come and I will forgive you.'"
>
> "But you say, 'We have never even gone away!'"
>
> "Will a man rob God? Surely not! And yet you have robbed me."
>
> "What do you mean? When did we ever rob you?"
>
> "You have robbed me of the tithes and offerings due to me. . . . Bring all the tithes into the storehouse so that there will be food enough in my Temple; if you do, I will open up the windows of heaven for you and pour out a blessing so great you won't have room enough to take it in!"
>
> "Try it! Let me prove it to you! Your crops will be large, for I will guard them from insects and plagues. Your grapes won't shrivel away before they ripen," says the Lord of Hosts. "And all nations will call you blessed, for you will be a land sparkling with happiness. These are the promises of the Lord of Hosts" (Malachi 3:6–12, TLB).

God is saying: "Put Me first. Obey Me. I will bless you." This promise of God is as true today as the day He first gave it to His people. God does not change—before the Law, during the Law, of after the Law.

JESUS AND THE TITHE

At the appointed time, Jesus Christ came. Did He throw out the Mosaic Law? No, He fulfilled all of the Law. He never once rejected what had been established. But He raised the bar: To who much is given, much is required. He provided a way for mankind to meet the requirements of the Law. Only through accepting Jesus Christ as Savior can one put God first.

Jesus gives us the freedom to be all God planned for us to be. No longer are we in bondage to sin. We are no longer under the rule of the Mosaic Law. God's Holy Spirit sets us free to respond to Him by faith. Giving generously then becomes a joyful testimony of our faith. Your ten percent should be the place to begin giving; not your goal to be achieved! Generosity exceeds a percentage.

REAL PURPOSE

In Deuteronomy 14:23, we learned the real purpose of the tithe—it hasn't changed and never will: "The purpose of tithing is to teach you always to put God first in your lives."

Tithing is to be your tutor. God is not going to starve to death if you don't give Him His rightful agency fee. He won't lose out, but you will.

Consider this: If you don't give to Him at least 10 percent, I can guarantee that you will very soon forget you are an Authorized Wealth Distributor. You will forget you are free to live a victorious and abundant life.

Look at tithing this way: Generous giving of 10 percent or even more becomes your regular refresher course that reminds you who you are and what you are to do. As you set aside and give God an agency fee on a regular basis, you are recognizing Him to be first in your life. This helps you, not Him. When you recognize Him to be your number one priority in the area of money, all the other areas related to life and stewardship fall more easily in line. This is not a legalistic obligation. This is a free-will tithe that helps you keep Him first in all things.

Pat and I started tithing as a couple the first week we were married. At that time, I must admit, we did see this as a duty or an obligation to be fulfilled. This was our duty. As we began to understand our steward responsibilities, our obligation we felt changed to gratitude to give. We now gave because we wanted to; not because we had to.

We chose to put Him first in our giving. In all our years of marriage, we never went hungry. I am still giving far beyond my agency fee because I want to. I continue to live very comfortably. I have never been caught up in hoarding, nor have I been preoccupied with materialism. I continue to recognize God to be my first priority in life, starting with the income God provides me as one of His stewards The more I give to Him, the more I always seem to have to give to causes that align with my life and mission.

PUTTING TITHING TO THE TEST

A young couple with two children lived in a small, northern Colorado town. They owned a small appliance business, but the business wasn't good.

Times were tough for the little community in the mid-1950s. Like many others, the young couple had their backs against the wall. Their financial problems overwhelmed them. No matter what they tried, there wasn't enough money to meet even the family's basic needs.

Then, on a cold and wet October day, they met a Christian businessman who was in the area on a business trip. They shared their despair with him. After they told him how tough things were, he asked them one simple question, "Are you tithing to God from what you now make?"

"No," they responded, "there's no way we can give to a church when we are not sure we can even feed our kids!"

"Well," the businessman replied, "if you're not giving God what's rightfully His, it's no wonder you're about to starve."

Then he proceeded to explain how tithing was designed to help them. He challenged them to give God His agency fee first out of whatever income—large or small—they received. "Try tithing for eight weeks and see if you don't see a difference in your financial position," he challenged the couple.

After the businessman left, the young couple decided to try this wild idea. After all, on what they were making, 10 percent wasn't going to make that much difference. They decided to take 10 percent off the store profits each day and set it aside in a jar.

After a few days, they had collected several dollars. They decided to attend the small church down the street and give their tithes there. They seldom attended any church, but it seemed reasonable that God's money should be taken to a place of worship. They had sent their kids there on occasion, so they decided they would go during their eight-week experiment with God.

At first, things seemed to go from bad to worse financially. Nevertheless, on the days they sold something in their small store, they set aside God's 10 percent agency fee.

Four weeks went by. From their perspective, they were losing 10 percent and not gaining a thing. Their thanksgiving feast was beans and potatoes.

Then it was three weeks before Christmas. Surely, they thought, people would come to the store to buy gifts. December had always been a good sales month. This time, however, most people just looked and wished. Some days there wasn't a single customer.

The couple's frustration now turned to anger. "Why is this happening? It's not fair," they cried. The wife was ready to wring the businessman's neck!

The husband had similar feelings but responded, "We made an eight-week commitment. The eight weeks are over in two weeks—December 24. When it's over, that will be the end of this experiment; but we've got to stick to our word till then."

Christmas that year was hardly one to look forward to. The husband went to the nearby woods and cut a small tree. His wife made paper decorations with the kids—but there wasn't a single gift to go under the tree. For Christmas dinner, there would be more beans.

On the morning of December 24, they opened the store. Throughout the day, people stopped by to look, but not to buy. When it was time to close that night, only a couple of dollars of profit had been made. God got a quarter that day.

That night the couple bundled up the kids to go to church for the special service. They trudged through the blustering cold, snowy night—and to put in their last tithe.

At the close of the service, they greeted the church friends they had made over the course of the last eight weeks. Then they headed home. The kids ran ahead, full of excitement for what they would find under the tree on Christmas morning. The young parents walked home without speaking. They knew there nothing was under the tree.

As the parents walked up to their home, just behind the store, the kids were waiting. Dad pushed the door open, and the kids rushed in.

"Mom, what is this?" they yelled. The kitchen table was covered with every kind of food you could imagine. The kids opened the refrigerator, and, to their amazement, it too was full of food. On the center shelf was a big turkey with all the trimmings, just waiting to be put into the oven.

The kids dashed from the kitchen to their small living room. "Look at this," they screamed. The tree was beautifully decorated with lights and glass ornaments. Under the tree were more than a dozen wrapped gifts for everyone in the family.

The parents were overwhelmed and confused! Where did all of this come from? Never once did they tell anyone in their community of their need or of their tithing experiment.

The next morning, after the gifts were opened, the husband received a phone call. "Merry Christmas!" greeted the caller. "Do you still have that electric range in your store? My husband gave me the money to buy it. If you still have it, could you deliver it tomorrow morning?"

That was just the beginning. In the first three weeks of January, the young couple did more business in their store than they had done during the previous three months! And to this day, they have no idea where the food and gifts came from that Christmas Eve.

Yes, this is a true story. They knew the businessman didn't provide their Christmas that year. When they told him of their tithing experiment over a month after Christmas, he was not even aware that they had started tithing after his challenge to them. In fact, he had all but forgotten about their conversation that day in October.

Some will say that their tithe experiment and the events on Christmas Eve and the days following were just a coincidence. But I think not. I believe that God prepared a blessing for them because they chose to put Him first.

God did use an Authorized Wealth Distributor to fulfill this need—but the couple will have to wait until they are in heaven to learn the name of their benefactor.

Although they understood little of what was happening, God was true to His Word:

> "'If you do,' says the Lord of Heaven's Armies, 'I will open the windows of heaven for you. I will pour out a blessing so great you won't have room to take it in. Try it. Put me to the test!'" (Malachi 3:10).

TRY IT

There is a biblical principle here for you! If you have never experienced God's return through tithing your income, why not initially try it faithfully for eight weeks? There is nothing magical in the length of time, but an eight-week period allows you to watch God do some amazing things. The principle here works!

As you do, let God be original in how He chooses to bless you. Don't play games with God with an I'll-do-this- if-You-do-that attitude. Put Him to the test. Watch Him keep His promise.

As you take the tithing challenge, remember that you are not doing this to get ahead or to help God out of a financial crisis. You are not paying a 23 percent tax as the children of Israel were required to do.

The purpose of tithing is to teach you always to put God first in your life!

CREATIVE GIVING

Tithing is a place to start—not a place to stop. In addition to giving God His agency fee, there are other creative ways to give financially that can stretch your faith. I have listed four.

1. **Faith promise giving.**

   The concept of faith promise giving has become popular today because of the testimony of Oswald J. Smith, of the Peoples Church in Toronto, Canada. Today, tens of thousands of stewards throughout the world are experiencing the adventure of giving by faith.

   Faith promise giving has its roots in 2 Corinthians 8:5. Paul wrote of how the Macedonia Christians, despite their hard times and limited financial resources, gave by faith to meet the needs of the church in Jerusalem. These stewards in Macedonia were the first to give witness to faith giving:

   > "Now, brethren, we wish to make known to you the grace of God which has been given in the churches in Macedonia, that in a great ordeal of affliction their abundance of joy and their deep poverty overflowed in the wealth of their liberality. For I testify that according to their ability, and beyond their ability they gave of their own accord, begging us with much entreaty for the favor of participation in the support of the saints, and this, not as we had expected, but they first gave themselves to the Lord and to us by the will of God "(2 Corinthians 8:1–5, NASB).

   The Macedonian stewards wanted to be meaningfully involved in the needs of the Jerusalem church. They were already giving what they had. But they wanted to do more. They believed God for the ability to give beyond their human ability. Giving beyond your ability is what faith promise giving is all about.

   Faith promise giving is counting on God to provide a specific amount that is beyond your current ability to give.

   Faith promise giving is not cash resources. Cash is what you have now. Although your commitment must become cash to be given, faith promise giving does not rely on currently available assets.

Faith promise giving is not a pledge. A pledge is a horizontal commitment between a person and an organization with the objective of meeting a need. A pledge is based on the ability to pay out of known resources over a prescribed period of time.

Faith promise giving is:

- Based on a decision and a desire to participate in what God is doing;
- An act of faith, for the decision you make, is based on future resources that you do not currently have;
- A promise to God that you will give from your inventory as He supplies you with His resources;
- Believing God to supply from His resources as you make a decision to participate in meeting a need.

Two years after we were married, we were introduced to the concept of faith promise giving. Since then, I have participated every year in some faith promise challenge. God has been faithful to supply His resources time and time again.

And I also had the privilege of challenging well over 500,000 people with this principle of giving. Time and time again, God has rewarded those who trust Him by meeting their commitment.

In my experience, I have found there are only three reasons that an individual would not see a faith promise commitment realized:

- Failure to pray the commitment in (they forgot about it).
- Lack of sensitivity to God's provision (God provided it, but they chose to use His provision for something else).
- A faith guess was made (rather than a step of faith, it was a leap into the unknown, with no frame of reference to God's provision in the past).

If you are challenged to make a faith promise commitment, I encourage you to respond only if you sense God has given you a genuine desire to be involved in the need presented. Don't respond out of pressure. If you have the desire to be involved, then ask God what steps He would have you take that would stretch your faith.

The amount He lays on your heart may shock you but will likely be an amount that you can believe God for. As you sense God's leading about an amount, make the commitment. Then ask God to make you sensitive to His provision. Pray regularly for the need you are committed to helping meet, and watch God provide!

I shared the principle of faith promise giving at a banquet one evening in Orlando, Florida. During dinner, I met a young couple over dinner who had faced some difficult times in the housing construction business during the previous nine months. We had a good time discussing how God always provides for His children.

That evening I challenged the 200 attendees to join in the adventure of faith promise giving. I explained how, invited participation, and thanked them for coming. The young couple at my table came up and asked to talk further.

"We feel we should respond to your challenge to make a faith promise commitment, but this is new to us," the young husband said. "Could you explain the principle to us again?"

I replied, "If God has given you the desire to be financially involved in this way, then I encourage you to take a step of faith. I recommend that their commitment be a stretch of their faith so that they could visualize God meeting the need.

"OK," they said together. "We really have the desire to see God use us and build our faith. We want to go for it." He sat down at the banquet table, took out his response card, filled it in, put it in the envelope I had provided them, sealed it, and gave it to me. "I'm trusting God to work through us," the husband told me. "We want to watch Him work through us. Thanks so much for helping us."

We shook hands, said goodbye to one another, and they headed out the door to their car.

An hour later, my associate and I were working through the many responses from the evening invitation to participate in faith-promise giving. As I opened the envelope from the young couple, I saw that they had committed $1,000 a month for the following twelve months! I was stunned. All I could think of was the difficult times they had experienced.

How were they going to see this faith promise realized? Oh, me of little faith!

A few weeks passed. Amidst a pile of mail awaiting my attention was a personal note from my new friends from the Orlando banquet:

Dear Larry,

We want to thank you for introducing us to faith promise giving. We are already beginning to see God working.

Last night my partner and I were closing out last month's books. We were able to make a profit for the first time in eight months. My wife and I then sat down and paid all of our bills. When everything was paid, we discovered we had $1,000 left over. God impressed us to send this immediately—His first provision of our one-year commitment to Him.

Enclosed in the letter was a check for $1,000. Since then, they have not only met their commitment every month—but have also written numerous other generous gifts from God's provision over many years. They continue to have fun watching God provide through their stewardship.

Any believer, regardless of age or financial position, can join in this adventure that results in needs being met and unprecedented spiritual growth for the participant.

When you give in this manner, you begin to experience the true dynamics of principle five on the five-pointed star, "I can give from my Father's resources." Try it, you will like it!

2. **The Lord's account.**

   Have you ever considered opening a special account at the bank, separate from your personal operational account, where you deposit all funds that are available for God's kingdom business? Stewards who have done so report that it is one of the most exciting things they have ever done.

   One couple I know was able to set aside a triple tithe each month. From this, they pay 10 percent to their local church fellowship. Their second tithe is designated to missions organizations for projects and missionaries. The third tithe is kept in the account without designation so that they are free to give as a special need is brought to their attention—whether it be an emergency request from a missionary or a sack of groceries for a needy person in their community.

Whatever is deposited in this special bank account is used only for direct ministry for the Lord. Whenever they receive extra funds, they always triple tithe to this account before making other decisions with the remaining money.

Having a Lord's account is a tangible way to recognize your stewardship over God's financial resources. It becomes a constant reminder that God entrusts His resources to His stewards. Is God leading you to establish a special Lord's account?

3. **Planned giving.**

What plans have you made to manage your affairs after you have been called home to heaven? Every Authorized Wealth Distributor should have a plan for the future. If you don't plan for the future, you are not fulfilling your responsibility as a faithful steward.

Although most of your giving should be done while you are living, no doubt God will take you home to heaven before you do everything you would like to do. To ensure that stewardship responsibilities are handled properly, it is necessary for each adult steward to have a Last Will and Testament prepared. This often is included with a Living Trust that addresses how you want your assets used when you are finished managing them. Your will and your Living Trust document become the last words you have to say! These tools help you speak to others when you can no longer speak. What you choose to say and the directives you wish to give are, therefore, very important.

Through your will, you should give testimony of your faith in Jesus Christ. You should also declare your authority as an Authorized Wealth Distributor and give specific instructions as to who should be granted the authority to take the material and financial inventory that you are leaving behind and to continue to manage it for God's kingdom business. Next to your birth certificate and marriage license, your will, and Living Trust are the most important documents you will ever have. Don't leave for heaven without it!

If you die without a will and a trust, you are forfeiting all rights to distribute your stewardship responsibilities you leave behind. These tools allow you to speak with authority here on earth after you have entered heaven.

You will need help in preparing a will and a trust. Seek out a Christian attorney who understands biblical stewardship. With his assistance, make the decisions that would be an honor to your heavenly Father. The attorney will provide legal expertise that will help you wisely make your last authorized wealth disbursement here on earth.

4. **Other ways to give possessions.**

   You are not limited to giving only cash. You can give other possessions that can be sold by qualified recipients. Anything you hold in your inventory can be given. To maximize such giving, you need the assistance of people skilled in the areas of handling such gifts.

   For example, you can give art objects, automobiles, stocks and bonds, life insurance, stamp collections, land, jewelry, precious gems, etc.

   Seek out professional counsel to determine how best to give items of this nature. If you hold legal ownership of something, there is a way for you to give it away.

   If you are over sixty-five, what is your plan for liquidating the excess that you have accumulated over the years? If everything you own is His, who will receive what you no longer need? Isn't it about time to develop an intentional redistribution plan? I am working on this now myself!

Giving your money and your related possessions is where the rubber meets the road. Paul's instruction to young Timothy should be the standard of the wise and sensitive steward:

> "Teach those who are rich in this world not to be proud and not to trust in their money, which is so unreliable. Their trust should be in God, who richly gives us all we need for our enjoyment. Tell them to use their money to do good. They should be rich in good works and generous to those in need, always being ready to share with others" (1 Timothy 6:17–18).

Now go and be rich in good works and generous to those in need!

Key To Abundant Living

UNLOCKING YOUR LIFE OF CONTENTMENT

If you have never tithed, why not start setting aside at least 10 percent of your income, beginning with your next paycheck or allocated income?

TEST this truth for eight weeks and see what happens.

After eight weeks have passed, list the results of your experiment.

What did you learn about God?

What did you learn about you?

If you have already experienced God's faithfulness in giving Him his agency fee as an act of trust and faith, select one of the other options outlined in this chapter for giving.

Make a plan and work your plan.

For starters, a plan should include a goal, a process, anticipated results, and a few dates for accountability. Get started! If it is not in writing, the plan does not exist.

According to Deuteronomy 14:23, describe, in your own words, why it is important to give generously.

Chapter 13
LIVING LIFE ABUNDANTLY

God will make this happen, for he who calls you is faithful.
—1 THESSALONIANS 5:24

My father decided it was time I began to learn what responsibility and accountability were all about. In other words, at thirteen, it was time for my first summer job. Dad arranged for me to work for a friend of his who owned a motel. I was to clean the pool each morning, maintain the pool area throughout the day, mow the lawns, weed the flower beds, and be a "boy Friday" for the room maids as they cleaned the guest rooms.

On my first day I was introduced to Jim. He was five years older than me. I was taking over his job. He was assigned to train me. He explained how to clean the pool each day, how to back flush the filter, and how to vacuum the pool once a week. He showed me where the lawn and garden tools were and demonstrated the proper way to do the tasks that the owner expected to be done each day.

I learned my job by watching and working with Jim for a couple of days. His last words of instruction were the key to my success: "If you're not sure what to do or how to do something, don't hesitate to ask the boss. He wants things around here done right."

ON MY OWN

Two days later when I arrived for work, I knew that I was on my own! Within an hour, I ran into a snag with the pool filter. I had watched Jim flush the filter once, but for the life of me, I couldn't remember the order in which he did the procedure. At first, I started to experiment, but then I remembered Jim's last words: "Ask the boss."

I decided to find my boss. Little did I realize the importance of that decision. He was waiting to see if I would "do my own thing" or rely on his experience and insight. Throughout that summer his confidence in me grew as he saw that I would do my job effectively when I knew what was expected of me.

YOUR JOB DESCRIPTION

Are you aware that God has a job description for His children? As His representative you have an important assignment. God wants you to be successful at your "job," but unless you are certain of your job description, it's difficult to carry it out effectively. I have watched many Christians try their best to live the Christian life but often end up feeling a failure and frustrated because they are uncertain of their responsibilities.

I have found that people are happiest when they know what to do and what is expected of them. In my role as a management consultant, I've helped define and write at least 300 job descriptions. I've observed how liberated people are once they see in writing what they are to do and what is expected. A job description is a tool that helps us focus on our purpose and know when the job has been completed.

To help you be a steward I have a job description for you. This is my job description as well. As you review it, you will likely find ways to make it more personal and specific to your particular culture, season of life, and specific task.

Let's begin with a general overview.

Steward Of The King Of Kings

JOB DESCRIPTION

I. *Purpose*: To manage effectively all that God chooses to entrust to me so as to bring praise and glory to His name.

II. *Scope*: Everywhere I go during my time on earth.

III. Responsibilities:

- To *reflect* God's character, love and purpose to those I meet as an ambassador of His kingdom.
  Standard of Performance: Act.
- To *reproduce* God's love and power by multiplying His work in my life through the lives of others.
  Standard of Performance: Act and inform.
- To *reign* on God's behalf as He would reign, using His authority to advance His plan on earth.
  Standard of Performance: Act and inform.
- To *manage* the time, talent and treasure which God has entrusted to me each day so as to maximize His influence in this world.
  Standard of Performance: Act and inform.

IV. Expectations:

- To live in reliance upon the power of the Holy Spirit.
- To respond in obedience by trusting in God's leading and direction.
- To submit to God's judgment and leadership.

V. Reporting Relationship:

- I report to my heavenly Father.
- I am to work in harmony with other stewards so as to meet the responsibilities and expectations of my Father.

Your job description defines you to as a "Steward of the King of Kings." To fully understand the implications of your job description and the various parts of the job description, we need a few definitions.

You know I often refer to you as a steward. What does this word mean to you? You are not assigned to a cruise line! Perhaps you think of a steward/stewardess on a passenger jet, speedily serving drinks and snacks at 35,000 feet and generally tending to each passenger's comfort. These twentieth-century views illustrate how far we've veered from the dynamic of the biblical meaning of steward.

When God's Word was penned, a steward was one entrusted with great responsibility. Occasionally New Testament church leaders were referred to as stewards. The treasurer of the city of Corinth, which had a population of over 600,000, carried the title of steward.

In the New Testament, two different words are used for steward. One is a guardian, whose responsibilities include *guardianship* of children and *administration* of a household. In Matthew 20, Jesus speaks of the steward who was responsible to pay the workers for the tasks they performed. This steward was in charge of administrating the bringing in of the harvest. Today, we who are parents are stewards in that we are held accountable for a child's well-being and supervision until they become adults.

The other New Testament word for steward stresses the role of *manager*, dealing primarily with property on behalf of the owner. The owner would entrust his steward with the management of his affairs. The task included handling receipts, disbursements, and related financial matters. The steward was a trustee of another person's property. He was vested with specific responsibilities and expected to meet the owner's expectations.

Jesus referred to stewards in several of His parables. Modern translations often use the word servant. The exact duties of a steward varied, depending on the master's needs; but almost always, they involved overseeing the management and operations of the master's estate.

It should not surprise you that a Christian is called a steward. God has entrusted the responsibilities of His kingdom to you! All you have belongs to Him. You are a steward of EVERYTHING you have been given. This is overwhelms me. "MY" house is not mine; it's His. The car I drive is not mine; it's His. My fun camping trailer belongs to Him. The clothes in my closet are not mine; they are His. The food in my kitchen pantry was purchased by His money and I am able to enjoy what was purchased. Nothing is mine; everything I steward is His. My Father holds me accountable for managing EVERYTHING that he has entrusted to me. You are responsible for what He has entrusted to you!

There's no getting around it: you *are* a steward. The question is, what *kind* of a steward will you be? You can choose to be effective in your responsibility, always endeavoring to represent your King faithfully and honestly, or you can choose to be sloppy, inefficient, and unreliable in your stewardship. How effective you are is a decision you make; either by a conscious act of your will or by default.

Let's look at a parable Jesus gave us to illustrate stewardship responsibility. Use your favorite translation and look to Matthew 25: 14–29. Here, a steward is called a servant. Answer these questions as your read:

- Who is taking a trip?
- Who is entrusted with financial responsibility?
- How much is each steward given?
- Is the amount for each steward the same amount?
- What did each steward do with what was entrusted to him?
- How long was the owner gone?
- What did the owner do upon his return?
- What was the reward for faithful stewardship?
- What were the consequences for indifferent stewardship?
- What did the owner do to maximize the use of his possessions?

My translation ends this passage with these words: "To those who use well what they are given, even more will be given, and they will have an abundance. But for those who do nothing, even what little they have will be taken away" (Matthew 25:29).

Here is the big picture summary of this lesson from Jesus: It is evident that the master expects His stewards to manage and invest wisely. The master knew that there would be some risk involved. The first two stewards managed and invested what was entrusted to them, took risks, and produced a multiplied return. They were wise, prudent, accountable, and responsive. The third steward made another choice: to ignore his responsibilities. He reaped severe discipline for his decision and negligence.

There is a lot here to digest. What other observations did you glean? What choices are you making? How can you make wiser choices? Your Master has high expectations for you as one of His stewards.

IMPLICATIONS OF YOUR JOB DESCRIPTION

Let's dig a bit deeper into your job description.

First, you will find a purpose statement—a one-sentence summary of why you are being called to carry out the task. Your purpose is *to manage effectively all that God chooses to entrust to you so as to bring praise and glory to His name.*

You are called to enhance the image and clarify the focus of God's kingdom on earth. He will choose to entrust things to you that He will not entrust to others, and vice versa. What He gives to you is not the issue, but what you do with what He gives to you to manage will make all the difference in the world.

Your management should produce results: praise, glory, honor, the lost finding Jesus, and thanks. Everything you do should be done with this question in mind: "How will what I am doing now bring glory and praise to my Father's name?" If what you are doing will not accomplish this, you'd better find a way to make a correction in what you are doing.

Next you will find your scope. This focuses you on where your job description will be carried out. Your scope: *everywhere you go during your time on earth.* As a steward, you don't get a day off. You are on duty twenty-four hours a day, seven days a week. This realization should influence what you do and determine what decisions you make. At times you will need to use careful discipline and establish boundaries in order to accomplish your purpose.

Being a steward full-time does not mean you've got to be a "stuffed shirt" with no time for relaxation and pleasure. We are talking about an attitude of your heart. With the proper attitude, a steward can experience a life full of high adventure and joy all the time.

Now you find certain responsibilities that you have as a steward. Let's look at each responsibility.

RESPONSIBILITY #1: TO REFLECT GOD'S CHARACTER, LOVE, AND PURPOSE TO THOSE YOU MEET AS AN AMBASSADOR OF HIS KINGDOM.

What do you see when you look into a mirror? You see a reflection of your image. A mirror is designed to produce an exact representation of what is before it. That is its only purpose.

Similarly, your first responsibility is to live your life so as to reflect the very nature and heart of God Himself. You are to love as He loves. You are to express compassion as He does. You are to be an agent for unity and peace. You are to give freely as He has given to you. Whatever God would do, you are to do.

When people see you, do they see a reflection of your heavenly Father? Are you walking and talking as an ambassador of the King? Are you expressing His thoughts, His actions, and His attitudes in your home, in your business, in social times, and in times of leisure?

RESPONSIBILITY #2: TO REPRODUCE GOD'S LOVE AND POWER BY MULTIPLYING HIS WORK IN YOUR LIFE THROUGH THE LIVES OF OTHERS.

The ability to reproduce after our kind is indeed a miracle. My two daughters are a daily reminder to me of the amazing miracle of reproduction. From our marriage union, my wife and I have reproduced two beautiful mothers who are developing and extending our purpose through the raising of their kids to be godly stewards as well.

Your second responsibility as a steward is to reproduce after your kind. You are in the business of influencing others in their spiritual growth. You were born into God's family to reproduce! There is no way to reproduce yourself without giving of yourself. To see God's family grow means that you and I as believers must give of ourselves to meet the needs of others.

This responsibility involves more than evangelism, although being ready to lead another to into a personal relationship with Jesus Christ is definitely a part of it. However, reproduction might also include giving a listening ear to understand a friend's concern, taking a baked goody to a lonely neighbor, and offering an extra pair of hands to help one in need complete a task. Reproduction demands a concentration of time and commitment.

SENSITIVE AND FLEXIBLE

One Saturday afternoon, while waiting for my associate to wrap up a seminar on wills and investments, I decided to use my free time to get some work done. I headed for a quiet spot off in the corner of a lounge. For fifteen minutes, I enjoyed peace, quiet and focus. I was making progress on a stewardship responsibility!

Then I was interrupted by a young man asking questions of another person at the far end of the room. I tried to ignore their conversation, but I couldn't. It seemed as though God were saying, "Larry, you've got the answers; I want you to give some time to answering Greg's questions. It's time for you to give; you were born to reproduce."

As I laid my work aside and went over to introduce myself to the young man, I learned that Greg was the custodian of the facility where we were holding the seminar.

He was waiting for us to finish so that he could clean the building. Since he seemed interested in learning more about the seminar, I saw an opportunity to share with him why it was so important to those in attendance.

From that point, it seemed very natural to share with Greg how he could be a part of God's family by trusting Christ as his Savior. As we talked, I saw the light go on, and within fifteen minutes, Greg invited Jesus into his heart as his personal Savior!

Greg seemed to be born to reproduce. Once he understood that he was now a child of God, he demonstrated a new countenance. We talked for a while, and then he was called away to take care of the facility's needs. When I saw Greg again an hour later, he was explaining to his girlfriend how she too, could know Christ as her Savior.

By choosing to give time to Greg, I was carrying out my responsibility of spiritual reproduction. My responsibility was not to see Greg decide to receive Christ as his Savior; my responsibility was simply to give my time, my ear, my mouth—my life—to be used by God. Successful witnessing (sharing Christ with others) is simply sharing Christ in the power of the Holy Spirit and leaving the results to God Himself. Spiritual reproduction, like physical reproduction, can occur only when one gives to another.

RESPONSIBILITY #3: TO REIGN ON GOD'S BEHALF AS HE WOULD REIGN, USING HIS AUTHORITY TO ADVANCE HIS PLAN ON EARTH.

The King has given you the privilege of acting with His authority, and this privilege should not be taken lightly. To use this authority delegated to us demands discipline and faithfulness. Those who misuse this authority suffer serious consequences. God has entrusted aspects of His business to His children, and He expects us to manage with wisdom and understanding.

> "Jesus said, 'You didn't choose me. I chose you. I appointed you to go and produce lasting fruit, so that the Father will give you whatever you ask for, using my name'" (John 15:16).

Jesus is emphasizing that the use of His name is the key to the believer's authority. This transferred authority means that we are expected to speak, act and make requests as if Jesus were taking the action personally. We are to act on His behalf in all our dealings.

My brother served as a government attorney for thirty years. When he first graduated from law school, he referred to his "fiduciary capacity." At the time, I had no idea what he meant (and was too proud to ask!). But later, I looked up this legal term. Fiduciary capacity refers to the degree of trust and confidence that one party can put in another to act in good faith on behalf of the first party.

When Jesus gave us authority to act using His name, He expressed His trust and confidence in us to act faithfully on His behalf. His delegated authority to us has created a fiduciary relationship with Him. And the failure to carry out the expected obligations of this relationship has serious implications. You are his fiduciary! Act like it.

Let's suppose a friend of yours decides to take a three-month vacation overseas and asks you to write his checks, pay his bills and represent him officially while he is away. You agree, and your friend gives you the power of attorney to act on his behalf. You have now entered into a fiduciary relationship.

Suppose that after your friend has been gone six weeks, you find yourself short of money. You then decide to "borrow" from your friend's resources by paying one of your own bills from your friend's checkbook. The moment you misuse your power of attorney, you commit perjury!

You also commit forgery when you misuse the authority given to you by your heavenly Father. The authority that comes with reigning as a child of the King carries tremendous responsibility! We are to live lives that are above reproach. God is light and in Him there is no darkness at all, so stay out of the shade! Set your goal to live in the brightness and warmth of the SON!

RESPONSIBILITY #4: TO MANAGE THE TIME, TALENT AND TREASURE HE ENTRUSTS TO YOU EACH DAY SO AS TO MAXIMIZE HIS INFLUENCE IN THE WORLD.

In this responsibility lie the dynamics of God's stewards working together. None of us can carry out God's plan alone. He never planned for solo operators. We are expected to work as a team, seeking to advance the kingdom of God as a body of dedicated believers who choose to work together in harmony.

The word manage means to get things done through other people. God has designed His children to work in partnership with one another. As I put my time, strengths, acquired education, years of experience, natural abilities, wealth, and income-generating capabilities into circulation, another steward takes what I have given and—through the stewardship accountability of his time, talents, and treasure—is able to multiply the harvest.

Managing one's time, talents, and treasure demands intentional planning, investing, analyzing needs, providing leadership, and following up on matters. We are not to "wing it." You should evaluate where your time, talents, and treasures can best be maximized. You are accountable for multiplication. You will be rewarded according to how wisely you invest what God entrusts to you.

I've observed that many stewards prefer to give from their financial treasure but guard their time and talents—almost as an act of selfishness. There was a time when churches could count on volunteers with skills from their congregation to come out for workdays and take care of needed repairs, participate in neighborhood visitation, and do other tasks that required an investment of time and talent. But more and more, it seems easier to hire someone else to do the work.

When we as stewards lock arms and freely give our time, talents, and treasure to one another and to address the needs of the unsaved world, we will impact the world dramatically for Christ. Are you ready and willing to manage all you have been given? Are you available for a new assignment from a steward that needs your help? Effective stewards do not sit around, soak up good Bible teaching, and sour with a critical attitude. They pitch in and work together.

You will note that each responsibility has a standard of performance, which simply tells you how to carry out that responsibility.

As you *reproduce*, you are to act and also inform God in prayer as to what is happening—you are involving Him in the process of reproduction, for it is His Spirit that ultimately is the multiplier.

As you *reign*, you are acting on His authority; thus, keeping Him informed as to how you use His name is only reasonable.

Managing your time, talents, and treasure is acting by faith, so it is appropriate to let Him know what you've given or in what you have invested so that His hand can be involved in the multiplied return.

You will also note that your job description includes expectations. At first glance, these expectations may seem almost overwhelming, but the first one is the key to the other two. It is: *to live in reliance upon the power of the Holy Spirit.*

The disciples spent hundreds of hours of personal time with Jesus; and when they felt confused and despairing, Jesus has some special instruction and reminders for them:

> "I tell you the truth, anyone who believes in me will do the same works I have done, and even greater works, because I am going to be with the Father.
>
> You can ask him for *anything*, in my name, and I will do it, so that the Son can bring glory to the Father. Yes, ask *anything*, using my name, and I will do it!
>
> If you love me, obey my commandments. And I will ask the Father, and we will give you another Advocate, who will never leave you. He is the Holy Spirit, who leads into all truth. The world cannot receive him, because it isn't looking for him and doesn't recognize him, but you know him, because he lives with you now and will later be in you" (John 14:12–18).

What Jesus said to them is a powerful promise for you and me as well! Jesus committed Himself not just to walk *with* us but also to work His plain from *within* us.

We are not left on our own to figure things out. We have his instructions. Like my first boss, He wants things done correctly. We are destined to be successful in our stewardship because of the supernatural power of the Holy Spirit that is available to us.

If you are still challenged by this promise and expectation, I encourage you to go back to Chapter 9 and review this powerful truth again. Accessing His power is the key to the Christian life as one of his stewards. He wants you to be plugged into His power.

TRUST AND OBEY

It is virtually impossible to obey someone you do not trust. To trust someone is to have confidence in his judgment. Therefore, *before you're willing to transfer your affairs to another, you want to see him in action.*

God has left us with a record of how He handles His affairs. God's Word is the testimony of His character. He is worthy of our trust. He never has and never will do something that will create a breach of confidence.

Have you ever observed how young children respond to their parents? I'm sure the reason God gave us parental authority is to help us learn to respond to Him in loving obedience. As parents demonstrate love and confidence to their children, there is a reciprocal response from the children as they reflect their parents' attitude.

Learning obedience is a process. Have you ever heard a parent say, "Johnny, it's time to pick up in your room," and then seen young Johnny jump up from his game and eagerly run to tidy up his room? Not too often. Usually, the response is, "OK, I'll be there in a minute." But 30 minutes later, Johnny still has not moved one inch toward his room, unless Mom or Dad has "encouraged" him to do so.

Why does this so often occur? Johnny is not trying to be disobedient—he's preoccupied with circumstances that cause him to be disobedient. Obedience is a matter of the will and of discipline to go in a direction that moves us away from our circumstances.

I'm sure there have been times when God asked you to do something, and, rather than being obedient, you chose to do something else that seemed to you a better alternative. Learning to obey is a life-long adventure. At times it means stepping out into unknown territory, but the only way you will grow is to step out and see what God has for you. Disobedience will bring only emptiness and frustration as your priorities become disoriented.

Remember the Old Testament prophet, Jonah? Because he chose disobedience over obedience, he had to live with the consequences—three days alone in the belly of a great fish. That experience no doubt soured Jonah's taste for seafood for the rest of his life. His willful decision to disregard his stewardship responsibility cost him dearly. Although it was a whale of an adventure, it wasn't worth it!

SUBMIT

No doubt one of the most misunderstood words in our twentieth-century vocabulary is the word submit. Submit means to defer to another's judgment or to yield to the action, control or power of another. I will never forget the pony race I described earlier, where Prince and I "won" third place. That day as Prince satisfied his appetite for the alfalfa clumps, I tried desperately to get his attention and redirect it toward our original goal—to win the race! My prodding, however, was a waste of time. In no way would Prince submit to my leadership. He chose not to yield to my judgment.

In contrast, I've watched trained racehorses run winning races. A winning racehorse is a submissive racehorse. The jockey on his back gives instructions that the spectators seldom recognize. The jockey's position in the saddle and his every move while on the horse's back communicate directions to the horse. The responsive horse yields his dynamic power to the jockey's will. The horse, though much stronger and more powerful than the lightweight jockey, chooses to yield his ability and power to the wisdom and insight of the jockey.

REPORTING RELATIONSHIP

The last section of your job description defines your reporting relationship: ***You report to your heavenly Father.***

Your chain of command is to almighty God Himself. You don't work through some up-and-coming assistant. You report to the creator of the universe!

Why? Because He paid the price for your salvation. It cost Him the life of His Son to have you join His family as a steward. He doesn't want you reporting to anyone else. We will avoid getting mixed signals as to our responsibilities if we report to the one who designed our job in the first place.

We report to our Father by talking to Him in prayer. This toll-free line of communication is direct and never busy. You will never get a recording or be put on hold. You are to tell Him what you are doing, how you see things, and how you feel. You are to ask Him for insight, wisdom, and understanding. He is ready to give counsel as you are ready to listen to Him.

His primary means of communicating to us is through His written Word. God's Word is an instruction manual for His stewards. An understanding of the manual allows you, the steward, to take decisive action that is in accordance with His will.

WORK TOGETHER

YOU ARE TO WORK IN HARMONY WITH OTHER STEWARDS TO MEET THE RESPONSIBILITIES AND EXPECTATIONS OF THE KING.

You are not the lone Ranger! God never intended for one steward to do everything. Many hands working in harmony can accomplish far more than one or two of doing their own thing.

Once farmer's house burned down. He and his family had to build a new home from scratch. To accomplish the task by himself would have taken weeks of work, causing his other farm chores to suffer. So, he decided to host a "house raising." On an appointed day, all of the neighboring farm families got together—the men to raise the house, the children to play, and the women to visit and prepare the food for the rest of the crew.

With fifteen to twenty ringing hammers and twice that many strong arms, what would have taken weeks or even months for one man was completed in a matter of hours. Why? Unity, harmony, and focused objective. How much more we could accomplish in proclaiming the gospel and meeting the needs of others if more "house raising" activities took place within the body of Christ today! God intends for stewards to work together to accomplish His mission.

You now have a job description. You now have a choice to make. Choices always have consequences. What kind of a steward will you choose to be?

The following Key to Abundant Living will help you better understand how working together in harmony with other stewards is critical to success. Lock arms with others and experience exceptional impact for God's Kingdom.

Key to Abundant Living

UNLOCKING YOUR LIFE OF CONTENTMENT

In each of the following categories, list some way in which you can work in greater harmony with other stewards:

1. Your church:

2. Your community:

3. Your home:

4. Your job environment:

As you think about this, what do you see to be the greatest barrier to your success in living out your job description?

What can you do to address this barrier?

After eight weeks have passed, list the results of your tithing experiment. What has this taught you about God?

Chapter 14
JUMPSTART YOUR GIVING

In thus giving his life he enriches the other person, he enhances the other's sense of aliveness by enhancing his own sense of aliveness. He does not give in order to receive; giving is in itself exquisite joy. But in giving, he cannot help bring something to life in the other person . . .

—ERICH FROMM, *THE ART OF LOVING*

The only place you can find a genuine old-fashioned general store these days is in rural America. The days of the dusty, smelly, and crammed old store with an old potbellied stove are rare today. To see this relic of the past you likely need to visit a high-priced tourist attraction that has a replica of what community commerce looked like in the past.

Our lifestyle today is dependent on one-stop shopping at mammoth supermarkets or giant "big box" stores. It is here that you can purchase about everything your heart desires—food, clothing, sporting goods, medicines, cosmetics, jewelry, garden supplies, office supplies, and home goods. You know what I am talking about and likely visited one within the last week.

And now you have online shopping! If you can name it you can find it and never leave your home. You now have unlimited options—delivered to your door in less than twenty-four hours. We have come a long way since the general store you saw on Little House on the Prairie.

Our heavenly Father also operates an international online resource center for his stewards. He has everything pertaining to life and godliness available for you. His inventory is unlimited. He delivers faster than Amazon Prime.

His inventory is free. No payment is required. Over 2,000 years ago, Jesus Christ personally paid the price for your lifetime membership. There is one catch. To receive more you need to distribute what you have already received. God planned for you to touch the lives of others so giving is the trigger to more withdraws.

He has the ultimate distribution network: God to people and people to people. It is through this network of Authorized Wealth Distributors that the needs are to be met. However, because of our self-centeredness and falling short of his standard (sin), the vast majority of us use only a fraction of what is available to us.

A few years ago, I asked members of a couples class I was teaching to help me to develop a list of what can be given. They had just thirty minutes to brainstorm giving options. With this time constraint over 100 different options were suggested. I could give you the list but I will jumpstart your creative thinking with thirty-five of the 100 this group came up with ways to give. This is just scratching the surface:

35 WAYS TO GIVE YOURSELF AWAY

1. ADVICE. Have you taken time lately to share your insights or recommend directions with a person who needs a wise steward's point of view on a complex matter?
2. AFFECTION. Have you taken time to express tender feelings through a touch or a kind word to a person who is down? When was the last time you hugged someone outside of your own family?
3. APPRECIATION. When was the last time you told someone how grateful you are to know him and what your friendship means to you? Have you ever written a text, email, or even a handwritten note to someone, expressing the ways that person has ministered and encouraged you?
4. BENEFIT OF THE DOUBT. Have you demonstrated faith in someone by giving him the benefit of the doubt, by looking at the person in a positive way, rather than in a negative way?
5. CARING. When did you last go out of your way to remember someone by showing genuine concern—perhaps a card, a text or a call—maybe

by taking the tiime to mow someone's lawn or buy groceries? Are you aware that the way children develop empathy is by seeing parents care for others?

6. COACHING. Have you been willing to stand quietly on the sidelines, encouraging someone else to excel while you get no credit?
7. CONFIDENCE. Have expressed your confidence in someone so that he could have renewed courage to face the challenges of his life? How have you helped someone to believe in themselves?
8. COUNSEL. Have you provided biblical input and wise perspective to a friend who is trying to work through a major decision of life?
9. EYE CONTACT. When you talk with people, do you give them your attention by looking them in the eye? Your eyes can tell the other person how you really feel.
10. FAITH. Do you seek to give your faith away in such a way that people will recognize you as a Christian who walks in the power of the Holy Spirit?
11. FOOD. Do you share with others what God has provided for your physical nourishment? A loaf of freshly baked bread or a sampling of homegrown vegetables, accompanied by a thoughtful note, can be a ministry in someone's life.
12. FORGIVENESS. Have you forgiven someone who has hurt you? Have you told them that you do not harbor resentment—and that all is forgiven?
13. GENTLENESS. Are you mild in your manners and in how you deal with circumstances and people? When in a heated or complex discussion, do you give a quiet response rather than a harsh retort?
14. GUIDANCE. Are you providing leadership and direction to others in such a way as to stimulate them to grow? Do you provide personal insights or helpful boundaries?
15. GRACE. You were given undeserved favor by God. How are you expressing grace to others when they don't deserve it?
16. HOPE. Do you demonstrate favorable and confident expectations about the future? Does your attitude stimulate others to have hope as well?
17. HOSPITALITY. Do you often go out of your way to make someone else feel needed and wanted? Are you willing to set an extra place at

your table for someone who drops in unexpectedly? How about inviting a person to stay at your home for a few days?

18. INTEGRITY. Does your life overflow with consideration for others, and with high character and stability? Do you tell the truth despite the circumstances?
19. JOY. Does your life overflow with inner contentment and peace, even in the midst of difficult circumstances? Do you radiate joy?
20. KINDNESS. Do you give preference to others and show concern for others by reaching out to meet a need? Do you go the extra mile in helping to meet a need?
21. KNOWLEDGE. Do you use what you have been taught by others to encourage others to grow? Do you use the sound mind that God gave you in determining the course of action to take?
22. LISTEN. Do you give your full attention to others so that you can sort out wisely what you hear and provide insight and encouragement?
23. LOVE. Do you regularly express your affection for others, letting them know that God loves them and that you love them too? How many ways can you show love today?
24. LOYALTY. Can others count on you to stand by them? How do you demonstrate your loyalty to your spouse? Your boss? Your pastor? Your friends?
25. MERCY. Are you there when someone needs you? When someone does something that hurts you, do you show mercy, just as the Lord has shown mercy to you? Do you extend kind, compassionate treatment to those who have not earned it?
26. MONEY. How free are you with the money you have? Are you prepared to give the cash you have to a person in need? Do you regularly use what you have to help others?
27. PRAISE. Are you always ready to give compliments for a job well done? Do you regularly go out of your way to express appreciation to others for what they do? How are you expressing praise to God?
28. RESPECT. Do you give honor and esteem to those with whom you work? Are you courteous at all times? Do you give preference to those older than you?
29. RESPONSIBILITY. Can you give a task to someone and express your trust that he will complete the task satisfactorily? Giving responsibility

helps a person grow. Do you delegate authority to others to help them mature?

30. SELF-CONTROL. Do you exercise self-discipline at times when you would like to demand your way? Do you guard your words so that what you say does not cause disharmony and hurt?
31. SHARING. Do you ask others to join you in an opportunity to see something special? Do you give preference to others' needs when you have a need yourself? Are you willing to cooperate with others to accomplish an objective?
32. STRENGTHS. Do you know what your strengths are? Are you utilizing them to help others? Do you use your strengths to uphold another's physical, spiritual, or mental needs?
33. TEARS. Are you willing to give your tears to show that you too feel for the hurting? Are you free to laugh with those who laugh and weep with those who weep?
34. TRUST. Do you demonstrate to others that you can be trustworthy?
35. WISDOM. Do you make decisions based on your walk with God, or do you act only in light of your circumstances? Can people recognize you as one who continually trusts God for His wisdom?

Has this list of thirty-five ways to give opened up new vistas of creative giving for you? Use this list to jumpstart your giving as an Authorized Wealth Distributor.

Did you notice that you often can mix things together? Effective giving is like baking a cake; it is the right combination of ingredients and steps that produce the best results.

THREE WAYS TO BE GIVING

There are three ways to initiate giving. Here is where you can "mix and match" to meet the needs of others.

> 1. *Through person-to-person contact.* The immediate reward comes from genuine person-to-person, face-to-face contact. You see what the benefit of your giving produces. This is the most effective way to give yourself away because you can get instant feedback and gratification.

2. *Through voice contact.* Although circumstances do not always permit you to have face-to-face communication, the phone allows you to give even when you can't be with someone. There are times when a text or an email will meet the need but hearing a voice is the next best thing to being there. Many of the ways to give listed above can be distributed via your phone. Leaving a message is all that is often needed, although voice interaction is by far the best.
3. *Through the written word.* Letters, texts, and emails often can give encouragement, love, commitment, affection, wisdom, and advice, more effectively than any other communication approach. A person receiving something in writing can read what you have written time and time again. God has chosen to use His written Word as His prime means of instruction to us so we can read it often. Be liberal in using your written word as you give to others.

BALANCE FOR BEST RESULTS

Make your aim to be between these three approaches. If all three are being used effectively, you will enhance the distribution of God's inventory to others.

Ask God to make you a blessing through the ways you give. Ask Him to show you how you best can carry out your job description. Allow Him to be original in your giving. You've got a lot to give!

You will never run out of things to give. Even when you feel you are in need, you have Jesus waiting to give to you and to others. You will never deplete God's warehouse. You name it, He's got it. As an Authorized Wealth Distributor for the Lord, you will always have what you need when you need it!

"Let us, therefore, draw near with confidence to the throne of grace, that we may receive mercy and may find grace in time of need."
—Hebrews 4:16, NASB

Key To Abundant Living

UNLOCKING YOUR LIFE OF CONTENTMENT

Review the list of thirty-five ways to give. Now jot down five specific ways that you can give in the next week. You are not limited to these thirty-five. You know what you have to give. Define your plan and work your plan!

Who are some people who may especially benefit from what you have to give? Ask God to give you specific opportunities to give to those people.

Chapter 15
DISSECTING DECEPTION

For a time is coming when people will no longer listen to sound and wholesome teaching. They will follow their own desires and will look for teachers who will tell them whatever their itching ears what to hear. They will reject the truth and chase after myths.

—2 TIMOTHY 4: 3–4

Deception: The act of causing someone to accept as true or valid what is false by misleading or omitting the truth to achieve personal gain.

When I first joined the Cru staff I met a very unassuming professional couple that was also joining the ministry staff. Whereas I would be serving on the campus at the University of Pennsylvania, they were joining the ministry staff to travel—using their years of experience in the entertainment industry to attract crowds, entertain, and then share how they had become believers in Jesus. Andre and Aljeana Kole were a team. Aljeana was not only his wife but also his assistant on stage. They were both pleasant, quiet, and unassuming. They were passionate about helping lost people find personal peace in knowing Jesus.

Andre was acclaimed internationally as the magician's magician. Without question, he was known worldwide as THE top living illusionist of our time.

Every magician saw him as their gold standard. While very friendly, I discovered I had to work to gain any information about them and their profession. They both knew how to keep secrets!

He was the magician's master teacher and creator of illusions. He was the innovator and original creator of many of the world-renowned illusionist tricks that are still performed today. If you have ever seen David Copperfield, Siegfried and Roy, Tim Kole (their son), or Kirby Van Birch perform, you have witnessed an Andre Kole illusion. When the world's magicians met annually behind closed doors, they all expected Andre Kole to perform his magic and introduce a new illusion that he had created.

You can learn all about his extensive professional career at AndreKole.com. You can see him perform some of his famous illusions—like the Table of Death, The Squeeze Box, sawing a lady in half, shrinking a person down to one-fifth the size, levitating a person in the air, and making the Statue of Liberty levitate and then disappear.

Six months after we met, I saw Andre again, but this time in Dayton Beach during college Spring Break. I had brought a busload of fifty college students from the northeast to this event Daytona Beach. Andre Kole was there to perform his magic to thousands of college students in the famous outdoor beach bandshell.

Soon after we reconnected, I learned he was interested in visiting the space launch site in nearby Cape Canaveral. I borrowed a friend's car one morning, and four of us headed for the Kennedy Space Center. Only if you asked Andre questions would you get answers, so my three friends and I decided to probe and see what we could learn from him.

That day I came away with a handful of gems about the life of a seasoned world-renowned illusionist:

1. Know more than your audience. That day he said casually, "Anyone can do what I do if you know what I know."
2. People are open to being deceived; it is our nature to believe what is not true.
3. To be good at this art, one must practice every day. As skilled as Andre was at his craft, he was disciplined to practice every day.
4. Always be very careful in what you say. Words matter. The less one says, the better the outcome.

5. Control everything that happens on stage. Andre insisted that those on his team do exactly what he instructed them to do. The majority never knew why but obeyed without question.
6. Stay away from rabbits! Andre has never pulled a rabbit out of a hat—he was allergic to rabbit hair.

Andre Kole was known as an illusionist, but you could also call him a professional deceiver. He knew what he was doing was not what it was perceived to be. In a matter of minutes, with costumes, music, lights, and props, he could transport thousands of captivated and spell-bound observers into a world far from their reality. He just knew more about what he was doing than his audience did!

One day I asked Andre if he had a performance that did not go as planned. He thought for a minute and then said, "Yes, one." He went on to explain that he once was invited to perform for an annual gathering of the leaders of tribal nations as they met annually in Window Rock, Arizona. He recalled a nighttime outdoor venue where a few thousand tribal leaders were in attendance. He was the featured entertainment for the evening. He explained to his audience many times during his show that everything he was doing was an illusion—nothing he was doing was as it was perceived.

He proceeded with his next new illusion. This included removing his assistant's head from her body—and then having her head float out over the audience of tribal leaders. Within minutes, most of the audience left the show. They had too much deception for that night!

Why are we attracted to things that we don't understand? Why were so many of us caught up in the saga of Harry Potter movies or books? Why are we attracted to magic and fantasy? Why do so many today get caught up in conspiracy theories? What makes us vulnerable to deceit, the "dark side," and believing what is not true is true? What causes many believers to embrace false teachings?

BE ON THE ALERT!!

Back in Chapter 10 we listened in on a casual conversation with Eve, a guest who stopped in for a chat, and Adam at their beautiful garden home. Their residence was truly heaven on earth. Imagine a perfect climate, a pristine tropical garden, and sinless surroundings. They lived in the first clothing-optional all-inclusive resort! Adam and Eve went on evening walks with God himself and had many intimate conversations with Him. They were God's first stewards of Eden. Their responsibility was to care for His creation.

In Genesis 3, you find the actual account of Eve's conversation with her drop-in guest. Lucifer's spirit chose to engage Eve through the most beautiful of all creatures, the serpent. She had no reason to think that she and Adam would play into a scheme of his deception. He appeared safe!

Lucifer knew that Adam and Eve's senses were the way to their hearts. If by using their senses, he could corrupt their hearts, he could alter their worldview. He knew that their sight, smell, touch, taste, and feel were the five pathways to their destruction. They did not. If he could get them to question their Creator and create distrust in His guidance and His boundaries He had established to protect them, Lucifer knew he would gain a win over his greatest enemy. His deceptive plan was to take them down. His deception technique was to focus on their experiences rather than God's truth.

Lucifer cunningly deceived them by appealing to their self-interests. He misled them by twisting what God had said, redefining a few words, and omitting the truth to achieve his plan for personal gain. He enticed them with a spiritual counterfeit—something not true but sure sounded to be true. His counterfeit had all the trappings of truth, but it was a lie.

They both took the bait! He utilized their senses that day to attack their heart. And what he did in the Garden he is doing today. He knows we are easily self-deceived. He is out to put a wedge between God's best plan for us through his deceptive message of truth. Things have not changed! He is still working his plan.

Remember the definition of deception:

> Deception is the act of causing someone to accept as true or valid what is false by misleading or omitting the truth to achieve personal gain.

For starters, let's look at just five Bible passages that talk about the end result of this deception:

> "The human heart is the most deceitful of all things, and desperately wicked. Who really knows how bad it is?" (Jeremiah 17:9).

> "Those that trust in their own insight are foolish, but anyone who walks in wisdom is safe" (Proverbs 26:26).
>
> "Jesus said, 'For from the heart come evil thoughts, murder, adultery, all sexual immorality, theft, lying, and slander. These are what defile you'" (Matthew 15:19–20a).
>
> "Since they thought it foolish to acknowledge God, he abandoned them to their foolish thinking and let them do things that should never be done. Their lives became full of every kind of wickedness, sin, greed, hate, envy, murder, quarreling, deception, malicious behavior, and gossip. They are backstabbers, haters of God, insolent, proud, and boastful. They invest in new ways of sinning, and they disobey their parents. They refuse to understand, break their promises, are heartless, and have no mercy" (Romans 1:28–31).
>
> "Everything is pure to those whose hearts are pure. But nothing is pure to those who are corrupt and unbelieving because their minds and conscience are corrupted. Such people claim they know God, but they deny him in the way they live. They are disobedient and worthless for doing any good" (Titus 1:15–16).

Are you aware that almost every letter in the New Testament addresses the dangers of deception and false teaching? If the first-century believers had to face this chronic problem creeping into the new church within a matter of years after Jesus' resurrection, you and I need to be on the alert that deception and false teaching are bombarding us today. We need to be alert to the clever ploys that are being used today to get us into a position of compromise and, ultimately, ineffectiveness. When our focus becomes our well-being, comfort, and personal gain, we are not focusing on God's plan for us. Lucifer still is a master at the self-deception craft!

HEART PROBLEMS!

Wouldn't you say that we have a serious heart problem? We need to admit we actually like to be self-deceived and are vulnerable to attack. We need to be intentional in being on alert about how easily we can get off track and become ineffective.

You and I are quite good at finding, and even battling, "the big bad ones"—those shortcomings or sins that blatantly ignore God and live lives with no regard for him. The deception you will be faced with regularly is the kind that looks as innocent as Lucifer did to Adam and Eve that day in the garden. That day Lucifer did not wear a red suit, have little horns and a tail, or carry a pitchfork. He was attractive, appealing, warm, conversational, looked trustworthy, showed sincere compassion, and shared new truths and insights that God had failed to share with them. It is easy to conclude that Adam and Eve liked this deceiver! He gained their trust. He then caught them in his web of deceit by enticing them with selective false information. And, like Andre Kole, he knew more than they knew.

He used Adam and Eve's senses to derail them and get this off course. He knew how to achieve his desired outcome: refocusing from God's direction to something that attracted appealed to self-interest—smelling the aroma, touching the texture, and tasting the flavor. It wasn't about the fruit. It was about not trusting God and his word. They had no clue they were being deceived until it was too late. He used what they had to put a wedge, called sin, between them and their Creator.

Here is the bottom line: As a steward, you must be intentional and careful. You and I are prime candidates for deception and a takedown when we least expect it. The goal of your enemy is to create an environment where you end up being neutralized in your responsibility as an Authorized Wealth Distributor.

Over fifty years ago, I was introduced to *The Screwtape Letters* by C. S. Lewis. If you have not read this insightful short read, this is a must for you. Screwtape is a cunning and insightful demon that oversees the minions of junior demons. Wormwood is one of these junior demons, and his job is to derail his assigned believers so that they are useless for serving God and fulfilling His plan. Screwtape instructs Wormwood with creative ways to keep his assigned believers off balance, useless, and defeated through subtle, deceptive means. If you know Jesus, your wormwood is out to mess you up. Watch out!

In Roman Catholic theology, there is some excellent teaching on what is known as the seven cardinal or deadly sins: pride, greed, lust, envy, gluttony, wreath, and laziness (indifference). These sins directly impact a person's capacity to live life as God designed a person to live. You can find a trove of books written on each of these sins.

Pride and greed are the two sins that help catapult us toward self-serving deception.

> **Pride:** a feeling of deep pleasure or satisfaction derived from one's own achievements, the achievements of those with whom one is closely associated, or qualities or possessions that are widely admired.
>
> Do you notice the first phrase of the definition has one focus: me! Pride is all about you and your accomplishments.
>
> **Greed:** an intense and selfish desire for something, especially wealth, power, or food. This is pride on steroids to satisfy who? Me!

These two sins focus on what one can get from others: **my** comfort, **my** way, **my** health, **my** happiness, **my** personal fulfillment, and **my** prosperity. Our nature is to aggressively search out ways to meet **my** wants in life, regardless of how these desires impact someone else.

BOMBARDED!

Deception is rampant and everywhere today—no culture has avoided this attack. You will find deception aggressively creeping into solid Bible-teaching churches. It is subtle but it is there! Yes, New Age cult teaching and tools are creeping into studies. "Progressive Christianity" movements are full of this without apology. Subtle deception is taught with fervor through feelings-focused independent and charismatic oriented churches. You will find deception proclaimed in formal and traditional churches through legalism on steroids. The result is total confusion, polarization, emotional stress, and debilitating depression.

The enemy's goal is to get healthy and growing believers to seek self-centered gratification through performance-based faith wherever possible. Remember, the message will look and sound very much like God's truth, but it will be a few degrees from the truth. If you are not regularly into God's Word—you are at risk of accepting and embracing false teaching. What is true is now false. What was once false is now true.

This is impacting every aspect of society. It is not limited to just the church. Watch your culture and you will see how deception is now in every aspect of society.

But for now, please focus with me on how you can be caught up in false teachings and be rendered useless to what God has planned for you. You are called to be a trusted steward in managing and distributing what God has entrusted to you to redistribute to others—even in culturally challenging circumstances. Come to grips with this reality: Your enemy is out to neutralize and destroy you. He wants you to be a failure. It is important for you to learn how to identify deception by those that look godly but are, in fact, deceivers.

WHAT DECEPTION LOOKS LIKE.

Without even knowing it, you can be pulled into the snare of deceptive thinking and soon be embracing and expounding on false teaching. You need your guard up and know your Bible in order to avoid deceptive thinking. Deception is lurking around in every community of believers. When caught, you become impotent and useless.

In the past, deception seemed to be veiled and thus more difficult to identify. But today, it is not unusual to see arrogant false declarations proclaimed by even trusted definers of truth. If you know what it looks like, how it sounds, and where it could be hiding, you can be better prepared to face it or flee from it.

There are two unassuming ways you can get caught in a snare of deception:

1. **Performance-based faith deception:** This form is the most subtle. You are not expecting this attack. Performance-based faith focuses on what you feel you need to better yourself. If you are good enough God will reward you. Your heart is telling you that you need to do more to prove your worth. The focus is on ME. When your focus is on your need, you are being set up to fail. Because of our sinful nature, we want to believe those that promise us a personal reward, good health, more wealth, and cozy comfort, with a feeling of peace and happiness.

   And you are being set up! Product marketing today conditions you for this take-down, Every day, through clever advertising, we fall for the ploy for self-fulfillment. We feel if we make the purchase, our needs will be met, and we will be more fulfilled. We end up making decisions based on false or half-truth evidence presented or taught, and spending money on something we do not need!
2. **Deceiver-driven deception:** This usually comes from someone with authority that has gained your trust. These individuals are masters at identifying with one's felt needs. They appear to have God's authority, blessing, and insider insight. You believe the deceiver has your best interest in mind and will help you get what you think you need. Actually, you are receiving carefully filtered information so as to get you to

> believe in something that is not true. They are relying on you to trust them—so that they get what they want from you. Like professional illusionists, they know more than you know!

Every steward is at risk of being deceived, and if you think you are above this, you are already deceived! If you are unfamiliar with what the Bible actually teaches, you will likely end up depending on your new trusted authority. You are being set up to fail.

Deception often is disguised and appears to be the answer to your longing or felt need. It always looks legitimate, honest, and God-honoring. It is a very close truth, but the degree it is off is where the danger lies. Just as in Adam and Even in the garden, you can be caught off guard by the cunning way the pitch appeals to your senses.

A deceiver's message to be full of new insight or understanding that you somehow missed. The message will include some Scripture to justify the declaration. Be alert. Know your Bible. Listen and process carefully. Challenge the thought. Never agree without studying the Bible and getting input from others with insight and wisdom. With some practice, you can learn to spot deception and help others escape entrapment.

16 CHARACTERISTICS THAT CAN HELP!

To help you get a jumpstart on identifying deception, here are sixteen characteristics worth reviewing. Think of these characteristics as tools in a tool chest. You will not see all sixteen used at any one time. A seasoned deceiver will use whatever tactic it takes to derail your effectiveness as a steward.

A deceiver will introduce you to new definitions of words or new concepts that you never thought about, and new things you must do. This is all intentional to get you to trust their deception. There will always be something that you must do to receive the outcome you want.

Deceivers are masters in manipulating your emotions. A good deceiver will find your weaknesses and then leverage this against you. Once you place trust in the deceiver's authority, he or she will begin reprogramming your thinking so that you believe the new cunning logic.

Watch and listen. A deceiver:

1. *Plays to your need or weakness.* A good deceiver will find your weaknesses and then leverage those weaknesses against you. He will convince you that he will help you solve "your problem."

2. *Appeals to your senses.* Just as Lucifer did with Adam and Eve, the deceiver wants you to connect with new truths by seeing, hearing, touching, tasting or feeling something.
3. *Builds on a felt need of personal prosperity or comfort here and now.* He will focus on immediate outcomes you feel you need or want to make it in life—after all, you deserve what you can get in this life as a king's kid. There is very little eternity in mind. If you perceive you have a need, he likely can fill it!
4. *Focuses on your desire for self-improvement rather than repentance, salvation, confession of sin, or eternity.* The appeal focuses on easy solutions to address your immediate need.
5. *Locks you in by getting you to give to him.* The deceiver will tell you that the key to being blessed now is your giving—almost always to his or her ministry. A deceiver will teach that generous giving is the trigger that unleashes God's prosperity, solutions to your need, and blessing in your life. Giving to get is the objective. This is a subtle but substantial difference of God wanting you to be generous to others. The intent is to bind you to this "new" message.
6. *Knows exactly what she is doing to snare you into deception.* A deceiver is a master manipulator. He knows with the right environment and setting, you will succumb to his plan for you when you least expect it. His subtle invitation looks very close to genuine truth. He will focus on what you feel you are lacking.
7. *Appeals to your self-focused need for personal gain and money, health, and resolution of a crisis you are facing.* The deceiver will empathize with your hurts and hang-ups. Deceivers do and say what the audience wants to see and hear.
8. *Appears to have an exceptional understanding from God Himself.* The deceiver's message is the answer you have been looking for. And yes, Scripture will liberally be used to build your confidence. Jesus will be mentioned often. Your ignorance of what the Bible teaches will lead you to believe the deception—and quote the verses out of context.
9. *Utilizes Christian language that you want to hear.* She will often say words that give you a feeling of inner peace.
10. *Knows that carefully chosen words matter.* A deceiver masterfully says what you want to hear, so you will act as he wants you to. Every word

and even every move is artfully planned. Deceivers are masters at leveraging mind control.

11. *Uses God's Word out of context to reinforce their authority.* The interpretation or application is typically not biblical, but the deceiver will convenience you that what is being said is from God himself. The message will often be couched in "here is new truth that has not been revealed to you until now."
12. *Depends on your being open to new revelations and special anointing.* Deceivers always have new truths to share with you that you have never considered before. God is now revealing himself to you through new insights.
13. *Has unvarnished pride in being exceptionally successful.* Deceivers are not embarrassed to show or talk about how God has blessed them and their teaching with impressive material rewards. Deceivers must demonstrate to you that they are directly in touch with God, as evidenced by the way God is demonstrating his blessing on them.
14. *Knows how to totally control the environment.* Few watching or hearing deceivers ply their craft actually know what is really going on "behind the curtain." If you are in a healing service, as an example, you never see or hear about those who truly needed healing but were screened out and not allowed into the environment. She effectively uses emotions to prepare you for deception.
15. *Appears to be spiritually mature, concerned for your well-being, and above reproach.* What they are off stage is rarely what one sees on stage. With rare exceptions, a deceiver's private life is not honoring the Lord, whom the deceiver proclaims as his authority. Personal lives of deceivers, that you rarely ever see, are typically a sham.
16. *Appeals to your need to do something in order to gain a deeper understanding of God.* The focus will be on what you can do to please God. This is legalism on steroids. The focus is getting you to do something to prove your faith.

Reflect on these characteristics for a moment. Could one of these tactics be used to unlock your weakness in the next day or two through a rally you attend, podcast you watch or a book you are reading? Be on guard. Never assume. Question. Knowing your Bible is your best defense against getting caught in the web of deception.

WORDS REVEAL DECEIVERS' HEARTS!

To help you identify deceivers, listen to what they say. Over the last few years, I have had fun collecting quotes from "reputable" deceivers. If you hear similar phrases coming from seemingly articulate messengers, you are likely hearing a deceiver speak. Have you heard declarations that sound like the following?

- "Today, God clearly told me to tell you something very important. Listen to me. This is for you."
- "God has revealed new truth to me that I am compelled to share with you." God has anointed me to declare hidden truths to you. God spoke to me this morning and told me to tell you…"
- "You exercise the power of faith through your words. Speak it out. Articulate what you want to receive from God. Your words will move God to act."
- "Name it and proclaim it. It is yours as you apply your faith to receive His provision. Your words have the power to create, heal, destroy, and kill. God is bound to act on what you say."
- "God has the power but you have the permission. God cannot act without your permission. You need to do your part for God to do his part."
- "God made you in his image. You are like God. He said it. Believe it! Begin acting with your God-given authority. You are his creation; you are god."
- "Your lack of faith is limiting God from hearing you. Name your health need. Declare you are healed, and you will be healed. Your lack of faith in God's ability will keep God's best from you."
- "To receive, you must give. Your giving is the seed that you must plant to receive his gift to you. You must give first to activate his blessing—and then receive what God wants to give to you."
- "Exercise your faith so that God can exercise His power. Don't let your lack of faith derail God's plan for you."
- "Jesus was a man who made a choice to be empowered with God's divinity, and he lived this way as an example of how we can live life as well. You have God's divinity."
- "Jesus was human, and he reached his potential to be God-like. We can be just like Jesus. We are sons of God just like he was the Son of God."
- "You are struggling because of what you have learned in the past. You need to unlearn old teachings to understand the new teachings."

- "Yes, the Bible is true. But God has more to say. He is working today as He did before. He is calling out apostles and prophets for this day to complete what He started. We are living in the latter days; He speaking to you right now.
- "God is always revealing his will for each generation. I am humbled to be called to help you with expanded understanding never before revealed."

A DECEIVER'S MOTIVATION.

Are you beginning to realize that deceivers are masters at what they do? Sadly, they have convinced themselves that what they declare is actually true. They feel anointed and empowered. They, too, are deceived! Most know that much of what they say is not totally true. However, they cannot back down from the deception they proclaim because it will cost them what they love the most—power, money, influence, and control. They are addicted to their schemes.

A deceiver loves:

- **Power:** Deceivers thrive on being the perceived authority on a new truth. This position of power feeds the deceiver's dark soul.
- **Money and "sustaining the family business."** The vast majority of deceivers are wealthy. They cannot afford to cut off their income streams. They are codependent on their acquired wealth and lavish lifestyle. Deceivers in today's culture live in excessive abundance: homes, cars, private planes, luxury accommodations, excessive bank accounts, and extensive hidden assets. Their wealth comes from those that they are deceiving. There is no remorse in this. After all, this is proof of God's blessing to them. The scheme works!
- **Influence and reputation.** Deceivers love their following. Their influence means more to them than anything else. They thrive on accolades and cannot live without a dedicated, but deceived, following. Their image is paramount to them.
- **Control.** To survive they must keep the system they created going. they must sustain their authority over those who follow them. Once they articulate their deception into messages they cannot back down. The message must continue to fulfill their income. The goal is to sustain control over messaging and thought as long as possible.

BE INTENTIONAL!

Jesus said that your heart is deceitful and wicked. The culture today tells you to "follow your heart." DON'T! This is the worst thing you can do. When you do, you are playing with fire. Your enemy wants you to "follow your heart" so that he can keep you from being an effective steward.

Rather than follow your heart, guard your heart in three ways:

1. **Know your Bible.** Read it. Study it. Memorize it. Spend time in it. The more you know what your Bible says, the easier it will be to identify a counterfeit teaching. When you know what the Bible says about a matter you will be prepared to counter the deceptive teaching. Deceptors are masters at using Scripture out of context so expect to hear them to often quote select Scriptures. They will be trying to get you to "see things in a new light."
2. **Keep your focus on giving what you have been given away.** As an effective steward is to be a distributor, not a taker. Be intentional in giving; not passive. Look for opportunities to meet a need. Become an instrument in helping others and reflecting God's character.
3. **Walk in the Spirit and master breathing spiritually.** Your sustaining power is to allow God's spirit to work in and through you. Master spiritual breathing that we discussed in Chapter 9. Understanding this truth was a game-changer for me. This will be a game-changer for you. When you do, you will be empowered to identify and confront deception. You cannot counter the enemy without His promised power.

Be assured, deception is not something new to our time. It started in the Garden of Eden. You can see this throughout both the Old and New Testaments.

Jesus warned his followers to watch out for false teachers. He knew counterfeits would be in the culture. Here are two examples:

- In Matthew 7:15–18, he said: "Beware of false prophets who come disguised as harmless sheep but are really vicious wolves. You can identify them by the way they act. Can you pick grapes from thornbushes or figs from thistles? A good tree produces good fruit and a bad tree produces bad fruit."
- In Matthew 24:24–25 he said: "For false messiahs and false prophets will rise up and perform great signs and wonders so as to deceive, if possible, even God's chosen ones. See, I have warned you about this ahead of time."

Paul was so concerned about deception and false teaching in the new church of his day that he wrote to the believers he was mentoring with these words:

- In Romans 16:17–18, he writes: "And now I make one more appeal.... Watch out for people who cause division and upset people's faith by teaching things contrary to what you have been taught. Stay away from them. Such people are not serving Christ our Lord; they are serving their own personal interests."
- In 2 Corinthians 11:13–15, he writes: "These people are false apostles, They are deceitful workers who disguise themselves as apostles of Christ. But I am not surprised! Even Satan disguises himself as an angel of light. So it is no wonder that his servants also disguise themselves as servants of righteousness . . ."
- In Ephesians 4:14, he writes: "Then we will no longer be immature like children. We won't be tossed and blown about by every new teaching. We will not be influenced when people try to trick us with lies so clever they sound like the truth."
- In Colossians 2:8, he writes: "Don't let anyone capture you with empty philosophies and high-sounding nonsense that comes from human thinking and from the spiritual powers of this world, rather than from Christ."
- In 1 Timothy 6:20–21, he writes: "Timothy, guard what God has given to you. Avoid godless, foolish discussions with those who oppose you with their so-called knowledge. Some people have wandered from the faith by following such foolishness."
- In 2 Timothy 4: 3–4, he writes: "For such a time is coming when people will no longer listen to sound and wholesome teaching. They will follow their own desires and will look for a teacher who will tell them whatever their itching ears want to hear. They will reject the truth and chase after myths."

There is no vaccine for this sin virus. False teaching is now raising havoc in every culture today. Well-meaning believers never intentionally planned to link up with deceptive teaching. It happened subtly. Perhaps it crept in through an entertaining visiting speaker, via a small group study by a respected leader, or through a collaborative community campaign. Take the warning of Jesus and the cautions of Paul seriously. Be aware!

Deception always starts with seemingly innocent circumstances. You will never see a sign that welcomes you to deceptive teaching. If you are not careful you will end up supporting and cherry-picking nuggets you like from false teachers. When you embrace any deceptive teaching, you become a part of the deception yourself.

IF YOU WANT TO GO DEEPER . . .

If you feel you need to go deeper into this destructive and polarizing subject, I encourage you to read and listen to some of the whistleblowers that are currently speaking out against deception. You will find a few recommendations in the Digging Deeper section of this book.

Key To Abundant Living

UNLOCKING YOUR LIFE OF CONTENTMENT

REFLECT ON A SITUATION WHEN YOU HAVE INNOCENTLY BEEN CAUGHT UP IN DECEPTION.

When was this?

What were the circumstances?

How did this impact you?

What did you learn as a result?

REVISIT THE 15 CHARACTERISTICS OF A DECEIVER THAT ARE OUTLINED IN THIS CHAPTER.

Identity five characteristics that you know can likely trip you up and make you vulnerable to being deceived.

1.

2.

3.

4.

5.

Now list three actions that you can take so that you can counteract deceptive tactics and keep you from being neutralized as an Authorized Wealth Distributor.

1.

2.

3.

Chapter 16

INDIFFERENCE: THE BIGGEST OBSTACLE TO GIVING

If you will live like no one else, later you can live like no one else.
—DAVE RAMSEY

A Chapter from *Performance-Driven Giving*[7]

By David L. Hancock and Bobby Kipper

What you are about to read will be liberating and helpful to you! Developing new habits are never easy. Even when we want to do so, taking the next step can feel risky and uncomfortable. But not responding as a steward could reflect indifference.

While working on *Intentional Living and Giving* I was introduced to *Performance-Driven Giving* by David Hancock and Bobby Kipper. You will find this book very helpful as you begin to chart your journey as an effective steward. The book is packed with some practical insights for you.

One chapter will be especially helpful for you right now. This subject is so important that I asked permission from the authors to reprint an entire chapter for you here.

In our fast-paced world, it is easy to become indifferent to needs around us. Too often, it seems easier to ignore a situation and do nothing than to respond to a need placed before us. Responding often requires you to rearrange your plans and give time and attention in a way you never anticipated.

When we don't respond, for whatever reason, we almost always miss a God-ordained opportunity to have a personal impact on others. What you are about to read helped me. You will find timely insight, wisdom, and practical tips that will help guide your thinking as you deal with indifference. Don't allow indifference to stop you from thriving as an Authorized Wealth Distributor.

Go for it!

You can order *Performance-Driven Giving* from your favorite book supplier or use the QR code below.

CHAPTER 4

Indifference: The Biggest Obstacle to Giving

If you will live like no one else, later you can live like no one else.
—Dave Ramsey

In the classic children's book *Pierre*, written by Maurice Sendak, we meet a young boy who doesn't care about anything. No matter what his mother or father says, no matter how they try to motivate him, he always responds with "I don't care!"

When a hungry lion pays a call and ultimately eats Pierre, it is only then that he starts to care. (Fortunately, the doctor was able to retrieve Pierre from the lion.) The story ends with these words: "The moral of Pierre is: CARE!"

Pierre may be a book for children, but it contains a lot of wisdom for adults. Many people in our culture today are indifferent to the needs of others and the opportunities they have to give. The *Merriam-Webster.com Dictionary* defines "indifferent" this way: "marked by a lack of interest, enthusiasm, or concern for something."

There are many obstacles that prevent people from giving. Most people believe the enemy of giving is "taking." But the biggest enemy is indifference. In this chapter, we will look at the reasons for it, how to handle it, as well as the symptoms of indifference.

The Roots of Indifference

Before we look at solutions for helping people overcome their indifference, we must first understand the reasons for it. There are several important roots that cause our indifference.

Distractions

In recent years, movie theaters have undergone many different kinds of transformations. They have upgraded projection systems, installed new sound systems, and offered new kinds of dining experiences. And oddly enough, they have cracked down on people using their cell phones.

You would be hard-pressed to go to a theater today and not see someone using their cell phone during the movie. This is a big problem because it distracts both the moviegoer and everyone around them from the main event.

This is a perfect metaphor for the world today: We are distracted and missing the big picture of life. On any given day, we spend two to three hours on social media, in addition to work, family, church, hobbies, and social obligations. How do we fit it all in? The truth is that we often don't. We are like squirrels who are constantly distracted, moving from one thing to the next. The result is that we don't have the mental capacity to notice the needs of others around us.

This not only applies to our productivity. It also applies to our giving. Whenever we are trying to juggle too many things in life, not to mention all of our distractions from social media, it is nearly impossible to think about anything but ourselves.

Denial

When we do see genuine needs, it is not difficult to deny them. It is easy to believe that the wealthy, the government, social programs, or churches will take care of the needs of other people.

We continue to be influenced by media outlets, which are focused on the urgent. They are most interested in stories and information that creates hype and results in the most clicks or views. The most important needs in the world don't always make for the most exciting stories.

We are also in denial about other people's needs because we simply don't realize they exist. Most of us live a life that is carefully curated to produce the most favorable image. We select the right photographs and social media posts to show to the world. It is hard to admit our real needs because we don't want to look weak. Therefore others may not know what our needs are, and we may not know other people's real needs.

Doubt

When people give to causes or charities, it is easy to doubt whether their gift is making any difference. There are two reasons for this.

First, it is sometimes hard to tell how your giving directly impacts lives. Most organizations create charts and reports detailing all kinds of data about their giving. But at the end of the day, people don't care about data—they care about the humans that the data represents. It's hard to feel engaged in giving unless you know the stories of at least some of the people your giving impacts.

The second reason that people are sometimes in doubt about giving is because they can mistrust the organizations themselves. In the last few years we've heard many stories of corporate greed and abuse of power. Of course, this is nothing new. As long as there have been people in power, there has been bad behavior. As long as we are fallen, broken human beings, leaders will fall short.

However, the bad behavior of a few high-profile individuals hurts everyone. Trust in the government and other organizations is at an all-time low. It can be hard to convince donors that they are making a difference if the donors don't trust them in the first place.

Despair

News outlets have reported recently that suicide rates are on the rise. With the current climate of world upheaval and an unpredictable economy, no one would be surprised to see this increase even further. We are in the middle of a mental health crisis. Many people have simply given up hope.

Anyone who has experienced depression or other mental illness knows how debilitating it can be. If you have a loved one who has suffered from mental illness, that can be equally as draining. Despair, hopelessness, and depression not only send the person down a dark path within themselves, but they also prevent them from bringing their true value to the world. You cannot give what you do not have.

It has been said that "hurt people, hurt people." It is also true that hurt people ignore others because they do not have the emotional capacity to pay attention to other people's needs. Although mental illness is rarely mentioned in connection with giving and generosity, it deeply affects a person's ability to fully show up in every area of their life.

Debt

The average American has four credit cards and nearly $40,000 of debt, excluding their home mortgage. This is a major factor that impacts people's ability to help others, but not just from a financial standpoint. When people are in debt, they are stressed and consumed with fear. This can lead to despair and, in the worst cases, people losing so much hope that they consider taking their own lives.

There are many reasons for a family's debt, but generally we can attribute it to two reasons: consumerism and a lack of discipline. When they are brought together, it is a deadly combination. We desire all the objects that other people, but if we lack the discipline to save, invest, and give, it's a deadly cycle.

This is a picture of the typical American family: Both parents go to jobs where they feel underpaid and undervalued. They are stressed about money and worried about paying their bills. They don't have much in savings. To deal with the stress, they buy more things and distract themselves with their media and entertainment. They don't face their financial problems head-on, which leads to more stress, more debt, and often to despair, since they don't believe they will ever get out of their hole.

This paints a pretty gloomy picture of the average American family—one where most people are simply indifferent to giving. Perhaps it describes *your* family. If so, don't be discouraged. We have some suggestions not just for your family, but for anyone who wants to help others give more.

Keys to Handling Indifference

Indifference takes on many different forms, and therefore you can deal with it a variety of different ways. However, these suggestions can help almost any situation when taken together.

Connect with the humans on the other side of giving.

Although our giving does not take place in a vacuum, sometimes it can feel that way. When we are giving to organizations, we often don't see the result of our volunteer efforts or the financial help that we offer. When possible, try to discover the human beings who benefit from your giving.

One example is World Vision, an organization that provides relief to children around the world. They do a fantastic job of helping their donors make a personal connection with the children they support. The donors and recipients can send letters back and forth, and they have also sent cards featuring a short video of supported child. This has a powerful effect of seeing the difference you have made in a real person's life.

You can also get personally involved with recipients by serving in a homeless shelter, food bank, or soup kitchen. These are wonderful opportunities to connect face-to-face with people whom you are serving. It is easy to see people as a faceless sea of humanity, but each one of these people has a story and a name.

If time and resources permit, you can also take a mission trip or serve abroad. Not everyone has the opportunity to do this, but a mission trip can be a powerful and life-changing experience that can give you a broader perspective on other people's needs.

Limit your distractions.

Technology is a force that can take over our whole lives if we allow it. This is what the creators of our gadgets and social media intend! The more time we spend on our devices and entertainment, the more they profit.

Limiting your distractions starts with being intentional. It doesn't mean you get rid of all your devices or you never watch movies or TV shows. But it does mean that with a little effort, you can free up a lot of mental space.

A great place to start is by turning off devices past a certain time of night, for example 9 p.m. The blue light from your device is not only interrupting your sleep pattern, but the notifications and distractions on those devices wreak havoc with your ability to rest and relax. If your brain is always engaged in your technology, it never has a chance to do a deeper reflection and to develop creative ideas.

We also suggest shutting off unnecessary notifications when you are doing important work. You can put your phone on airplane mode or and shut off other alerts such as email and apps. If need be, work in a different place so you do not have to deal with as many interruptions and distractions.

Sometimes it is very simple things that can help us get free from distractions and have a healthier life so we can breathe emotionally and mentally.

Stay emotionally healthy.

When we talk about mental health, we don't just necessarily mean those who suffer from clinical depression. Mental health is important for everyone, even if you don't consider yourself depressed or have not been diagnosed with a mental illness.

Let's start with the basics. Are you taking care of yourself? Do you take one day off per week at least? Do you do things that are relaxing? Are you getting enough sleep? Are you eating healthy and exercising? Those are all important aspects of being emotionally healthy.

It's also vital to maintain a group of close friends. A big part of mental health is knowing that you are part of a community of people who care for you. If you're not, reach out to someone in your circle and invite them to lunch or get on a call with them. You would be surprised at the number of other people in your life who are feeling isolated and lonely as well. You might just be the solution to your own problem.

Of course, if you are suffering symptoms of depression or going through a personal crisis, consult a doctor who can prescribe the correct pathway forward for you to deal with any serious issues in your life. We want you to be healthy, whole, and energized so you can show up and give your best self to the world.

Pay attention to the needs around you.

When we use the phrase "pay attention," we do so very intentionally. Paying attention literally means that it's going to cost you something. The attention you give to others must be taken away from something else, and that's a good thing. We have to intentionally choose to break out of a distracted mode and begin to really see the needs of those around us.

It doesn't mean you necessarily have to go to a foreign country to do this. In fact, you can do it right now wherever you are. Who is around you? Your family, team members at work? Those on social media or others you have contacted today? Do you know what they need? Do you know what's going on in their lives?

Giving is not always a big flashy affair. In fact, sometimes the most meaningful giving is what we give of ourselves. It could mean listening to your child or spouse who's had a bad day, and being empathetic with them. It could be listening to a colleague's suggestion at work. But it could also mean giving to a homeless person or responding to a call for volunteers at church.

It doesn't take much to become aware of the needs around us. It just means that we are intentional and that we choose to not be sucked into all the distractions around us.

Reduce your debt.

This is a far more complicated topic then we can address in detail here. But the main point is this: Most people know what they need to do to get out of debt, but it is difficult to do it because it is an emotional issue. For example, everyone knows that they need to save money, invest, make more money, and get rid of debt to have a better financial footing. But if it were easy, nobody would have debt.

A great first step to dealing with debt is to track your finances and make a budget. You can use a simple spreadsheet, an app, or a computer program. The tool does not matter as much as the regular discipline of seeing where your money actually goes. As Dave Ramsey says, make sure every dollar has a job. This means planning in advance how much you're going to spend on various categories for the coming month.

It is also helpful to have a conversation with your spouse about money and how you can begin getting out of debt. If you are single, enlist the help of a good friend who can help keep you accountable. Money conversations are among the most difficult to have, but if these conversations can put you on a better financial path, they are absolutely worth it.

You can also reduce the amount you are spending on nonessential categories such as entertainment, new clothes, or eating out. Those are fantastic ways to save money and free up income to pay off debt and give to other people as well.

We would also suggest getting more intentional around paying off debt. In today's digital economy, the types of side hustles and extra jobs you could get are almost limitless. How badly do you want to get out of debt and have a better financial future? Remember that it's not just about you; it's also about your family and ultimately being a channel for a blessing.

Remember that your children are watching you.

As parents, we sometimes get so wrapped up in our own problems that we forget others are watching everything we say and do—especially our children! You may not think of yourself as a teacher, but you are. Your kids learn how to manage conflict, overcome problems, handle money, and more by looking at what we do (or don't do).

This should not feel intimidating. Instead, it's a blessing. We get to impact our kids not just during the time they live at home, but for the rest of their lives. If you are a grandparent, you can still continue to have a massive impact on your kids, and their kids as well. Everyone who comes behind you is watching and learning—not from what you say, but what you do. So take the opportunity to give and serve others, because that will set the example others will follow.

Keep an eternal perspective.

If you are a person of faith, you see everything you do in light of eternity. We are not just finite creatures who cease to exist one day. When we step through death's door, we simply step into a different type of existence. Knowing this impacts our daily lives in two ways.

First, it is a reminder that the frustrations we face on a daily basis are nothing compared to the expanse of eternity. As Paul wrote in 2 Corinthians 4:16–18, "So we do not lose heart. Though our outer self is wasting away, our inner self is being renewed day by day. For this light momentary affliction is preparing for us an eternal weight of glory beyond all comparison, as we look not to the things that are seen but to the things that are unseen. For the things that are seen are transient, but the things that are unseen are eternal."

Second, we know that our giving can have an impact far beyond what we experience on a daily basis. You can save a life, assist a friend in need, help build a house in another country, support your church and community, establish a better financial future for your family, and so much more when you give. You can *literally* change the world with your giving.

But if we want to change the world…it must begin with us. It begins with our attitude. It begins with stepping out of the familiar comfort of our everyday lives and taking a risk. It begins with caring enough to give, serve, and see things from an eternal perspective.

Keys to Performance-Driven Giving

In order to reduce indifference in your own heart, consider the following:

- Ask yourself honestly if you feel distracted. (The answer is probably yes!) What can you do to begin limiting these distractions? Even one small change can make a big difference.
- If you struggle with depression or other mental illness, what can you do to get healthier? Have you seen a professional?
- Assess your personal debt. Is it keeping you from giving as much as you could? How motivated do you feel to reduce your debt?

For Leaders: Five Symptoms of Indifference

Indifference can kill the effectiveness of a team and the organization's mission. However, it can be hard to spot, because it is not always as obvious as other destructive forces like gossip or dishonesty. However, it's just as destructive.

Indifference is like a virus. You can't see it directly, but you can see the symptoms. Below are five symptoms of indifference, along with questions to help you spot it.

1. **Conflict.** Does the person in question get along with others? How do they handle disagreements? Do they seem to lift up the team or tear down the team

2. **Negativity.** Do they have a positive attitude? How did they handle tough situations and disappointment? Does the emotional energy of the room go down when they walk in?
3. **Cynicism.** When they speak, do they have a sarcastic or bitter tone? Do they have a sense of hopefulness or despair toward the world in general?
4. **Anger.** Do they have a pleasant disposition, or do they make others uncomfortable? How do the team members respond to them? Do they handle setbacks well?
5. **Tribalism.** Are they a team player? Do they look out for the good of the whole group or just their own department or group? Do they see other coworkers as colleagues or competitors?

A Conversation with Andy Storch, Talent Development Consultant

In this chapter, you have learned to overcome indifference within yourself and others by increasing your passion, focus, connections, and other important qualities. We are thrilled to bring you this interview with Andy Storch, a business leader who embodies these qualities and much more.

Andy is a consultant, coach, speaker, and facilitator specializing in the talent development space. He is the author of *Own Your Career, Own Your Life: Stop Drifting and Take Control of Your Future* and the host of two podcasts: *Talent Development Hot Seat* and *Own Your Career*. And if that's not enough, Andy also heads up the Talent Development Think Tank Conference and Community.

We asked Andy to close out this chapter because he is the least indifferent person you will ever meet. Andy is full of passion and well known in entrepreneurial circles for being an amazing connector. We began our conversation with Andy by asking how we can better use social media to connect with people and add value.

> *We live in a time where we have the opportunity to have our voices heard by tons of people on social media. Our content can be available everywhere. That is the best way to connect because not everyone will go to conferences and events.*
>
> *One important way you can be a giver on social media is to create content and engage with content. So instead of just promoting you and your brand*

> *or business all the time, find ways to give value to others. You can entertain them, inspire them, or educate them.*
>
> *I like to create a lot of content that is inspiring for people in my network. I try to help them take some action that will improve their life. The easiest way for me to think about doing that is to focus on things I'm struggling with, or the things that help me.*
>
> *Although we are all unique, most of us have very similar challenges. We all struggle with basically the same things. If I can share things I know are helpful for me, then I know they'll be helpful for other people. And I often hear from people who says, "Hey, thank you for sharing that. I needed to hear that today."*
>
> *Another important way to use social media is to connect with people on a personal level. I do this all the time on LinkedIn and Facebook. I also have friends who do this really well on Instagram, where you can send people direct messages. You're just checking in with people and asking, "How are you doing? What are you working on? Is there any way I can support you?"*
>
> *It's all about giving people value, whether it's advice, a referral, a recommendation, or something else that will help them. There are so many opportunities to do that, and a lot of that is facilitated by social media.*

You can probably imagine our natural follow-up question: How do you keep from getting distracted by so many things going on and focus on what is most important? Andy shared some helpful words of advice.

> *I used to be a lot better at this. I still do a decent job, but there is always room for improvement. There are three factors to limiting distractions.*
>
> *The first is planning my day and understanding what's important. What do I need to get done? What's on my schedule? Where do I have open time in my schedule? That's where I really value having a good journal. I use that to let me plan ahead and figure out when and how I'm going to do that.*
>
> *The second is scheduling time for things that you need to get done. That can be global, like scheduling a block for getting things done that I said I was going to do. Or it can be really miniscule where every single little thing that you need to do, you put in your schedule. It might be things like calling the doctor at a certain time, talking to your spouse and having a conversation, or scheduling family game night or a date night.*

The more you can schedule stuff and follow your schedule, the more effective and productive you're going to be.

The third piece is noticing how you are distracted by things and finding ways to cut down on those distractions. The biggest offender is the notifications on your phone and your computer. I really try to minimize those. As much as I love social media and am on it every day, I have all notifications from social media turned off on my phone.

Think about all the apps we use. Every single one of them is run by a company who has a group of employees whose single most important job is to make their app as addictive as possible so that you keep coming back to it again and again. If you want to take control of your time and your schedule, you've got to take control of how you operate.

Andy provides training for lots of companies and comes from a corporate background himself. It's easy to think that companies are only interested in profit, but he reminded us that there are a lot of great companies that care about their people. He had a few tips to put into practice.

I run a community for talent development professionals, and one of the topics on a recent call was, "How are you taking care of your people?" There is a study out there that shows 82 percent of employees say they are burned out or near burnout. How are we taking care of them?

The first piece is recognition. That's a really big one. Most people don't get the recognition or affirmation they really want. That is actually the number one thing many people care about: knowing their work is making a difference and getting those words of affirmation. Of course, the financial part of taking care of employees is a big deal, but this affirmation piece is very important.

There is also a lot of talk these days about how companies are helping people with health and wellness. They are incentivizing exercise, mindfulness, meditation, gratitude, and other related practices. Many companies are also looking for ways to give people more time off.

Another factor that will become more important in 2021 and beyond is the social justice movement. Forward-thinking companies are looking for ways to create more psychological safety and a more inclusive culture where people can show up, be themselves, and have equal opportunities so they're not discriminated against. Focusing on diversity, equity, and inclusion is huge right now.

Thanks, Andy! We are grateful for your leadership and efforts to help companies treat their people well.

Andy's website is https://andystorch.com. Make sure to check out his book, *Own Your Career, Own Your Life*, which will help you clarify your direction and seize the future. To listen to the entire interview, go to PerformanceDrivenThinking.com/Giving or scan the QR code to visit the page.

Key To Abundant Living

UNLOCKING YOUR LIFE OF CONTENTMENT

It's time for some reflection based on what you just read!

What has caused you to often be indifferent to needs or circumstances in the past? Facing your realities is a first step toward healing and moving forward.

As you think back to an illustratio or situation where you were indifferent, what need was not met or what blessing did you miss?

What are two practical steps you believe you can take that will help you become less indifferent in the future?

Chapter 17
LEVERAGED RETURNS

Give, and it will be given to you. A good measure, pressed down, shaken together, and running over, will be poured into your lap. For with the measure you use, it will be measured to you.
—LUKE 6:38, ESV

Are you ready for graduation? There comes a time in each of our lives when we've got to graduate from one stage in life in order to experience another. The time has come for you to begin to apply the insights and understanding you have gleaned about intentional living and giving.

Do you feel that you are ready to face the world as a Spirit-filled Authorized Wealth Distributor? There is no comprehensive exam to take. There is no cap and gown to be rented or worn. All you need to do now is walk boldly into your world and intentionally begin distributing what God has given to you. You are equipped for this journey.

Commencement is never the end. Commencement is the beginning of a new phase of life! Step out as a steward who is trustworthy in the task God has for him.

God has filled your life with an extensive inventory of His riches. You need nothing else. And more is available as you give what you have already received away. You have access to the needed tools to help glorify His name.

NEW PERSPECTIVE

Do you now have a new perspective on God-given desires?

Do you now have a different perspective of the world of greed and need around you? Are you now more sensitive to how easy it is to get trapped in the fog of circumstances and deception? Do you now know what to do to get free of that fog?

Where is your new focus? Do you now have a new sense of direction so that you no longer run from clump to clump like my miniature horse, Prince? Are you now aware of your mission and your goal?

Are you delighting yourself in the Lord and allowing Him to meet your needs, wants, and desires? Are you now comfortable in your submissive role to your heavenly Father?

And that job description—do you feel you have a better understanding of why you are here and what is expected of you as a steward of your the King? Do you now have a handle on how to reflect, reproduce, reign, and manage for your heavenly Father?

Do you have an understanding of God's principles of wealth distribution? Let us recall the five points of the star:

I trust that you have taken the time to complete each Key to Abundant Living. Reading a book does little for you unless you personalize its content in some personal way. The exercises at the end of each chapter have been provided to help you internalize the content you have read.

WHAT NOW?

If you don't begin to use what you've learned, you will soon lose confidence in your ability and will cease to be on the cutting edge of faith that gives you the dynamic flair so needed in our troubled, confused world. Use it, don't lose it!

Here are eight ways to develop your skills as an Authorized Wealth Distributor:

1. **Practice.**

You can never become really good at something unless you practice, practice. This means you need to develop habits of regular, systematic giving. You need to have a plan and work the plan. Practice will help you go from good to great as a steward.

My greatest concern is that you will treat your stewardship responsibilities as something you turn on or off like an electric light. I suggest you download a copy of the Authorized Wealth Distributor commitment from LarryONan.com. You can then sign, date, and frame this copy. Hang it where you see it every day. This signed commitment will help remind you of who you are. My original copy was signed on June 29, 1979. It still hangs on my wall in front my desk. This framed copy reminds me often of my responsibilities and who I am.

If we were haphazard in living, we would either starve to death or go bankrupt within a month. What would life be like if you decided to get up each day whenever you felt like it? What if you only went to work when you were in the mood? What if your kids went to school only when they wanted to and stayed home the rest of the time? Without plans, goals, and some defined processes, life would be chaotic. Define your plan and begin following it.

Make plans to give. You need to be intentional. Decide what to give and follow through as a regular practice. The more often you give, the more effective you will be in giving.

As you practice, think about quality! Don't give table scraps. Remember: What you sow, you will reap.

2. **Give your best.**

As a preacher's kid, I once heard my dad tell a story about a wealthy man who desired to be a genuine giver. One day he decided to ask a poor builder he knew to build him a beautiful home overlooking the valley below. It was a lovely setting—a grand location for a mansion. It was his choice location of all the property he owned.

He explained to the builder what he wanted. He gave him plans and specifications. He told the builder he wanted the very best materials that money could buy and the highest quality workmanship he could deliver.

"I want this to be an exceptionally fine home that will last for years. Spare no cost in building the very best possible," he explained.

The man then told the builder that he was going on an extended trip and would not return until after the elegant home was completed. The builder reasoned with himself, "What an opportunity to get rich! With him gone, I can cut corners and come out ahead!"

The builder proceeded to build; but rather than using the best materials, he cheated in every way possible. He used inferior products and did shoddy work. He was able to pocket a considerable sum as he did far less than his best.

After some time had passed, the rich man returned. The builder delivered to him the keys to the new home. He explained what a beautiful home he had built and referred to the quality of his workmanship to deceive the rich man.

"I'm so glad to hear this report," the wealthy man said, "I am indeed glad it was built with such care and thoughtfulness because I have intended all along to give it to you when it was finished. The house is yours! Here, you take the keys. Move your family into your new, well-built home!"

As a steward, don't cut corners. Give your best for your Master. What you give will return to you. Practice, practice, practice!

3. **Tell others what you have learned.**

Share your testimony of how your life has taken on a new perspective since you've learned about way- of-life stewardship. Give your friends a copy of this book as a special gift. Help others become effective stewards.

4. **Become proficient in using the skills God has given you.**

What do you really enjoy doing? God's Word teaches that each person who accepts Jesus as his Savior is given one or more spiritual gifts. You may wish to read the two major passages in the Bible regarding these gifts: Romans 12:4-8 and 1 Corinthians 12.

God gives each of us special abilities specifically to help others and to build upon Christ. You may be blessed with the ability to teach. Someone else may have a special ability to lead or perform services of help or mercy. Learn about your spiritual gift(s) and then develop them to your full potential.

You are responsible to use your spiritual gifts as a steward to serve the body of Christ.

Some stewards have the gift of evangelism, for example, others do not. This, however, does not mean that the one who has the gift of evangelism need not be concerned with teaching or showing mercy. Likewise, the steward who does not have the spiritual gift of evangelism is still commanded to share his faith and should look for opportunities to do so. But as each of us develops a degree of specialization in doing one or more skills, we can then use that ability to multiply God's kingdom business here on earth.

How has God made you different from your peers around you? Do you know your primary strengths? Knowing your strengths will help you excel in your stewardship. I know my strengths and my weaknesses. Weaknesses are not bad; they are simply things that I do not do well. I want to major in my strengths and minor in using my weaknesses. If you are not sure what your strengths are, I encourage you to utilize the helpful resource that I have provided for you at Digging Deeper (page 265 of this book) and LarryONan.com. This will help immensely.

5. **Learn all you can about managing your finances.**

Every steward should work diligently to become mature in matters related to finances. Without helpful guidance in this area, you may feel inadequate and ill-prepared to help others. Coaching and some solid training will help you manage money wisely. Money management is a reflection of your ability to manage other things well.

Proper money management will allow you to do more with what has been entrusted to you. You will be recognized as trustworthy by your heavenly Father if He sees good stewardship in this critical area. In Digging Deeper (page 265 of this book), I provide you with three of the best money management resources available today. Small study groups are available in many locations. You don't have an excuse!

6. **Learn how to maximize your time.**

The best way to find tips on maximizing your time and talents is through reading. Become an active learner. Focus on books that help you grow in your stewardship responsibilities. I personally try to read a minimum of one educationally oriented book each month. We are blessed abundantly with books by Christian authors on every subject imaginable.

Begin a reading list. I have one and refer to it often. Ask friends what they are reading. When you hear of a good book on a subject, jot down the title and the author's name. Add it to your reading list. Make reading one of the ways to nourish yourself. Read, read, read!

For starters, I encourage you to visit my website: LarryONan.com. You will find a treasure of resources and practical recommendations to help you become a healthy steward. While what you read lays the foundation for you, there are many fine sources to help you in specialized areas.

7. **Become an intentional Authorized Wealth Distributor in your church and community.**

Share with others what you have learned. Share your testimony of how your life has taken on a new perspective since you've learned about intentional stewardship. Give your friends a copy of this book as a special gift. Offer to lead a small group study using this content. A leader's guide is available for you to download at LarryONan.com.

Will you allow God to use you to stimulate more stewardship awareness in your church? You may not be a born leader, but that doesn't mean you don't have an influence on those who give visible leadership.

Why not dedicate time each week for further personal study? There is a wealth of good material available today. Start by revisiting the many Bible passages referenced in this book and revisit the Key to Abundant Living worksheets and the end of each chapter. Visit LarryONan.com for recommended books, podcasts, and other helpful resources that will help you thrive in understanding. Many excellent resources are only a click away for you!

8. **Husbands and wives, work together as an Authorized Wealth Distributor team.**

Nothing is more rewarding than being involved as a couple in a worthwhile endeavor. This does not mean you do everything hand-in-hand, but it does mean you have common interests and continue to encourage one another. Pat and I were committed to common stewardship objectives. We were a team and encouraged one another and celebrated what we were able to see God do as we intentionally gave to others.

To be effective as a couple, let me suggest three ways to get started.

First, take a planning weekend together. If you have children, get a babysitter for two nights and three days (an entire weekend). Select a quiet resort-type area where you can be alone to think, talk, pray and relax together. The location should have nice restaurants nearby. Wives are not to cook on planning weekends!

Before you go, determine together what your agenda will be. What will you discuss—the discipline of the kids, frustrations in your communication, your schedule of activities for the next six months, ways to put into practice your responsibilities as Authorized Wealth Distributors, or other things? The list should not include more than three or four items.

Take a few appropriate materials that will be helpful in your planning. If, for example, you were going to focus some time on your stewardship as a couple, you may want to take your copy of Intentional Living and Giving so that you could discuss the Key to Abundant Living exercises together.

The purpose of a planning weekend is to enhance communication between husband and wife. Sometimes the process of communication is difficult, but it is always well worth it. Give yourselves to each other. Be transparent with each other.

Why not put one planning weekend into your schedule two or three times a year? This getaway time could be the most valuable investment you ever make in each other's lives. This is couple soul-time! And if you feel your marriage needs some special help, don't hesitate to seek professional Christian counsel. Get things back on track!

Second, attend a family conference. I recommend that you attend a Family Life Weekend as a couple. These are excellent conferences that are held throughout the United States and in many, many countries of the world.

Family Life is a special ministry of Cru. The content of these getaways is excellent. Don't hesitate to find a location and register for this life-changing experience. Family Life offers excellent resources on various topics that deal with family relationships.

Third, begin a Bible study together as a couple. Begin to study something together as a couple that will enrich your lives spiritually. I'm not talking about heavy Bible study where the husband teaches the wife. I suggest something simple that gives you a springboard to other discussions. I recommend finding Ha daily devotional guide on a topic of your choosing

Doing a study together will help keep you focused on what is important to your spiritual growth.

HOW YOU LIVE IS UP TO YOU

Isn't it great to know that God is original with each of us? He made only one of you!

You are to live your life for the glory of God. You are to seek first His kingdom. Recognize that everything you've been blessed with is still His. He is counting on you to use all His gifts for the furtherance of His plan on earth.

Edmund Burke once said, "All that is needed for evil to triumph is that good man do nothing." I believe you now know what to do to do something. It's now just a matter of trusting God and obeying His Word. Continue to evaluate your responsibilities as a steward. Continue to seek to bring men and women into a relationship with Jesus Christ. Continue to multiply your influence by giving your time, talents, and treasures.

You are a vital part of an expanding network of believers who believe they can make a difference for the Lord. If we, as members of this network, each choose to do our part, we can be assured of victory. United as a network of Authorized Wealth Distributors, we can see the world reached with God's love and forgiveness. In the process, we will be demonstrating that our trust in God is real.

As a steward, you are created to find your maximum fulfillment in living a life that is free from the cares of this world. As you give from your inventory by giving yourself away, you are free to give glory to God. You can experience heaven on earth as you trust and obey Him.

HELP BRING HOPE TO CONFUSED AND HOPELESS PEOPLE

We, as Authorized Wealth Distributors, have what it takes to help change our world. Our network has all that is needed. In our inventory is the technology, the materials, the strategies, the manpower, the expertise, the money—everything—that is required to meet the physical and spiritual needs of people within miles of you as well as the over eight billion people living on our small planet today.

GOD WANTS TO USE YOU TO REFLECT HIS POWER AND GLORY. ARE YOU AVAILABLE?

In the midst of the barren Mojave desert between Los Angeles and Las Vegas stand three giant 459-foot high towers. At the top of each tower are enormous black receivers. If you were to drive by this area at night, all you would see is a dark desert. Except for a few security lights, you would think nothing is there.

Each day tens of thousands of people drive Interstate 15 during daylight hours. As they near the border between Californian and Nevada, they cannot help but see the blinding light of solar generation on top of the three gigantic towers. As of 2014, the Ivanpah Solar Power Facility was the world's largest solar thermopower station. The solar generating facility sets on a six square mile area and includes 173,500 heliostats. Each heliostat cradles two giant mirrors.

Each day these heliostats track with the sun from when it rises in the East until it sets in the West. The sunlight strikes the giant mirrors. The mirrors focus the sun's energy onto the black receivers. The receivers generate 1,000 degrees of heat. The heat *in turn* drives specially adapted steam turbines. The anticipated outcome is one-million-megawatt hours of electricity each year.

How can these black receivers turn into a glowing ball of fire with a temperature exceeding 1,000 degrees F every day? The receivers themselves have no ability to generate power.

The secret is on the ground. It is the tracking of the sun's energy and the ability to transfer that energy to the receivers. Through this complex network of mirrors that power is thus generated from the sun.

REFLECTING THE SON

In many ways, you and I, as Authorized Wealth Distributors, are like heliostats and mirrors on the desert floor. Our responsibility is to receive from our heavenly Father. Our task is then to transfer what we have received to others. When we are available to receive, and we then give what we have received, we are obedient stewards.

We are reflectors of the Son. As we transfer what God freely gives to us to meet the needs of others, we fulfill His plan for our lives. By receiving and giving, we link a dynamic network together that has the power to change the world. Just think of what power can be unleashed for God's glory when the giving energy of a worldwide network of Spirit-controlled Authorized Wealth Distributors focuses on the needs of our messed-up world!

But such a network is going to be effective only when each of us personally chooses to become a giver, rather than a taker. Leave the completion of the networking up to God. Your priority concern should be to carry out your job description as a steward.

Are you allowing God to work His will through you? Are you willing to give yourself away through the strategic utilization of your time, your talent, and your treasure? If so, you are about to experience the freedom of an eagle as he soars in the heavens.

> *But those who trust in the Lord will find new strength. They will soar high on wings like eagles. They will run and not grow weary. They will walk and not faint. —Isaiah 40:31*

Key To Abundant Living

UNLOCKING YOUR LIFE OF CONTENTMENT

Reflect for a moment. You have completed Intentional Living and Giving. Now summarize in ~~a~~ just a sentence or two your thoughts about what you have gleaned from this book. What is your primary takeaway that will help you as your chart your course?

You were introduced to a number of practical suggestions in this chapter that you can develop as an Authorized Wealth Distributor. What three suggestions should be your focus over the six months or year? Selecting three and writing these down will go a long way to helping you achieve your desired outcome.

1.

2.

3.

Digging Deeper

Thanks for joining me on this intentional journey!

While you are now finished with this book, I encourage you to use what you have read as a springboard to new adventure of faith. Hopefully you are already experiencing transformation. I pray that you are now embracing your role as an Authorized Wealth Distributor. You were created for this purpose. You are fulfilling some of what God's desire for you.

Hopefully these pages have helped you gained new insights—have caused you to be thirsty for more. These pages have only scratched the surface of the potential of what is available to you to help you grow and thrive.

There is more available to you. I hope I have wetted your appetite for more. I encourage you to visit LarryONan.com. At this sight you will be able to access a few helpful tools that will help you spread the word about this lifestyle. One practical tool is a leaders guide that you can download. This will help you lead a small group through this topic. You can order books there as well. And there is more!

And do visit the Resources section. I have provided a listing of books, study materials, and podcasts related to stewardship, deception, managing money, and other related worthwhile topics. I update this regularly. I never recommend content without getting into the content first. I am providing you access to some of the best resources available to help you develop your thinking, manage your resources and combat blatant deception.

And I would love to hear from you! There is a place on this website for you to jot your reflections, tell a story, or share how you are seeing God use you as a lifestyle steward. As you share with me, I will post experiences from you and others. I will post these so that others hear from other Authorized Wealth Distributors.

So glad you spent some time with me. Your partnership as a steward means a lot.

Helping ignite abundance and blessing,

Larry O'Nan

Acknowledgments

My wife, Pat, who transferred her address to heaven in 2015, played a vital partnership role with me as we learned what intentional living and giving were all about. Her honest insights were a game-changer. She used her clerical and administrative skills in drafting the initial work. We became an Authorized Wealth Distributors team in 1980. This led us to a life adventure beyond our wildest dreams. We sensed God's daily blessing as we gave ourselves away. *Thank you, Pat, for being my best friend and partner for forty-five years! I am abundantly blessed today because of you.*

This book is the result of a team effort of outstanding young leaders that served with me over a thirteen-year period, as we were growing from nothing to something. These men and women contributed with biblical research, questioning and challenging what we were learning, and adding practical insight and wisdom. They helped ensure that this message penetrated all that we did to help resource funding to help fulfill the Great Commission. One of my treasures today is a list of over forty individuals that gave themselves as pioneers to this mission. Together we experienced breakthroughs in fund-developed applications for the worldwide ministry. *Thank you, team! You were vital to the success we saw as we learned to be stewards, used our strengths and helped involved partners in ministry.*

Dr. Bill Bright and the Cru leadership assigned me to the task of defining the "theology of stewardship" for the ministry and then provided me the freedom to implement the theology through the fund development office for Cru for over a decade. Without this assignment, this book would have never been written. *Thank you, leaders, for allowing me the opportunity to break new ground and have the freedom to fail.*

In recent years, I have benefited from the insight of my long-time friend, David Orris. He encouraged me to write *Giving Yourself Away* in 1984. He continues to be a source of creative insight and wisdom while revising and releasing *Intentional Living and Giving* for a new generation. Special thanks to Chuck MacDonald for his input and who reviewed every paragraph as editor. Cortney Donelson was especially instrumental in editorial formatting. The creative team at Morgan James Publishing has been an encouraging and valuable resource for getting this book in print and into worldwide distribution.

It has been an honor to partner with business leaders and many hundreds of dedicated stewards worldwide for over forty-five years as a professional fund development mentor and consultant. These individuals have been blessed with significant resources and have caught the vision that you have been introduced to on these pages. They continue on the joyful journey of giving themselves away. *Thank you, faithful stewards, for wisely managing what God has entrusted to you and being willing to give yourselves away. Because of you, there is hope!*

About the Author

Larry W. O'Nan is a 1966 graduate of the University of Colorado. He and his wife Pat, served on the full-time staff of Cru (Campus Crusade for Christ) for eighteen years. During this time, Larry dedicated thirteen years to developing and overseeing the accelerated growth of many fund development initiatives. These efforts resulted in more than $150 million raised for evangelism and development programs worldwide during this time.

In 1984, Larry joined the Management Development Associates team as vice president of stewardship strategies. He invested thirty years in providing counsel to Christian ministries by advising and helping clients implement stewardship-focus programs that helped raise additional tens of millions of dollars for a variety of ministry purposes. He stepped down from full-time consulting 2012.

He continues to speak in the United States and abroad about lifestyle stewardship and fund development practices. As an active volunteer, Larry serves on numerous community and Christian nonprofit organization boards. He is a recognized specialist in non-profit board governance, non-profit management, major gifts strategy design and implementation, and funding campaigns.

Larry is the author o*f Giving Yourself Away (1984)* and *Intentional Living and Giving.* Larry is the co-author of practical assessment tools like the *Church Stewardship Inventory*, the *Organization Stewardship Inventory*, the *Personal Stewardship Inventory*, and the *Success Probability Inventory.* He has written over 300 funding proposals for many nonprofit organizations.

In addition, Larry has a life-long passion to help children learn biblical values and virtues. He is the president of Andy Ant Productions Inc. and the creator of Andy Ant—a fun-loving fourth-grade ant who, along with his family and ant friends, teaches young children (like Andy's best friend, Joey) biblically based virtues that lead to living a life of integrity. Eight virtue-focused adventure books for children, featuring Andy and Joey, are currently in this collection and available at AndyAnt.com.

Larry resides in Highland, California. He has two daughters, two sons-in-law, two delightful granddaughters, and four adventuresome grandsons.

Larry says: Encouraging individuals to become effective lifestyle stewards and utilize what God has entrusted to them is a privileged and a blessing. Healthy stewards help accelerate God's work to redeem a lost, confused, and broken world. I believe that asking people to live and give to help lost people meet Jesus and help meet genuine needs in communities is doing something ***FOR*** *them, not* ***TO*** *them. As partners, we have equally the same impact as the person who is called to physically go to the lost and help the needy.*

Email: Larry@LarryONan.com

Endnotes

1 Thompson, Barbara R. Interview with chaplain Richard Halverson, "Evangelicals' Subtle Infection," *Christianity Today*, November 5, 1982, p 47.

2 Bonham, Tol D. 1975. *God Doesn't Want Your Money*, Oklahoma City: Vary Idea Press, p. 28.

3 Ardala, Thomas R. 1981. *Hearst Castle—San Simeon*, New York: Hudson Hills Press, p. 229.

4 Bright, Bill. "How to Insure a Bountiful Harvest," Worldwide Challenge (September 1981), p. 5.

5 Used by permission of Bright Media Foundation.
From How You Can Filled with the Holy Spirit, ©2003-2023 Bright Media Foundation (BMF). All rights reserved. Previously ©1971- 2003 Campus Crusade for Christ, Inc. All rights reserved. Bright Media Foundation® is a registered trademark of The Bright Media Foundation, Inc. Cru®, Cru Global®, Campus Crusade for Christ®, CCCI®, and Campus Crusade for Christ International® are registered trademarks of Campus Crusade for Christ, Inc. No part of this book may be used in another work, posted online, stored in a retrieval system, or transmitted in any form or by any means, except in the case of brief quotations printed in articles or reviews, without prior permission in writing.

6 From a speech by David Jackson, *Los Angeles Times*, (June 1, 1981).

7 Hancock, David L. and Bobby Kipper. 2022. *Performance-Driven Giving: The Roadmap to Unleashing the Power of Generosity in Your Life.* New York: Morgan James Publishing, reprinted by permission Morgan James Publishing.

A free ebook edition is available with the purchase of this book.

To claim your free ebook edition:

1. Visit MorganJamesBOGO.com
2. Sign your name CLEARLY in the space
3. Complete the form and submit a photo of the entire copyright page
4. You or your friend can download the ebook to your preferred device

A **FREE** ebook edition is available for you or a friend with the purchase of this print book.

CLEARLY SIGN YOUR NAME ABOVE

Instructions to claim your free ebook edition:

1. Visit MorganJamesBOGO.com
2. Sign your name CLEARLY in the space above
3. Complete the form and submit a photo of this entire page
4. You or your friend can download the ebook to your preferred device

Print & Digital Together Forever.

Snap a photo

Free ebook

Read anywhere

Printed in the USA
CPSIA information can be obtained
at www.ICGtesting.com
JSHW082145110524
62932JS00002B/16